THE BRITISH ISLES

Becky Burton
David Penrose
Simon Burton
Mark Penrose
Sarah Dixon
Kim Dixon
Jenny Leinert
Robert Croft

LEARNING ENGLISH

GREEN LINE NEW 1

Ausgabe für Bayern

von

Rosemary Hellyer-Jones
Marion Horner
Robert Parr

Ernst Klett Verlag
Stuttgart Düsseldorf Leipzig

LEARNING ENGLISH **GREEN LINE NEW 1**
Ausgabe für Bayern

von
Rosemary Hellyer-Jones M.A., Ehingen (Donau); Marion Horner M.A., Cambridge;
Dr. Robert Parr, Vaterstetten sowie Wolfgang Funk, Bamberg

Beratende Mitarbeit
Dr. Thomas Becker, Nürnberg; Harald Fischer, Nürnberg; Renate Leive, Sonnefeld;
Andrea Martin, München; Gerhard Nickl, Nürnberg

Visuelle Gestaltung
Elsie Lennox, London (Zeichnungen); Christian Dekelver, Weinstadt (Grafik)

CDs

1 Begleit-CD zum Schülerbuch für zu Hause und für den Unterricht mit Texten, Liedern, Ausspracheübungen (Klettnummer 547218)

1 CD mit den Hörtexten für den Unterricht (Klettnummer 547219)

Lernsoftware

Zu diesem Band gibt es ein multimediales Lernprogramm. Dieses Programm bietet abwechslungsreiche Übungsformen zu Vokabular und Grammatik, Leistungs- und Lernzielkontrollen und ein Lexikon mit dem Wortschatz des Lehrwerks.

1. Auflage 1 15 14 13 12 | 2015 2014 2013 2012

Alle Drucke dieser Auflage sind unverändert und können im Unterricht nebeneinander verwendet werden. Die letzte Zahl bezeichnet das Jahr des Druckes.

Internetadresse: http://www.klett.de

Redaktion: Peter Cole M.A., Heinz-Peter Gerlinger (Projektleitung),
Dr. Claudia Handwerker, Monique Kunhar M.A.
Gestaltung: Marietta Heymann

Umschlaggestaltung: Christian Dekelver, Weinstadt
Reproduktion: Meyle + Müller, Medien-Management, Pforzheim
Druck: Firmengruppe APPL, aprinta druck, Wemding
ISBN-13: 978-3-12-547210-5
ISBN-10: 3-12-547210-5

9 783125 472105

Hallo und herzlich willkommen
bei LEARNING ENGLISH GREEN LINE NEW 1, Ausgabe Bayern!

Damit du dich in deinem neuen Englischbuch gut zurechtfindest, erfährst du jetzt erst einmal, was alles in ihm steckt.

Auf Seite 8 heißt es **Let's start**. Das bedeutet so viel wie: Jetzt geht es los. Dann folgen sieben längere **Units** (Lerneinheiten) mit verschiedenen Themen.

Zwischen den **Units** findest du abwechselnd entweder **Focus on ...** mit Informationen zu Land und Leuten oder **Revision** mit Übungen, die dir zeigen, was du jetzt schon alles kannst.

Extra line im Anschluss an den **Unitteil** bietet dir zusätzliche Texte zum Lesen, aber auch zum Spielen mit der neuen Sprache.

Der Übersetzungsteil ab S. 122 heißt **Translation & Mediation.**

Es folgt dann der Grammatikanhang **Grammar** auf S. 130 mit vielen Beispielen, Regeln und Tipps.

Am Schluss des Buches gibt es dann noch ein Vokabular **Vocabulary**. Hier sind die Wörter für jede **Unit** aufgelistet. Es ist zum Lernen gedacht und enthält zahlreiche Lerntipps, wie du die Vokabeln am besten lernen kannst. Besonders empfehlenswert ist die Mittelspalte mit Beispielsätzen und sehr nützlichen Hinweisen zu den einzelnen Wörtern. Also die Mittelspalte bitte immer mitlernen!

Das **Dictionary** ab S. 198 listet die Vokabeln alphabetisch auf. Es ist zum Nachschlagen gedacht, wenn du einmal ein Wort vergessen hast.

Alles klar? Also, dann kann es ja losgehen.
Viel Spaß und viel Erfolg beim Lernen!

Zeichenerklärung

1 Alle Texte und Übungen, die auf der Begleit-CD zum Schülerbuch aufgezeichnet sind, erkennst du an diesem grünen Zeichen.
■ Hier beginnt ein neuer Track auf der CD.

1 Übungen mit diesem blauen Symbol verweisen auf die CD zum Hörverstehen. Die Hörtexte sind nicht im Schülerbuch abgedruckt.

Übungen mit diesem Symbol kannst du am besten in Partnerarbeit lösen.

Alle Übungen mit diesem Symbol könnt ihr gemeinsam in Gruppenarbeit lösen.

G10 Dieses Symbol verweist auf den Grammatikteil.

Inhaltsverzeichnis

let's start

1 Hello

PUBLIC SUBWAY
UNDERGROUND
PUBLIC SUBWAY
MONUMENT STATION
Public subway
District and Circle lines
Docklands
SCORE BOARD
TOILETS
MUSEUM SHOP
CENTRE COURT
NO 2 COURT
14-17 · COURTS 14-17
EXIT GATE 5 · EXIT
Hi. I'm Robert Croft.
I'm twelve and I'm from London.
I'm new in Nottingham.
Hi. My name is Monny the Monster. What's your name? How old are you? Where are you from?
Hello. My name is … I'm ten / … I'm from …

2 Friends

1
Look, Robert. It's Becky. She's my best friend.
Yes.
2
Is that her dog?
3
Hello, Robert. I'm Becky Burton.
Hi, Becky. This is Robert Croft.
4
Robert's new here. He's from London.
From London? Wow!
Woof!
5
Hello, dog. What's your name?
His name is Barker.
6
You're a nice dog, Barker.
7
Come on, Barker. Let's go.
8
Bye, Becky.
My cat Tabby is nice, too.
9
I'm at Haywood School.
Hey, that's my new school. And Becky? Is she at Haywood School?
Yes. She's in my tutor group.
10
Hi!
And that's David Penrose. He's in my tutor group, too. Hi, David!
11
Ow!

1 His name is Robert

1. His name is Robert. He's twelve. He's from London.
2. Her … Sarah. … eleven. She's … Nottingham.
3. … Becky. … twelve. … Nottingham.
4. … David. … eleven. … Nottingham.

Your turn:
This is my friend.
Her / His name is …
She's / He's …
She's / He's from …

2 About you

Write in your exercise book.

My name is Anna.
I'm ten.
I'm from Augsburg.

3 Make sentences

1. Sarah / cat
2. Robert / new school
3. Becky / dog
4. David / friend

Example:
1. This is Sarah. That's her cat.

4 What's missing?

1. This is Robert. … twelve. He's … London. He's … in Nottingham.

2. That's Becky. … twelve. She's … Haywood School. Barker is … dog.

3. My name is … . … eleven. Becky is … best friend. … in my tutor group.

4. That's … . … in my tutor …, too. He's … Nottingham.

5 Sound practice

a) Listen and say the numbers.

1 one 2 two 3 three
4 four 5 five 6 six
7 seven 8 eight 9 nine
10 ten 11 eleven 12 twelve

b) What's your telephone number?

My number is 85670 (oh) 91.

6 Listening: Telephone numbers

Listen and write the telephone numbers.

Becky: … David: … Sarah: … Robert: …

4 3 David and Robert

Robert: Wow! Hi, David. I'm Robert Croft.
David: Hello. How are you?
Robert: I'm fine. But what about you? Are you hurt?
David: No, I'm not hurt. I'm OK, thanks.
Robert: I like your skates!
David: Yes. They aren't new, but they're really fast.
Robert: Great!
David: Are you new here?
Robert: Yes. We're from London. That's our house over there.
David: Welcome to Nottingham, Robert.
Robert: Thanks. Nottingham isn't London, but I like it. – Er, are Sarah and Becky your friends?
David: I'm in their tutor group at school. They're girls, but they're OK.

1 What's missing?

Put in: *'m, 's, is, isn't, 're, are, aren't*

1. I … new here. We … from London. We … from Nottingham.
2. No, this … our house. Our house … over there.
3. Sarah Dixon and Becky Burton … nice. They … girls at my new school.
4. David … in their tutor group. They … his best friends, but they … OK.

2 Long and short forms of *to be*

Say the sentences.

1. I am ten. ➜ **I'm ten.**
2. She is my friend. ➜ **She's** …
3. They are new here. ➜ …
4. You are at Haywood, too. ➜ …
5. He is not from London. ➜ …
6. I am not in your tutor group. ➜ …
7. We are friends. ➜ …
8. It is a nice dog. ➜ …
9. They are not from Nottingham. ➜ …
10. It is not his dog. ➜ …

Long form	Short form	
I am	I'm	(I'm not)
you are	you're	(you aren't)
he is	he's	(he isn't)
she is	she's	(she isn't)
it is	it's	(it isn't)
we are	we're	(we aren't)
you are	you're	(you aren't)
they are	they're	(they aren't)

3 Friends

Put in: *my, your, his, her, our, their*

1. He's the new boy. **His** name is Robert.
2. She's my best friend. … name is Becky.
3. I'm Sarah. Tabby is … cat.
4. … cat is nice, Sarah.
5. They're the Burtons. That's … house.
6. We're at Haywood. That's … tutor group.
7. Are you new at Haywood? What's … name?
8. This is David. I like … skates.
9. Is that … dog, Becky?
10. We're new here. That's … house over there.

4 Role play

a) Hello. I'm … . What's your name? → Hello. My name is … → How old are you? → I'm … → Oh, I'm … (, too). Where are you from? → We're from …

b) Hi, … . How are you? → Fine, thanks. And you? → I'm OK. → Great! Bye. → Bye.

5 Sound practice

[aɪ] **I**'m f**i**ne. That's n**i**ce. B**ye**.
[e] My b**e**st fri**e**nd B**e**cky is tw**e**lve.
[æ] Th**a**nks. Is th**a**t c**a**t T**a**bby?

[ɜː] The g**ir**l and h**er** friend are h**ur**t.
[r] Whe**r**e‿is **R**obert f**r**om?
[ð] Is **th**at **th**eir tutor over **th**ere?

6 A song: I can sing a rainbow

Red and yellow and pink and green,
Purple and orange and blue.
I can sing a rainbow, sing a rainbow,
Sing a rainbow, too.

Listen with your eyes,
Listen with your eyes
And sing everything you see.
You can sing a rainbow, sing a rainbow,
Sing along with me.

Words: Arthur Hamilton

- yellow
- orange
- red
- pink
- purple
- blue
- green
- white
- grey
- black
- brown

7 What colour are the monsters?

Example: Number 1 is blue and yellow. / Number 1 is the blue and yellow monster.

4 Robert! Where are your school things?

Oh dear! OK, my school bag is on the floor. There's a black pencil case next to it, with a yellow folder and a red ruler. Great. – But where are my exercise books? Hm, let's see … These are my football magazines. Oh dear! Maybe in those drawers over there? Under those comics? – No. Or in my school bag? There's one book in my school bag. There are four books on my desk, and three brown pencils, a black pen and a rubber, too. OK, but where are my exercise books? – Ah! There, under the chair. And where's my blue folder? Here, on the bed. And there's a blue biro next to it. But where's my green biro? …

1 What's this in English?

What's this?
It's a …

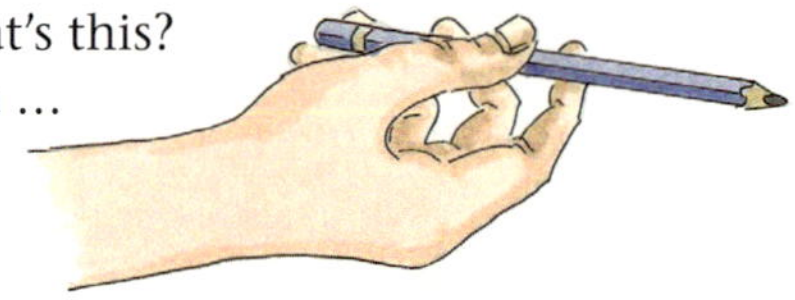

What's that?
It's a …

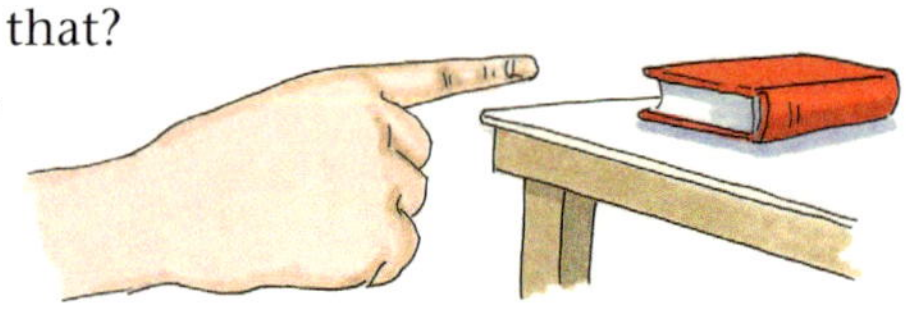

2 Listening: Cats and dogs

Listen and find the right sound. Make lists.

[s] – cats	[z] – dogs	[ɪz] – exercises
…	…	…

3 What's in your school bag?

There's a pencil case in my school bag. There are three books, a biro and …

4 Where is it? Where are they?

Your teacher:	You:
Where's the biro?	It's under the …
Where are the pencils?	They're …

5 A game

Your turn: Play the game!

6 Listening: Sarah and her school things

What's missing? Listen and draw the picture again.

7 *These* and *those*

1. These pencils are red. Those pencils are blue.
2. These books are on the chair / under bed.
3. biros in pencil case / on desk.
4. folders green / yellow
5. boys from Nottingham / London
6. skates in drawer / on floor

8 Pairs

Girl and boy, you and I,
Yes and no, hello and goodbye,
Her and his, desk and chair,
Words are easy in a pair!

Make pairs.

my – **your**	this – ?	these – ?
our – ?	here – ?	black – ?
cat – ?	he – ?	under – ?

9 Put in: *this, that, these* and *those*

1. … is David. He's my friend.
2. … is my book. Your books are on your desk.
3. Is … Sarah over there? Is she at our school?
4. … boys and girls here are new at Haywood.
5. Are … your new pencils? They're great.
6. … aren't my pencils. My pencils are here.
7. I'm in your tutor group. – … 's great!
8. What's in your bag? – Oh, … and …

8 5 School!

In the playground at Haywood School.

Sarah: Is Robert in 7MD, too?
Becky: Yes, he is. There's the list.
Robert: 7MD? What's that?
Sarah: Our tutor group, silly!
David: Great. Are you good at Maths, Robert?
Robert: No, I'm not. Maths? Ugh!
Sarah: Becky's good at Maths.
Becky: No, I'm not.
David: Oh yes, you are. You're good at everything.
Robert: What about the teachers at Haywood? Are they OK?
Sarah: The teachers? They're, er –
Mr Cooper: "Guten Morgen!"
Robert: Who's that?
Becky: That's Mr Cooper.
Robert: He's the German teacher, right?
David: Brilliant!
Robert: Is he OK?
Becky: Yes, he is. He's very nice.
Robert: And who's MD?
Sarah: MD is Margaret Dane. That's Mrs Dane, our tutor.
Robert: And is Mrs Dane nice?
Becky: Yes, she is. And she's our English teacher, too.
Robert: So MD is our ET, right?
Sarah: ET? What's that?
Robert: English teacher, silly!

1 Answer the questions

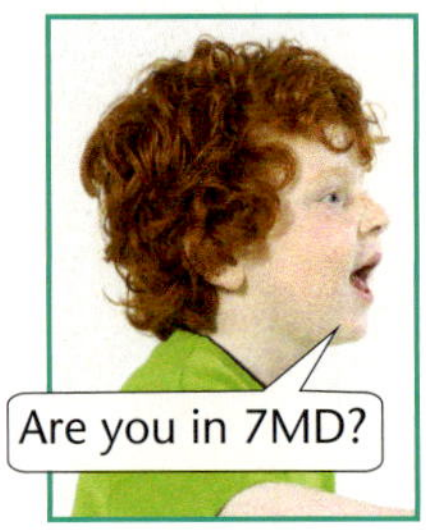

1. Are you in 7MD? **Yes, I am.**
2. Is Sarah in your tutor group? **Yes, …**
3. Are you good at Maths? **No, …**
4. Is Becky good at Maths? …
5. Is Mr Cooper the German teacher? …
6. Are you in his tutor group?
7. Who is MD?
8. Is she your tutor?

2 Your turn

Ask and answer questions.

Are you … | Is your teacher … | Am I … | Is Monny … | Aren't you …

German? | a monster? | English? | nice? | good at Maths? | from London?

3 Watch out!

He's or ***his***? ***You're*** or ***your***? ***They're, their*** or ***there***?

1. David's here. ... in ... room.
2. Are the Burtons ... ? – Yes, ... in the house with ... dog.
3. ... really fast on ... new skates, David.
4. David's ... . And Robert, too. ... friends.
5. Becky, ... good at German. Who's ... teacher?
6. Robert is new here. ... from London. Sarah, Becky and David are ... new friends.

4 Word power: A mind map

What's in your pencil case?
Make a mind map.

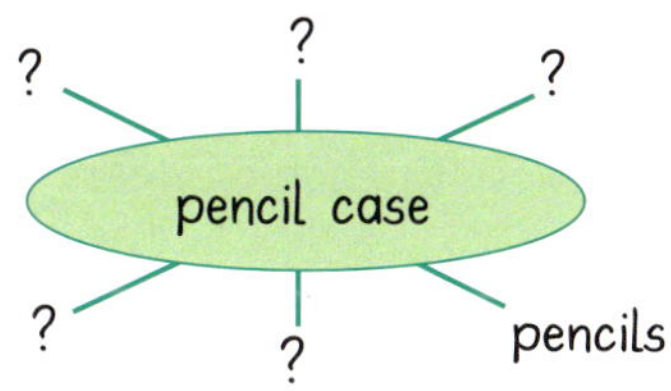

9 5 Sound practice

[aɪ]	I'm fine. That's nice. Bye.
[eɪ]	Let's play that game, David. It's great.
[əʊ]	Hello. Oh, no! A yellow folder.
[aʊ]	The brown house? Wow! How nice.
[eə]	They're there, but where are their books?
[ð]	Is that their tutor over there?

10 6 Alphabet Rap

A – B – C D E
We are all in 7MD.
F – G – H I J
We're at Haywood every day.
K – L – M N O
Come on in and say hello!
P – Q – R S T
Listen to our ABC!
U V W – X Y Z
Hear us rap the alphabet!

a) Spell your name.

My name is Lisa Meyer.
L-I-S-A M-E-Y-E-R.

b) Who's your favourite star?

"R-O-double B-I-E"

"It's Robbie Williams!"

6 Pictures in the classroom

Robert: Is that your picture, Becky?
Becky: Yes, it is.
Robert: I like its colours. And is that your dog in the picture?
Becky: Yes, it is. It's Barker.
Robert: Wow! It's brilliant. Not like that picture over there! Look at those dogs. Ha, ha! They're really funny.
Sarah: No, they aren't.
Robert: Yes, they are. That's a terrible picture.
Sarah: No, it isn't. Those dogs are nice.
David: Er, Robert – don't laugh too loud. Look at the name under the picture.
Robert: Er – Sarah Dixon. Oh dear.
Sarah: Yes, it's my picture. Thank you very much, Robert Croft. You're so nice.

1 Match the sentences

1. Look at that picture. ----→ b)
2. This is Barker.
3. Wow, Becky!
4. Thank you, Robert.
5. This is our classroom.

a) You're so nice.
b) It's great.
c) We're in 7TC.
d) You're really good!
e) He's our dog.

2 Is that your picture, Becky?

1. Is that your picture, Becky?
   – **Yes, it is.**
2. Is that your …?
   – **No, it isn't.**
3. Is that …?
   – **…**

Your turn: Is that your …? – …

3 That's not true!

1. Robert isn't new at Haywood. – **Yes, he is!**
2. That picture is terrible. – ...
3. The boys aren't OK. – ...
4. That girl is funny. – ...
5. My pencils aren't in the pencil case. – ...
6. My picture isn't good. – ...
7. It's my pen. – ...
8. It's not his dog. – ...
9. The girls are in the classroom. – ...
10. Barker isn't nice. – ...

4 A question game

What's the number? Find the words and make questions. What are the answers?

Example: (3) + (4) Are Sarah and Becky at Haywood School? – Yes, they are.

(1) David and Robert	(4) Mrs Dane and Mr Cooper
(2) Barker and Tabby	(5) David and Sarah
(3) Sarah and Becky	(6) your friends

+

(1) nice	(4) at Haywood School
(2) ten	(5) English
(3) German	(6) teachers

5 Let's play "Simon says"

Stand up.

Sit down.

Shut ...

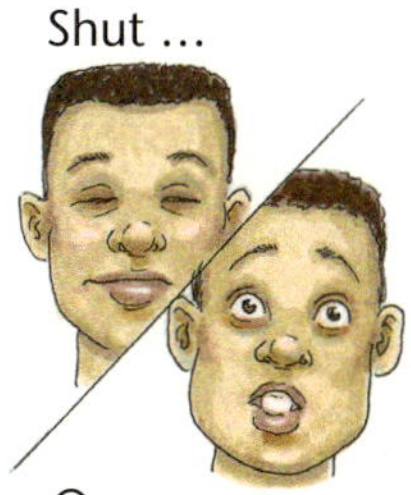
Open your eyes.

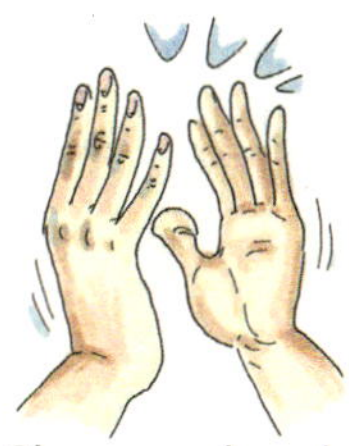
Clap your hands.

Touch your nose.

Teacher: Simon says, "Stand up."
Simon says, "Sit down."
Shut your eyes. – You're out, Daniel!

6 Don't ...

Don't
↓
sit • stand • play • touch
laugh • sing • clap • write
↓
that game • down • too loud
a song • your nose • up
your hands • in your book

7 The lesson

The girls and boys are in the classroom.
Mrs Dane is late.

Sarah: Let's play a game! I'm your teacher. I'm – er – Mrs Dixon.
David: You? You're a very young teacher, Mrs Dixon!
Sarah: Sit down and be quiet, please. Now, where's the new boy?
Robert: Here, Mrs Dixon. My name is Robert Croft.
Sarah: Where are you from?
Robert: I'm from London.
Sarah: From London? Wow! Thank you, Robert. – Now, are you ready, boys and girls? Here's your homework.
Becky: Our homework?
Robert: No, thank you, Mrs Dixon!
David: OK. Now it's your turn, Robert.
Robert: Yes. I'm the new teacher. David, what's that on your desk? Is it a book?
David: No, it isn't. It's a comic, Mr Croft.
Robert: What? A comic – in my lesson? Bring the comic here, please.
David: No, it's my comic.
Sarah: Yes, it's his comic!
Robert: Quiet, please, Sarah. David, don't be silly. Bring the comic here. Thank you. Oh, great! I like comics.
David: Hey, you aren't the teacher now. It's my turn –
Mrs Dane: Oh no, it isn't. It's my turn now!
Becky: Oh! Mrs Dane is here!
Mrs Dane: Yes, I am. Sorry I'm late!

1 Look at the text

Are the sentences true or false? Correct the false sentences.

1. The girls and boys are in the playground. – That's not true. The girls and boys are …
2. Mrs Dane is late. – That's …
3. 'Mrs Dixon' is a very young teacher.
4. The new boy is from Nottingham.
5. David is the new teacher.
6. His book is on the desk.
7. Mr Cooper is here. It's his lesson now.

2 In the classroom

You:

Good morning.
Sorry I'm late.
Where are we?
What's 'Tafel' in English, please?
Can you spell 'blackboard', please?
Here's my folder.
Can we open the window?
What's our homework?
Bye.

Your teacher:

Yes. B–L–A–C–K–B–O–A–R–D.
Yes, OK.
It's on the board.
We're on page 21, exercise 2.
Good morning.
It's 'blackboard'.
Thank you.
Goodbye. See you tomorrow.
That's OK. Sit down, please.

3 A team game: What's that in English?

What's 'Fenster' in English? → It's 'window'. → That's right. Now it's your turn.

What's 'Tafel' in English? → Sorry, no idea. → It's 'blackboard'. One point for our team.

13 4 A song: The Hokey Cokey

1. You put your left arm in,
   your left arm out.
   In, out, in, out,
   you shake it all about.
   You do the Hokey Cokey
   and you turn around.
   That's what it's all about.

Chorus: Oh, oh, the Hokey Cokey. (3x)
Knees bend, arms stretch,
ra ra ra.

2. your right arm
3. your left leg
4. your right leg
5. your whole self

Words: Jimmy Kennedy

8 Let's check

1 *Who, where* or *there?*

1. … are you from? – I'm from Nottingham.
2. …'s from London? – Robert.
3. … are two dogs in the house.
4. …'s Mrs Dane? – She's our tutor.
5. …'s Mrs Dane? – She's in the classroom.
6. …'s Mrs Dane. She's nice.
7. She's over …
8. …'s Robert? – He's the new boy.
9. …'s in the playground? – David's …
10. …'s …? – It's Becky.

2 Find the words: *my, your, his, her, its, our, their*

1. Is that your book, Becky?
   – Yes, and this is … book, too.
2. Is Mr Cooper your tutor?
   – Yes, I'm in … tutor group.
3. She's new. What's … name?
4. Are you in 7TC, boys?
   – No, we aren't. … tutor group is 7MD.
5. Are the girls in 7MD?
   – Yes, that's … tutor group.
6. Very good, girls! … poster is nice.
7. Is that your school?
   – Yes, … name is Haywood School.
8. What's that on the desk? Oh, David, you and … comics!

3 Where are Barker and Tabby?

1

2

3

4

5

1. Tabby is … the green folder. 2. Barker is … 3. Tabby is ….

4 *I'm, you're, he's, she's, it's, we're, they're*

1. Hello, … Becky. What's your name?
2. Sarah! Becky! Where are you? – … here!
3. Woof! Woof! – Oh, Barker, … terrible!
4. Are you and David friends, Robert? – Yes, … good friends.
5. Are you in 7TC, too? – No, … in 7MD.
6. Are we late? – Yes, girls. … late!
7. Robert is new. … from London.
8. Here are David and Becky. … at Haywood, too.
9. Our school is in Nottingham. … a nice school.
10. Sarah is eleven. … in tutor group 7MD.
11. Becky, David and Robert are her friends. … in 7MD, too.
12. Mr Cooper is funny. … the German teacher.

5 What's your answer?

1. Hello!
2. How are you?
3. What's your name?
4. Are you English?
5. Where are you from?
6. How old are you?
7. Who's your teacher?
8. Is your teacher German?
9. What's in your school bag?
10. What colour are they?
11. Where are your books?
12. You're late.

6 Yes or no?

1. Are you from London? – Yes, …
2. Is she thirteen? – No, …
3. Are they good at Maths? – No, …
4. He's good at Maths. – No, …
5. Is the pencil on the desk? – Yes, …
6. Are these skates fast? – Yes, …
7. Is this your house? – No, …
8. Robert and David aren't here. – Yes, …
9. Am I in your tutor group? – Yes, …
10. Is he nice? – No, …
11. Are you our English teacher? – No, …
12. She isn't from Nottingham. – Yes, …
13. Are you and Becky friends? – Yes, …
14. I'm silly. – No, …

7 What's in the picture?

Example: In picture number one there are two dogs, five cats, …, but there is only one …

8 Which sound?

Put these words in the right lists:

cats, dogs, pencils, exercises, friends, teachers, sentences, books, numbers, sounds, pencil cases, desks, windows, raps

[s]	[z]	[ɪz]
…	…	…

9 Mixed bag: What's missing?

1. … is the new boy. … name is Robert. … from London.
2. … is David. He … from London, he's … Nottingham. … skates … fast.
3. … girls are their …, Becky … Sarah. They are … Haywood School.
4. … tutor group … 7MD. … are 12 boys and 16 girls in 7MD.
5. Mrs Dane is … tutor. … nice.
6. Mr Cooper is their German … . There … a German book … his hand.

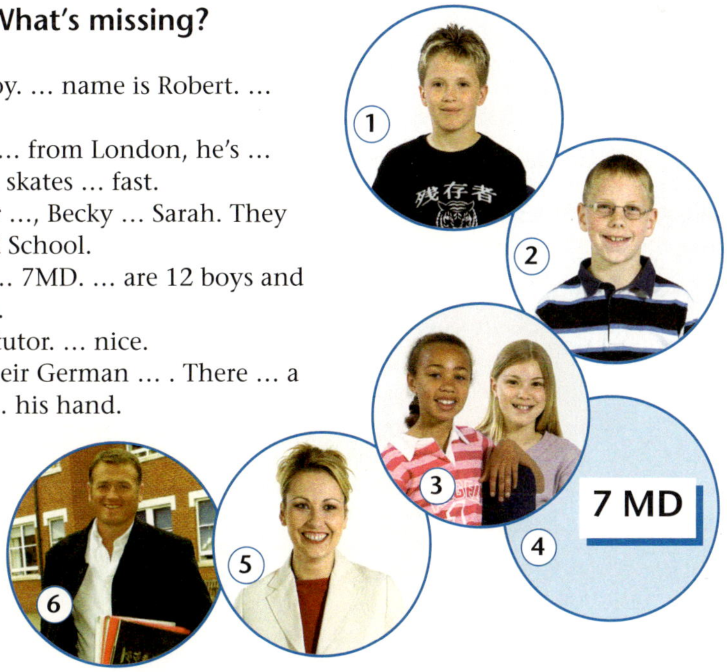

Focus on families

1 A family tree

This is Becky Burton's family.

Make sentences.
Example: Simon is Becky's brother.

Simon • Becky • Paul • Peggy • Arthur • Jack • Lizzy • Mary • Alan	is	Becky's • Paul's • Simon's	mother • father • sister • brother • aunt • cousin • uncle • grandma • grandpa

2 A puzzle: Who is where?

It's Becky's birthday. Look at these sentences. Match the names with the places at the table.

1. The boys next to Becky are cousins.
2. Paul is on his uncle's right.
3. Becky's brother is next to his mother's mother.
4. Peggy is on her mother's right.
5. The person on Jack's right is married to the person on Lizzy's left.
6. Jack is next to his brother.

Becky's:

mother • father • brother • cousin • aunt • uncle • Grandma Jones

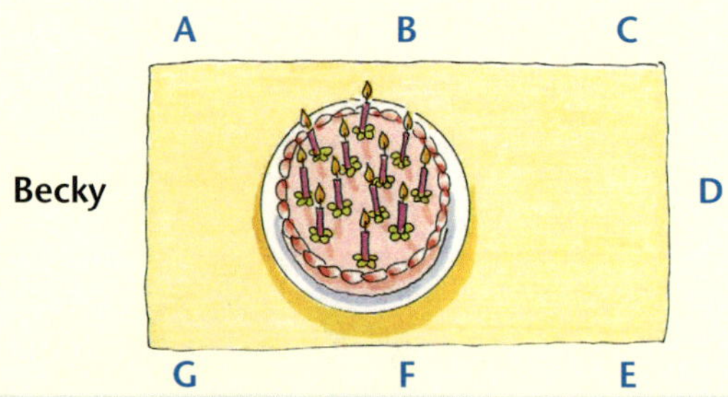

14 3 Sound practice

[s]	[z]	[ɪz]
Jack's brother	Peggy's name is Jones.	Grandma Jones's turn
My aunt's house	Aunt Lizzy's dogs	David Penrose's cousin
Robert's comics	My father's friends	

15 4 Anuja's family

Hi, I'm Anuja Singh. I'm 12 and I'm from London. This is my family.

Here are my parents. My father is tall and dark. His name is Rajiv and he's from India. My mother is English. Her name is Helen and she's tall and blonde.

That's my brother Anil, next to my father. He's 10 and he's terrible! But sometimes he's OK.

I really like my Uncle Balujee. He's so funny! He's my father's brother and he's Indian, too, of course. But he's married to an Italian woman, my Aunt Rosa. Their children are my cousins Tejinder and Rita. He's 15 and she's 12. They're both nice.

We're a very international family!

Match the pictures with the names. Example: Number one is Anuja's brother Anil.

4 5 Listening: Who are they?

a) Draw Anuja's family tree.

b) Now listen and write down the names.
Example: 1. Tejinder.

Uncle Balujee | Anuja | Rita | Helen Singh
Anil | Aunt Rosa | Tejinder | Rajiv Singh

6 Your turn: My family

What can you say about your family?

My ...'s name is ...
He / She is ...
... is my ...'s brother / sister / ...

unit 1 intro

The Burtons and the Dixons

17 This is the Burton family – Becky Burton with her mother, her father, her brother Simon and their dog Barker. Their house is in Nottingham, but it isn't in the city centre. It's in Arndale Road, in Sherwood.

This is Sarah Dixon's house. It's in Sherwood, too – in Larwood Grove. The man and the woman in the picture are Sarah's mum Janet and her dad Eddy. The girl on the right is Sarah's sister Kim. And the cat is Tabby.

1 Talk about these families

2 Sherwood

This is Sherwood.
Say where these places are.

1. Haywood School
2. Arnot Hill Park
3. The Burtons' house
4. The swimming pool
5. The Burtons' bike shop
6. The Dixons' house
7. The supermarket

Example: 1. Haywood School is in Edwards Lane.

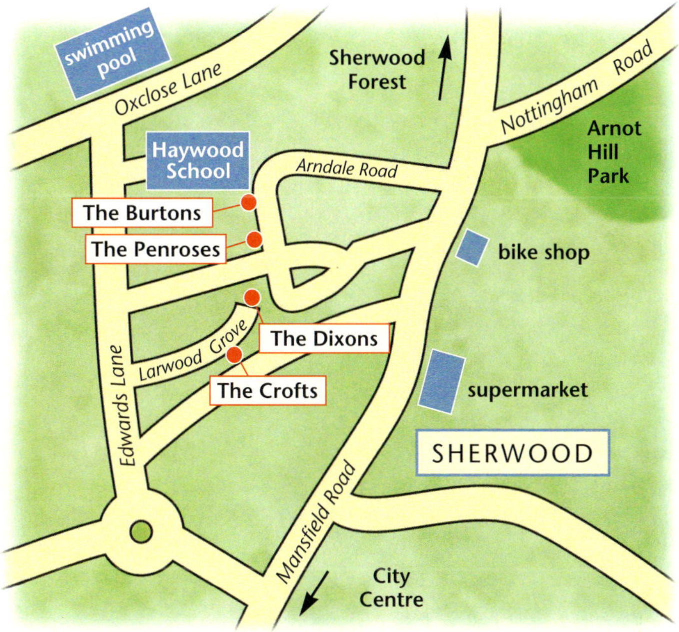

3 Listening: Inside and outside

Look at the pictures and listen to the CD. Is this David's house? Why or why not?

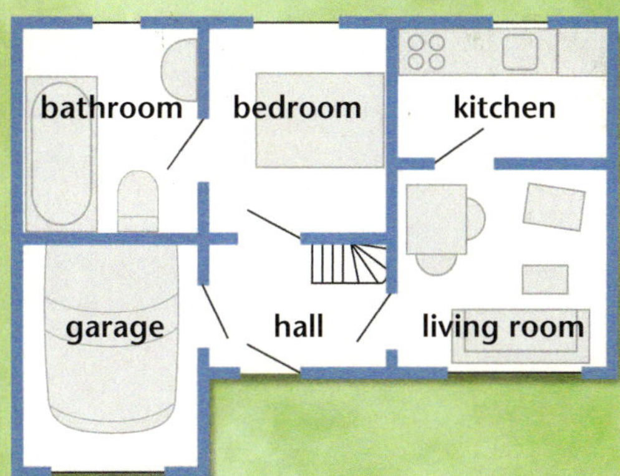

4 A plan

Draw a plan of your own house or flat.
Put in the words in English.

A We're busy

Simon and Becky Burton have got their own rooms.

Simon's room isn't very tidy. On the floor he has got magazines and clothes. There's an empty bottle on his desk. And there are comics and a skateboard on his bed. He has got football posters on his walls.

Robert: You must listen to this CD. It's by the Underdogs.
Simon: The Underdogs?
Robert: Yes, it's brilliant. Have you got a CD player?
Simon: No, I haven't.
Robert: Oh dear.
Simon: I've got an idea. Becky's got a stereo. Let's ask her.

Becky has got a tennis racket, a stereo and a computer in her room. She hasn't got football posters on her walls. She has got animal posters. Her favourite animals are horses – and Barker, of course!

Robert: Becky? Can we come in? I've got a new CD. You must listen to it.
Becky: Oh, what is it?
Robert: The Underdogs.
Becky: I've got it already.
Simon: Oh please, Becky! Can't we listen to it?
Sarah: No, you can't. We're busy.

1 The Burtons

a) Make sentences.
Example: Becky has got a tennis racket.

Becky • Simon • The Burtons	has got • hasn't got • have got • haven't got	a tennis racket • a garden • a stereo • a CD player • a skateboard • animal posters • a dog • a cat

b) Your turn. What about your room?
Example: I've got a stereo in my room.

2 Short forms

Say the sentences. Use short forms.

1. She has got her own room.
   ➜ She's got her own room.
2. They have got a big garden.
3. Anuja has got two black cats.
4. We have got five English lessons.
5. He has got a brilliant skateboard.

3 What's missing: *have, 've, haven't, has, 's, hasn't?*

1. *Robert:* I … got a great new CD here, Simon. … you got a CD player?
Simon: No, I … . Sorry.
Robert: What about Becky? … she got a CD player?
Simon: Yes, she … . She … got a stereo and a computer!

2. *Robert:* The Burtons … got a nice dog. … you got a dog, too?
Sarah: No, we … . We … got a cat.
Robert: What about David? … he got a dog or a cat?
Sarah: No, he … . He … got a brother and a cousin from Germany.

21

4 Sound practice

[ə]	[ən]	[ðə]	[ði]
a good‿idea	an‿idea	the dog	the‿old dog
a nice‿animal	an‿animal	the bottle	the‿empty bottle

Now put these words in the right lists:

a / an *English book* *good example* *dog* *answer* *old dog* *question* *book*

the *example* *football* *alphabet* *animal* *nice animal* *Underdogs* *right answer*

5 Who has got what?

Work in pairs. Ask and answer questions.
Examples: Have the Burtons got a cat? – No, they haven't.
Has Becky got a stereo? – Yes, she has.

6 Your room

Work in pairs. Look at the pictures on page 28. Ask and answer questions.
Example: Have you got a desk in your room? – Yes, I have. / No, I haven't.

6

7 Listening: David and his room

a) Listen to David. Which is his room – number one, two or three?

b) Draw your own room. Write a short English text about it.

G11–16

22 B Breakfast at the Dixons' house!

It's Friday morning. Sarah and her family are in the kitchen.

Kim: Where's my knife? It's your turn to set the table today, Sarah.
Sarah: My turn?
Kim: Yes, I haven't got a knife.
Sarah: It's always my turn. It's your turn today.
Kim: No, it isn't!
Mr D: Girls. Please! I've got the knives.
Kim: Thanks, Dad.
Mrs D: Where's your lunchbox, Kim? It isn't on the shelf.
Kim: I'm not sure. In my bag?
Mrs D: And where's your bag?
Kim: Over there, on the chair.
Sarah: You're so lazy, Kim.
Mrs D: Is this your lunchbox?
Kim: No, that's Sarah's lunchbox, Mum.
Sarah: What! My lunchbox in Kim's bag?
Mr D: Please! Let's not fight about lunchboxes. Er – how's your new bike, Kim?
Kim: Great, but I need a lock for it.
Mr D: I'm sure Becky's parents have got locks.
Sarah: Oh, yes. And I need a new pump. Let's go to the Burtons' bike shop together.
Kim: Together?
Sarah: Yes.
Kim: No. You go alone.
Mr D: Children, please!

1 Make sentences

1. It's Friday morning
2. Sarah and Kim are
3. Kim's lunchbox isn't
4. Sarah's lunchbox is
5. Kim has got
6. Becky's parents have got
7. Sarah and Kim aren't

a) in the kitchen.
b) in Kim's bag.
c) at the Dixons' house.
d) a bike shop.
e) always good friends.
f) a new bike.
g) on the shelf.

2 Find the odd word out

1. knife, glass, fork, spoon
2. plate, bowl, saucer, bottle
3. desk, cup, table, chair
4. skateboard, bike, CD, tennis racket
5. books, magazines, clothes, posters
6. dog, animal, cat, horse
7. brother, mother, monster, sister
8. garden, garage, house, flat

23 3 Sound practice

[f]	My **f**avourite kni**f**e is on the shel**f**. **F**unny **f**amilies always **f**ight.
[v]	I've got fi**v**e kni**v**es, but they'**ve** got twel**v**e shel**v**es.
[æ]	Th**a**t m**a**n **a**nd his two bl**a**ck c**a**ts!
[e]	T**e**n t**e**rrible m**e**n and their b**e**st fri**e**nds.
[ɪ]	L**i**sten to the **E**nglish w**o**m**e**n and ch**i**ldren.

knife – knives
shelf – shelves
man – men
child – children
woman – women

Now make plural forms and put them in the right boxes.

cat, dog, house, comic, bed, book, room, pencil case, magazine, racket, horse, desk, skateboard, bike, CD, computer, shelf, lunchbox, knife, family

[s]	[z]	[ɪz]
cats	dogs	…

4 Word power

What can you see in the picture? Start like this:
I can see two knives, …

5 Write sentences

1. Becky has got a computer. It's on her desk.
   → Becky's computer is on her desk.
2. The Burtons have got a nice garden.
   → The Burtons' garden is nice.
3. Barker has got a bed. It's in the hall.
4. The Penroses have got a house. It's in Arndale Road.
5. David has got a football. It's in his room.
6. Simon hasn't got a very tidy room.
7. The Underdogs have got a great new CD.
8. The Dixons have got a house in Larwood Grove.
9. Mr Dixon has got a folder. It is on the table in the hall.
10. Sarah has got a sister. Her name is Kim.

6 Watch out: Burtons, Burton's or Burtons'?

Example: 1. The Burtons are the Penroses' neighbours.

1. The **(Burton)** are the **(Penrose)** neighbours.
2. The **(Burton)** **(children)** names are Becky and Simon.
3. Mr and Mrs **(Burton)** bike shop is in Mansfield Road.
4. The **(Dixon)** have got a cat. The **(cat)** name is Tabby.
5. David **(Penrose)** cousin is from Germany.
6. Becky **(Burton)** favourite animals are horses.
7. The **(Croft)** house is in Larwood Grove.

G17

24 The frog (I)

1. It's Sunday afternoon. Robert and Simon are on their bikes in Arnot Hill Park.

Robert: Look! A frog!
Simon: Where?
Robert: There. Under that big tree.
Simon: Oh, there. Hey, I've got an idea. Let's take it home.
Robert: Home? Why?
Simon: We can play a trick on Becky!

2. Later. Becky and Sarah are in Becky's room.

Becky: Let's listen to a CD.
Sarah: Good idea. What about your new Underdogs CD?
Becky: Yes. Why not. – Oh, no!
Sarah: What's the matter?
Becky: Er … Sarah.
Sarah: What?
Becky: There's a frog! It's on your leg!
Sarah: Aaah! Becky!
Becky: It's a nice frog. Come here, little frog.
Sarah: It's under the desk now!
Becky: Come here.
Sarah: Under the bed!
Becky: It's OK, little frog. I'm your friend.
Sarah: That's funny. How can a frog get into your room?
Becky: Mmm. Good question.

3. It's teatime. It's Simon's turn to set the table.

Becky: What about the plates, Simon?
Simon: Oh, yes. They're in the cupboard.
Mrs B: Becky, can you call Dad? Tea's ready.
Becky: OK, Mum.
Simon: Aaah! Mum! Mum!
Mrs B: What's the matter, Simon? Are you OK?
Simon: A frog! In the cupboard! Look!
Mrs B: That's silly.
Simon: Really! Look!
Mrs B: But how can a frog get into our cupboard? Becky?
Becky: Ask Simon.

1 True or false?

Correct the false sentences.

Picture 1 1. Robert and Simon are in Arndale Park.
Example: That's not true. They're in Arnot Hill Park.
2. The frog is under a desk.
3. Simon has got an idea.

Picture 2 4. Becky is in Sarah's room.
5. Becky has got an Underdogs CD.
6. The frog is on Becky's leg.

Picture 3 7. Simon must set the table.
8. The frog is under a chair.
9. This is Simon's trick.

2 Who or what is it?

1. It's under the desk! (line 22)
2. I'm your friend. (line 25)
3. They're in the cupboard. (line 32)
4. Are you OK? (line 36)

3 Odd word out

a) Find the odd word out.

1. nice – silly – leg – good
2. bed – plate – desk – cupboard
3. home – take – get – ask
4. in – look – on – under

b) Find more examples and play 'odd word out' with your neighbour.

9 4 Listening: The frog (II)

Listen to the CD. Say where the frog is now. How many frogs, trees and bikes are there in the story?

27 5 A song: One, two, three, four, five

Listen and sing.

One, two, three, four, five,
Once I caught a fish alive[1].
Six, seven, eight, nine, ten,
Then I let it go again[2].

Why did you let it go?[3]
Because it bit my finger so[4].
Which finger did it bite?[5]
This little finger on my right!

Words: Traditional

[1]Einmal fing ich einen Fisch • [2]Dann ließ ich ihn wieder schwimmen • [3]Warum hast du ihn wieder schwimmen lassen? • [4]Weil er mich in den Finger gebissen hat. • [5]In welchen Finger ... ?

1 *Has got* or *have got*?

Ask and answer questions.

1. Have the Burtons got a house in London?
   – No, they haven't. They've got a house in Nottingham.
2. ... the Dixons ... a house in the city centre? – ...
3. ... David ... a cousin? – ...
4. ... the Burtons ... a dog? – ...
5. ... Simon ... animal posters in his room? – ...
6. ... Becky ... a sister? – ...
7. ... the Dixons ... a bike shop? – ...
8. ... Kim ... a new bike? – ...
9. ... Becky's parents ... locks? – ...
10. ... your teacher ... a bike? – ...

has got
have got

2 *a* or *an*?

1. *Sarah:* Have you got ... answer for this? ... green animal with long legs.
   Becky: ... animal? Well, it must be ... frog.
2. *Robert:* I've got ... idea. Let's listen to ... song.
   Simon: Oh yes, that's ... good idea!
3. *Kim:* I've got ... new bike. It's great!
   Sarah: I've got ... old bike. That's not fair!
4. *Mr Dixon:* There's ... empty glass on the table. It must be Kim's.
5. *Simon:* This is ... easy exercise.

a
an

3 Watch out!

a) What are the long forms?

1. This boy's Simon Burton. He's 10 years old.
2. He's got a sister. Her name's Becky.
3. She's got a computer in her room.
4. Simon's got a new skateboard.
5. Look who's here. It's Robert.
6. Hi, Robert. I've got two new football posters. – They're great.
7. Let's see what you've got there. – It's a new CD.
8. Let's go to Becky's room. She's got a stereo. – That's a good idea.
9. But Sarah's in Becky's room. They're busy.
10. The boys can't listen to the CD. It isn't fair.

b) *It's* or *its*?

1. This is the frog from the park.
2. ... nice and green.
3. ... got big eyes.
4. ... friends are in the park, too.
5. The frog is under ... favourite tree again.
6. ... good to be home again.

4 Word power

What can you find in the word snake?
Write the words in your exercise book.
Mark the plural forms.

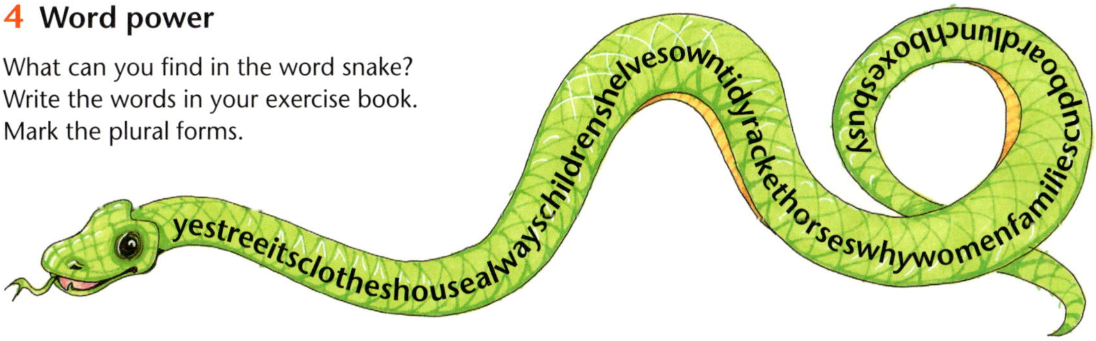

5 Write new sentences

1. *Becky:* Simon's got a new skateboard. ➜ Simon's skateboard is new.
2. *Kim:* My sister's got silly friends.
3. *Simon:* My sister's got terrible animal posters.
4. *Becky:* My parents have got great bikes.
5. *Sarah:* Kim's got a nice new bike.
6. *Mrs Dixon:* Our children haven't got tidy rooms.
7. *Mr Burton:* That child hasn't got a green bike.
8. *Becky:* Simon's got silly ideas.
9. *Frog:* The Burtons have got a cupboard. It's very big.

6 Word power: These words go together

1. boy – **girl,** false – ___, black – ___, new – ___, man – ___, open – ___, question – ___, together – ___
2. he – **his,** you – ___, I – ___, we – ___, they – ___, she – ___
3. knife – **fork,** cup – ___, table – ___
4. pictures – **look at,** CDs – ___, game – ___, table – ___, question – ___, trick – ___
5. room – **in,** shelf – ___, school – ___, bike – ___, bag – ___, Larwood Grove – ___, wall – ___

7 Put in: *can, can't,* or *must*

1. Can you play tennis? – No, I …
2. I … get a lock for my bike. But I … go to the bike shop today. … you go for me? – No, I … go today. I'm busy.
3. You … listen to this new CD! It's great. – OK, we … listen to it in my room.
4. … you write a story? – Yes, I …
5. Let's listen to the song again. You … sing along, OK? – Oh yes, that's a good idea.
6. Have you got a question? You … ask your teacher. She's really nice.
7. We … go home now. We're late already.

8 My family

Write about your family and your home.

parents? sister? house?

dog? garden?

Let's start – Unit 1

1 The Burtons

I • you • he • she • it • we • they •
my • your • his • her • its • our • their

What's missing?

1. *Simon:* Hey! ___ can't find ___ new CD! Have ___ got ___, Becky?
2. *Mrs Burton:* Where's Becky? It's ___ turn to set the table today.
   Mr Burton: ___'s in ___ room with Sarah. ___'re busy with ___ homework.
3. *Simon:* ___ like this little frog! ___ legs are really funny – ___'re so green.
4. *Becky:* Where's ___ bowl, Barker? Oh, ___ can see ___ now – ___'s over there!
5. *Simon:* Hey, David, let's ask Becky. Maybe ___ can listen to that new CD on ___ stereo.
6. *Mrs Burton:* Is Simon here, Becky? ___ isn't in ___ room.
   Becky: No, ___'s at Robert's house.
7. *Becky:* Look, Robert. This is ___ shop.
   Robert: What? Have ___ got a bike shop? Brilliant! ___ need a new lock for ___ bike.
   Have ___ got locks?
   Becky: Silly question! In ___ shop ___'ve got everything!

2 Who am I?

Now you are Becky, Sarah, Kim, David, Robert, Simon, Mark or Jenny. Play the game in pairs.

Are you **Have you got**	ten / eleven / twelve a girl / boy from London / Nottingham / … at Haywood School a house in … a dog / … a sister / a brother / …	?	Yes, I am. No, I'm not. Yes, I have. No, I haven't.

Example:

Who am I? → Are you a girl? → No, I'm not. → So, you're a boy. Have you got a little brother?
→ Yes, I have. → Oh, are you David? → Yes, I am!

3 Two rooms

Talk about the two rooms.
Examples: There's one window in Sarah's room. But there are two windows in Kim's room.
There are clothes on the floor in Sarah's room, and there are clothes on her bed.

Sarah's room

Kim's room

4 The new CD

Sarah is in Becky's room. What's missing?

Becky: I've got ___ great new CD, Sarah! It's ___ the Underdogs!
Sarah: Brilliant! Let's listen ___ it!
Becky: ___ dear! Where ___ it?
Sarah: ___ idea. Oh – is it ___ CD here ___ the shelf?
Becky: No, ___'s ___ old CD! ___ CDs over there ___ the right ___ old.
Sarah: Maybe it's under ___ books here. – No!
Becky: Hey! I' ___ got ___ idea. Maybe Simon ___ got it!
Sarah: Let's look in ___ room. Come on!
Becky: Yes, look! ___'s my CD – on ___ bed! Brothers ___ terrible.
Sarah: And look – next to ___ comics over there! Your ___ racket!

5 Watch out here!

Write the sentences in your exercise book. Put in the right forms:

-s -'s, -s' | **he's his** | **you're your** | **it's its** | **their they're there**

1. The ___ **(Burton)** house is in Sherwood, in Arndale Road. The ___ **(Dixon)** have got a house in Sherwood, too. But ___ house is in Larwood Grove.
2. Come on, Kim! ___ late for school. And what about ___ lunchbox?
3. Is that ___ **(David Penrose)** little brother? – Yes, it is. ___ name is Mark, and ___ four.
4. Are the ___ **(Dixon)** the ___ **(Penrose)** neighbours? – No, the ___ **(Burton)** and the ___ **(Penrose)** are neighbours. The ___ **(Dixon)** house isn't in Arndale Road.
5. Is this ___ CD, Sarah? Please put it in ___ box.
6. Where are the ___ **(children)** bedrooms? – ___ over ___.

6 Breakfast at the Penroses' house

Write the exercise in your exercise book.

It's breakfast time at the Penroses' . Mark is next to David. David is on his father's . Mrs Penrose is next to Mr Penrose. Everything is on the  for breakfast.

There are ,  and .

They've got cornflakes in their 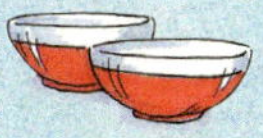. There are two 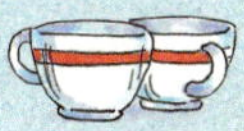 and 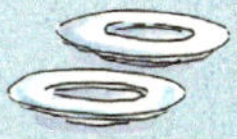 on the table for the  and three  for the .

There's a 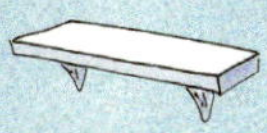 in the . David's 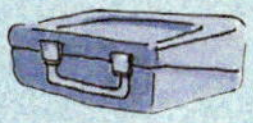 is on it.

unit 2 intro In town

1 Pictures of Nottingham

Listen and match texts A–D with the pictures.

1

2

3

4

A This is the Victoria Shopping Centre. It has got clothes shops, music shops, bookshops, supermarkets ... You can spend lots of money here!

B You can get from place to place by bus. A Day Rider ticket is for all buses in the city for one day.

C This is Old Market Square in Nottingham city centre. There are always lots of people here, but no cars.

D The Robin Hood statue is in front of the castle.

2 A poem: Let's go into Nottingham

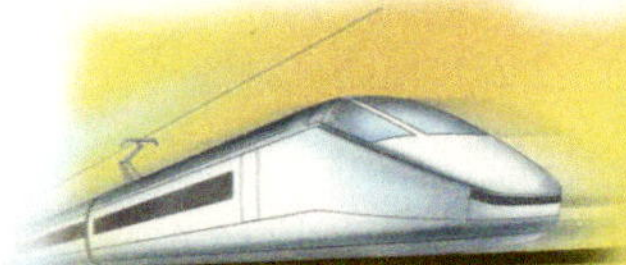

Let's go into Nottingham.
Can we go by train?
Or has it got an airport
So we can go by plane?

Oh no, let's take a taxi.
That's the thing for us!
But what about the money?
OK, let's go by bus.

3 Can you tell me the way, please?

30 a) Read the dialogues and make a list of phrases.

Excuse me. Can you tell me the way to the City Information Centre, please?

Yes, of course. Go down Long Row into Smithy Row. The Information Centre is on the right.

Excuse me. Can you tell me where I can find a supermarket, please?

Yes, there's a supermarket not far from here. Go down Long Row and turn left into King Street. It's on the left.

b) You're in Old Market Square. Find it on the map. Then make dialogues with your partner. Start with: Excuse me. Can you tell me the way to ...?

1. ... the Victoria Shopping Centre?
2. ... the cinema in Mount Street?
3. ... St Peter's Church?
4. ... the castle?

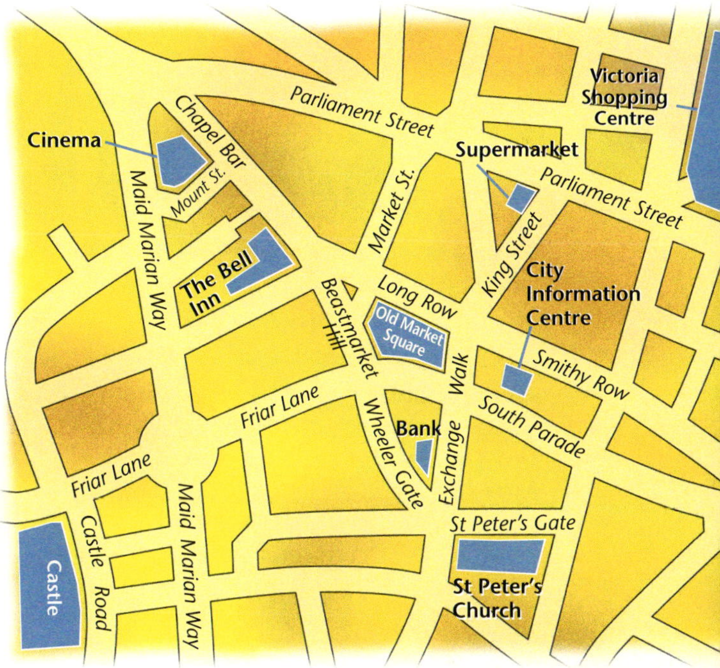

4 Listening: Word groups

10 Listen to these words and put them in the right lists.

people	places	things
...	...	...

5 Your town

a) Talk about your city, town or village.
Examples:

We've got a nice market square with lots of old houses.

There are three cinemas in our town.

We haven't got a castle, but we've got a big church in our town centre.

b) Make a poster about your town. Find pictures for it and write about them.

32 A Shopping

Becky and Sarah are at Martins Media, a big shop in Nottingham. They are spending their pocket money. Sarah is buying a book and Becky is looking at videos.
A young man is playing a guitar, but the people in the shop aren't listening. Two boys are watching a cartoon on a big TV. They are laughing.

Sarah: Let's go, Becky. Kim's waiting outside.
Becky: Just a minute, Sarah.
Sarah: What are you doing? Are you buying that video?
Becky: No, I'm not. Of course I'm not buying it – I'm just reading about it! OK. I'm ready now. We can go.

1 What are they doing?

Sarah • Becky • Becky and Sarah • Kim • The young man • The two boys	is • are	looking at videos. • playing a guitar. • laughing at a cartoon. • waiting outside. • buying a book. • spending their pocket money.

2 Is Sarah buying a video?

Ask and answer questions.

1. Sarah • buy a video? (**Is** Sarah **buying** a video? – **No, she isn't.** She's buying a book.)
2. Becky • look at videos? (Is Becky looking at videos? – **Yes, she is.**)
3. The boys • play the guitar? (**Are** the boys **playing** the guitar? – **No, they aren't.** They're …)
4. The young man • laugh at a cartoon?
5. Kim • wait outside?
6. Becky and Sarah • spend their pocket money?
7. The boys • read a book?
8. Becky • watch a video?

3 Listening: Who is doing what?

Listen and write down what the people are doing.

1. Becky and Simon
2. David and Jenny
3. David
4. Mr Burton
5. Robert and David
6. Mrs Burton

4 What is different?

Work with a partner. Partner A: Look at picture A. Partner B: Look at picture B.
Don't look at your neighbour's picture! Five things are different.
Talk about your pictures and say what the five things are.

Example: "A boy is reading a book. What about in your picture?"
"No, in my picture a ... is reading a book."
Or: "A ... is ... in my picture, too."

A

B

5 Word power: Make new words

Make words.
Example: **bedroom**

bed • cup • lunch • break • play • super • home • book • bath • black • birth • skate • class • foot

+

shop • fast • work • ground • day • ball • box • room • board • market

33 B Can you fetch us, Mum?

This is Sarah, Mum. Can you hear me? (...)
What? Sorry, I can't hear you. Er, Mum – can you fetch us in the car, please? – Becky and me. (...)
We're in Market Street. (...)
What are we doing here? No, we're not sitting in a café! Please, Mum. It's raining and we're getting wet! (...)
No, Kim's not with us. No idea where she is. She's got our bus tickets. (...)
I can't call her, Mum. Her mobile is engaged all the time. I'm sure she's phoning her boyfriend.
Oh, please, Mum. We've got lots of things and we can't carry them all. (...)
What about Dad? Can't you ask him? (...)
Writing e-mails? Can't he do it later? (...)
No? Oh, wait a minute – the rain is stopping now. Hey! The sun is coming out again. Oh, and here's Kim! My favourite sister!

Kim: Oh, yes?
Sarah: It's OK, Mum. We can take the bus. Bye for now.

1 Sarah and her mother

What are Mrs Dixon's questions and answers?

2 What are they doing?

Put in the right verb forms.

grammar
sit → sitting
phone → phoning

1. Becky and Sarah **(stand)** outside a shop.
2. It **(rain)** and they **(get)** wet.
3. They **(not sit)** in a café.
4. Sarah **(phone)** her mother.
5. She **(not write)** a text.
6. Ah! The rain **(stop)** now.
7. And the sun **(come out)** again.
8. The girls **(go)** home by bus.

3 No, sorry

Make dialogues with a partner.
Example: Can't Dad fetch us? **he • write • e-mails** – No, sorry. He's writing e-mails.

1. Hey, you two. Let's go to a café. **we • go • home now**
2. Dad, can you look at my bike? **I • get • tea ready**
3. Can Simon and Becky come to Arnot Hill Park with us? **they • do • their homework**
4. Where's Kim? Can I talk to her? **she • talk • on the telephone**
5. Can Robert come to the cinema with us? **he • play • tennis with David**
6. Let's go into the city centre, Jenny. **I • ? • ?**
7. Can't we go home now? **I • ? • ?**
8. Let's do our homework together. **I • ? • ?**

4 Put in the right words: *me, you, him, her, it, us, you, them*

1. I like these two videos, but I can't buy ____ – I haven't got the money.
2. Hey, there's a cartoon on TV. Let's watch ____ together.
3. Becky and I are getting wet. Please come and fetch ____ in the car!
4. I've got no idea where Kim is. I can't see ____ here.
5. Can you tell ____ the way to the cinema? I'm new here.
6. Sorry, can you say that again, please? I can't hear ____.
7. Look, there's Robert! – Oh, yes. I can see ____.
8. Hey, you boys. Can I play football with ____?

5 Make sentences

1. me • Can • the castle? • tell • you • the way • to → Can you tell me the way to the castle?
2. ask • us, • so we • with • her. • Kim's not • can't
3. lots of • They've • them • things • got • and • all. • they • can't carry
4. this video • and • Let's buy • with him. • watch it • for Dad
5. from Germany, • so she • you • Jenny's • with • can help • German homework. • your

6 Text puzzles

Kim's texts to her boyfriend Lewis (and his answers) are funny.

a) Read them. (What letters are missing?)

H, Lws,
m n th cty cntr. m wtng fr my slly sstr nd hr frnd. cnt fnd thm. v gt thr bs tckts. Nw ts strtng t rn. m gttng wt! Cn y ftch m n th cr?
S y ltr,
Km

Hi, Lewis, I'm in the city centre. I'm waiting …

Srry, Km. Mms gt th cr.
Wht bt yr sstr nd hr frnd?
S y tmrrw,
Lws

b) Write them out in good English.

7 Word power

Play this game with your partner.

Find a word and write it down. (No *ing*-forms, no plurals!) Your partner must start with the last letter and make a new word. Then it's your turn again.

You can play this game in class, too.

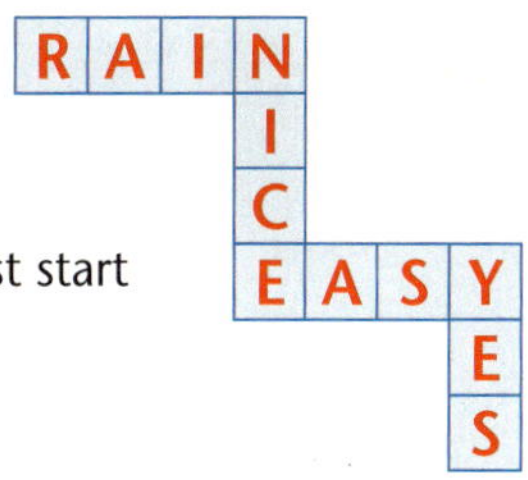

34 8 Sound practice

[ʊ]	[u:]	[ʊ] + [u:]
That's‿a good book.	She's‿in my tutor group.	Good‿afternoon.
Look‿at my football!	She's‿at school this‿afternoon.	Let's play football‿at school.
Kim's from Sherwood.	This‿is for you, too.	That woman has got two dogs.

The race

Driver: Four Day Rider tickets. Here you are, young man.
David: Thank you.

It is a sunny Sunday afternoon and David, Jenny, Sarah and Robert are getting on the bus in Sherwood. David has got money from his parents for their afternoon in Nottingham, so he can buy the tickets.

Sarah: We can use those tickets again. Don't lose them, David.
David: Of course not. I'm not stupid! I've got them in my pocket.

Twenty minutes later, the bus is standing in front of the Victoria Shopping Centre in Nottingham.

Sarah: Let's get off here.
Robert: OK. Let's go into Martins Media. We can look at the CDs.
Jenny: Oh, yes. Good idea.

■ But it's very busy in Martins Media. Lots of other people are looking at CDs.

Sarah: This is terrible. Let's go out again.
David: OK. Let's go to the castle gardens.
Jenny: Is it far?
Robert: Yes, but we can go by bus. We've got Day Rider tickets.
David: Come on, Robert. It isn't far. We can walk from here.
Sarah: OK, then. Let's have a race – from here to the Robin Hood statue! David and Jenny can walk. And we can go by bus, Robert.
Robert: What – go by bus with you? – Oh, OK!

So the race is on. David and Jenny are already running down King Street towards Old Market Square.

David: Ha, we can't lose, Jenny. It's Sunday. You can wait a long time for a bus today!
Jenny: Are you sure?
David: Of course I am. There's lots of time. Not so fast.

■ At the Victoria Shopping Centre, Robert and Sarah are waiting for their bus.

Robert: Which is our bus, Sarah?
Sarah: The 12. There's one in three minutes.
Robert: Ha! Easy! We can't lose. *(singing)* We are the champions, my friend ...

Now David and Jenny are at Old Market Square, but the sun isn't shining. There's a big black cloud in the sky.

David: Down Friar Lane now, Jenny.
Jenny: It's starting to rain, David.
David: Oh, no! Let's run again. Oops! Sorry!
Woman: Hey! Look where you're going!

A bus is stopping in front of the Victoria Shopping Centre.

Sarah: Number 12. This is our bus, Robert.
Robert: Great. And it's raining, too. Poor old David and Jenny, ha, ha.
Sarah: Er, wait a minute ...

■ David and Jenny aren't far from the castle now. But they can see a number 12 bus and it is going past them.

Jenny: Oh, no. That's their bus.
David: Yes, and it's stopping at the castle gardens. Oh, dear. We can't win the race now.
Jenny: Hey, but where are Robert and Sarah? I can't see them.

Ten minutes later, two very wet people are running towards the castle gardens.

Jenny: Look, David. It's Sarah and Robert.
David: Oh, yes. ... Hi, you two. Why aren't you on a bus?
Sarah: Good question, David. The answer is in your pocket!
David: Huh?

1 The story

Look at the pictures. Say what you can see in them.

2 Write two short dialogues

Look at lines 61 and 77. Go on with the dialogues.

1. *Sarah:* Er, wait a minute ...
   Robert: ...

2. *David:* Huh ?
   Sarah: ...

3 Find the odd word out

Find the odd word out in each group and put it in the right group.

1.	2.	3.	4.
car	walk	sun	street
bus	run	rain	cinema
train	plane	sky	go
shine	stop	castle	square
taxi	turn	cloud	church

4 Just for fun

39 5 A song: Singing in the rain

I'm singing in the **rain**,
Just singing in the rain.
What a **glorious** feeling[1],
I'm **happy**[2] again.
I'm laughing at **clouds**
So **dark** up above[3].
The **sun**'s in my **heart**[4]
And I'm ready for **love**[5].

Let the **stormy**[6] clouds **chase**[7]
Everyone[8] from the place.
Come on, with the rain,
I've a **smile**[9] on my face[10].
I'll[11] walk down the lane
With a happy refrain[12].
Just singing,
Singing in the rain.
Dancing[13] in the rain …

Words: Arthur Freed

[1] glorious feeling [ˌglɔ:riəs 'fi:lɪŋ] – grandioses Gefühl • [2] ['hæpi] – glücklich, fröhlich • [3] [ə'bʌv] – oben • [4] [hɑ:t] – Herz • [5] [lʌv] – Liebe • [6] ['stɔ:mi] – stürmisch • [7] [tʃeɪs] – jagen • [8] ['evriwʌn] – jeden • [9] [smaɪl] – Lächeln • [10] [feɪs] – Gesicht • [11] I'll [aɪl] – Ich werde • [12] [rɪ'freɪn] – Refrain • [13] [dɑ:nts] – tanzen

a) Listen to the song and read the text.

b) Make two lists with the **blue** words and phrases from the song.

c) Now listen again and sing along.

☺	☹
I'm singing	rain
…	…

1 Talk about the pictures

2 Object pronouns

Put in: ***me, you, him, her, it, us*** or ***them***

1. *Mr Penrose:* Mark can't find his pencils. Can you see …, David?
2. *David:* Jenny hasn't got the phone number for Germany. Can you tell … the number, please, Mum?
3. *Robert:* I can't do this German exercise. Jenny, can you do … with …?
4. *Sarah:* Can I play football with …, Robert?
5. *Mark:* Mum, where are my pencils?
   Mrs Penrose: Oh, David. They're on that shelf. Can you get … for …, please?
6. *Becky:* Sarah and I are going out with Barker. Who's coming with …?

3 Mixed bag: Who's that girl?

What words are missing?

It's a sunny Friday afternoon in the city [1], and there are [2] people in the streets. David and Robert are on their skates. They're [3] for Simon. He's in the music [4]. Robert is sitting outside. David is going [5] the street on his skates. What is Simon [6]? He's [7] a CD. Robert can see [8], but he can't go in on his skates. A [9] is stopping in [10] of the shop. A tall blonde [11] is [12] off. Now she's [13] into the shop.
"Wow! David! Can you see [14]?"
David is [15] to the shop window, too.
"Look. She's [16] to Simon. Is she his friend?"
David has got no [17].

Simon and the girl are spending a long [18] in the shop. There are lots of CDs, and the two are [19] at [20] all. They're talking and laughing.
"Let's have a [21], Robert. The sun is [22], and we can't sit here [23] the time and wait [24] Simon."
"Wait, David. I've got an idea. Let's call [25] on your [26]."
"OK. – Simon! We can't wait for [27] all day!"
"Sorry, you two. Just a [28]."
Simon is [29] out of the shop and taking his bike.
"And who's that girl?"
Simon is [30] to laugh.
"No idea. But she's [31] nice."

Focus on numbers

1 How many animals?

How many animals can you see in the big picture?

Example: "I can see three cats." – "No, that's wrong. There are four cats in the picture."

2 Read the numbers

13 thirteen	16 sixteen	19 nineteen	30 thirty	43 forty-three	70 seventy
14 fourteen	17 seventeen	20 twenty	32 thirty-two	50 fifty	80 eighty
15 fifteen	18 eighteen	21 twenty-one	40 forty	60 sixty	90 ninety

100 a / one hundred	1000 a / one thousand
101 a hundred and one	2,345 two thousand three hundred and forty-five
200 two hundred	1,000,000 a / one million

3 Can you read these numbers?

79 38 116 815

53 419 6,289

756 1,013 785

4 A numbers game

Take a number from each box. Work with your partner.

29 38 41 49 53 85 256 119 165 202	+ −	6 3 12 18 25 13 21 8 17 9

What's 29 plus 6?

That's easy! 29 plus 6 is 35.

What's 41 minus 12?

Oh dear! Let's see, er, 41 minus 12 is …

5 British money

There are 100 pence (p) in a pound (£).

1p	one p (= penny)	£2.80	?
25p	twenty-five p (= pence)	69p	?
£1	a / one pound	40p	?
£1.50	one (pound) fifty	£9.99	?
£2	two pounds	£17.85	?
£3.70	three (pounds) seventy	£5.68	?

40

6 How much are these clothes?

1. *Shop assistant:* Can I help you?
Customer: Hello. I need a pair of blue jeans, size 32 / 30. How much are they?
Shop assistant: They're £24.99.
Customer: Thank you. Can I try them on?
Shop assistant: Of course. Over there, sir.

2. *Customer:* I need a Haywood School uniform. How much is it?
Shop assistant: With skirt or trousers, madam?
Customer: With trousers, please.
Shop assistant: It's a special offer. It's only £44.50.
Customer: Good. I need size 9, please.

Make more little dialogues with your partner.

17

7 Listening: In the shop

Listen and say …
1. … what Kim, Robert and Mr Penrose are buying.
2. … how much the things are.

unit 3 intro

Free time

42

It's Monday evening, 6 o'clock. David is playing the guitar.

It's Tuesday, 4 o'clock, after school. Becky is going for a walk with Barker.

It's Wednesday afternoon. Robert is riding his bike in the park.

Sarah is in the playground. It's Thursday. She's playing football with the others.

Jenny is busy. The Penroses are having dinner, but she's writing a dialogue for the school theatre group.

1 Word power

Make sentences with these words. Sometimes you must put in more words.
Example: We're going **for a** walk.

I • We • You • They • Sarah • Becky • David • Jenny • Robert	play • go • have • ride • do	walk • guitar • breakfast • homework • bike • swimming pool • football • cinema • tennis • horse • bus • dinner • friend's house

43 2 A song: I met him on a Sunday

I met[1] him on a Sunday
And I missed[2] him on Monday.
Well, I phoned[3] him on a Tuesday.
Well, I dated[4] him on Wednesday.
And I kissed[5] him on Thursday
And he didn't come[6] Friday.
When[7] he showed up[8] Saturday,
I said[9] "Bye bye, baby."

[1][met] traf
[2][mɪst] vermisste
[3][fəʊnd] rief … an
[4]['deɪtɪd] ging aus mit
[5][kɪst] küsste
[6][dɪdnt 'kʌm] kam nicht
[7][wen] als
[8][ʃəʊd‿'ʌp] auftauchte
[9][sed] sagte

Words: Owens, Harris, Lee, Coley

3 Your week

Talk about your week.
Say what days are good or bad for you.

Example: Thursday is great / bad / my favourite day.

I like Mondays because there's … / because I can / must / have …

4 Weekend plans

Becky: Let's go to the zoo this weekend.
Jenny: Good idea. What about Sunday? When is it open?
Becky: It's open from 9 o'clock to 6.30 in the evening.
Sarah: Where can we meet? And when?
Jenny: We're usually at the swimming pool on Sunday morning. Can we go in the afternoon?
Becky: Let's meet at Sarah's house at half past twelve on Sunday. Is that OK?
Sarah: That's early. Our lunch is at quarter past twelve.
Jenny: Yes, and our lunch is at quarter to one on Sunday. What about half past one?
Becky: OK. That's fine.

Answer the questions.

1. When is the zoo open on Fridays?
2. When is the swimming pool open on Saturdays?
3. When are the Penroses usually at the swimming pool?
4. What time is lunch at the Dixons' house?
5. What time is Sunday lunch at the Penroses' house?

What time is it?

It's twelve o'clock.
It's half past twelve. (= twelve thirty)
It's quarter past twelve. (= twelve fifteen)
It's quarter to one. (= twelve forty-five)

5 What's the time?

a) Say what time it is.

1. **past**
   6.05: "It's five past six."
   8.22, 11.10, 2.28, 10.15, 7.26, 1.07
2. **to**
   7.36: "It's twenty-four minutes to eight."
   4.53, 6.40, 9.39, 12.55, 1.47, 12.36
3. **past or to?**
   4.05, 6.22, 11.35, 2.10, 3.29, 11.59

b) You can say the time like this, too:

1. 3.09: "It's three – oh – nine."
2. 10.15: "It's ten fifteen."
3. 5.30: "It's …"
4. 6.11: …
5. 7.03: …
6. 12.39: …
7. 4.48: …
8. 11.27: …
9. 10.45: …

45 A Jenny's day

Dear Katharina,

Thanks for your e-mail. This time I'm writing in English – but I'm sure you can read it. How are you? Is school really boring without me? It's different here. For example, we wear school uniform (!) and we have lunch at school. Usually school is OK, but sometimes it's boring, too.

The good thing is: We start at 8.45 every day, so I never get up before 8 o'clock in the morning. David and I always walk to school together after breakfast. Assembly is at 8.45, and all the teachers and pupils are there. Lessons start at 9.05 and finish at half past three. My favourite subject is English. (I hate Maths.)

After school we usually go home and do our homework, but on Tuesdays I play tennis and on Thursdays I have theatre group. Here in England you do these things at school in the afternoon. In the evening I usually play with David and Mark or we go and see Sarah, Becky or Robert. We go to bed at 9.30.

■ Weekends are different: On Saturday I often go to town with Uncle Colin. I help him with the shopping and we usually have an ice cream. On Saturday afternoon I meet my friends, and we go for a walk with Barker or ride our bikes. We can watch TV until 10 o'clock on Saturday. Aunt Pat and Uncle Colin sometimes go out and we can go to bed later!

Sunday mornings are nice – we can stay in bed! But David and I sometimes get up early and make breakfast for Aunt Pat and Uncle Colin. They love that!

That's all for now. I must finish my Maths homework. :(

Love,

Jenny

1 Look at the text

Read Jenny's e-mail to her friend Katharina in Munich.

a) Which words and phrases from the text go together with:

1. school? | 2. free time? | 3. time?

b) When? Put time phrases in the right places.
Example: I get up at 8 o'clock **in the morning.**

1. I get up at 8 o'clock.
2. We walk to school.
3. We start school.
4. We go home and do our homework.
5. I play tennis.
6. I have theatre group.
7. You do lots of things at school.
8. I play with David and Mark.
9. We go to bed.
10. I meet my friends.
11. We watch TV.
12. We stay in bed.

c) Your turn. Talk about your day. Use phrases like these:

I always get up at … | I go to school … | Every day … | After school … | At the weekend I …

2 Their free time

Say what they do in their free time. Start like this: 1. On Monday Robert and his mum go … .

Monday	Tuesday	Wednesday	Thursday	Friday
Robert • his mum	Jenny • Mark	Becky • Sarah	Sarah • the boys	Robert • Simon

20 3 Listening: Monny's week

Monday: guitar lesson
Tuesday: …
… …

4 Put in the adverbs

1. I have an ice cream in town. **(often)**
2. We wear school uniform. **(always)**
3. I meet my friends at the weekend. **(usually)**
4. They are boring. **(never)**
5. They go to the cinema. **(sometimes)**
6. We have breakfast early. **(always)**
7. We go to school on Sundays. **(never)**
8. I help my mum/dad in the house. **(?)**

5 Make correct sentences

1. I • play • every Saturday • tennis
2. in the evening • our homework • do • we
3. often • listen • they • to music
4. meet • we • every morning • at Assembly
5. to the city centre • go • I • by bus • always
6. have • sometimes • I • lunch • in the park
7. never • go • my parents • to the cinema
8. help • I • my mum • usually • in the shop

6 Your turn: Say when or how often …

1. … you play football.
2. … you stay in bed until 10 o'clock.
3. … you do your homework in the kitchen.
4. … you go to the cinema.
5. … you see your best friend.
6. … you watch TV after 9 o'clock.
7. … you go for a walk.
8. … you read a book.

7 Some days are different

Say why. Example: I **always go** to bed at 9 o'clock. But **today I'm watching** TV.

1. I usually … **(go)** to school by bus. But today I … **(walk)**.
2. I usually … **(play)** football in the afternoon, but today I … **(play)** tennis.
3. They often … **(lose)** a match. But look! Today they … **(win)**.
4. Today we … **(do)** our homework in the kitchen. We usually … **(do)** it in our rooms.
5. You always … **(go)** shopping on Sundays, but today you … **(not go)** shopping. Why not?
6. We … **(go)** for a walk now, but usually we … **(stay)** at home in the evening.

G22, 23

47 B In the park

It's Saturday afternoon and Robert has got a new scooter. He shows it to David. "This goes really fast," he says. Then David fetches his skates and they go up to the park. Robert does tricks on his new scooter. "Watch me," he says and starts to ride down the hill. He takes his right hand and right foot off the scooter, turns towards David and waves with his free hand and leg. "Yahoo!" he cries. Then things happen very fast. Suddenly something small and grey comes out of the trees and runs right in front of Robert. And something big and yellow chases after it. "Watch out!" shouts David. But it's too late. Robert turns left. His scooter hits a stone and stops, and Robert flies into a big bush.

Now Becky and Sarah are there. "Oh Barker!" says Becky. "It's silly to chase rabbits! They're too fast for you." Robert comes out of the bush and picks up his scooter. He isn't hurt, but he is angry with Barker. "Stupid dog!" he shouts. "Stupid you!" says Sarah. "Why can't you look where you're going?"

1 Put the sentences together

1. Robert has got a new scooter. → c)
2. David fetches his skates.
3. Robert says, "Watch me."
4. He takes a hand and a foot off the scooter.
5. He waves with his free hand and leg.
6. Suddenly a rabbit runs in front of him.
7. Robert sees them too late – and turns left.
8. Robert is angry and shouts, "Stupid dog!"

a) Then Sarah says, "Stupid you!"
b) Then the two boys go to the park.
c) He shows it to David.
d) But he hits a stone and flies into a bush.
e) And a dog chases after the rabbit.
f) Then he shouts, "Yahoo!"
g) Then he starts to ride down the hill.
h) Then he turns towards David.

2 Look at these forms and find rules

to show	he / she / it shows	[z]
to run	he / she / it runs	
to hit	he / she / it hits	[s]
to take	he / she / it takes	
to fetch	he / she / it fetch**es**	[ɪz]
to rush	he / she / it rush**es**	

to **fly**	he / she / it **flies**	[flaɪz]
to **carry**	he / she / it **carries**	['kæriz]
to **play**	he / she / it **plays**	[pleɪz]
to **say**	he / she / it **says**	[sez]
to **go**	he / she / it **goes**	[gəʊz]
to **do**	he / she / it **does**	[dʌz]

3 What they often do

1. *David:* I like music. I often play the guitar in my free time. ➜ David **likes** music. He often ... in his free time.
2. *Jenny:* I sometimes phone my parents in Germany, but I usually write e-mails.
3. *Robert:* I help my mum a lot. I often fetch things for her or carry them in from the car.
4. *Becky:* I go out with Barker every day. We usually go for a long walk in the park.
5. *Sarah:* I do lots of sport. For example, I always play tennis with Becky on Saturdays.

4 Tell your partner

a) Look at A. Your partner looks at B. Talk about what the people often do on Saturdays.

Example:
A Robert rides his bike in the morning. What about the Penroses?
B They ... And in the afternoon?
A Robert ...

A	Robert	Mrs Dane	Becky & Simon	The Penroses
morning	ride his bike	?	play tennis	?
afternoon	play football	?	go for a walk	?
evening	watch a video	?	play games	?

B	Robert	Mrs Dane	Becky & Simon	The Penroses
morning	?	go shopping	?	work at home
afternoon	?	correct homework	?	go out in the car
evening	?	go out	?	watch TV

b) Tell your partner what **you** do on Saturdays.

5 Robert's Saturday

Put in the verbs: simple present or present progressive?

chase (2x) | get up (2x) | go | have (2x) | work | like | look (2x) | play | ride (2x) | shout | stay | watch

1. It's 10.30 on Saturday morning. Robert **is getting up**. He usually **gets up** at 9 o'clock.
2. Robert's mum usually ___ at home on Saturday, but today she ___.
3. Robert usually ___ his bike on Saturday morning, but this morning he ___ TV.
4. Now it's 12.30. He usually ___ lunch then, but today he ___ breakfast!
5. He usually ___ football on Saturday afternoon, but this afternoon he ___ his new scooter.
6. Now he ___ down a hill. Oh no, he ___ back at David! He usually ___ where he's going.
7. Watch out, Robert! Barker usually ___ footballs, but now he ___ a rabbit right in front of Robert's scooter.
8. "Stupid dog!" Robert usually ___ Barker, but today he ___ at him.

G22, 24, 25

48 Barker's story

Hello.
I'm Barker.
My people are the Burtons – Peggy and Arthur Burton and their children Becky and Simon. I look after the Burton family. That's my job.

Becky is my pet. Every morning at half past seven I wake her up and wash her face. Then she washes her face again and makes my breakfast.
After that she has her own breakfast (muesli – yuk! no thanks).
Then her brother Simon comes down for breakfast. He's usually late.

■ At twenty past eight Becky and Simon go off to school.
Then I take Peggy and Arthur to the bike shop so they can earn some money.
That's their job.
I help, of course. When people buy things, I'm nice to them.

On Saturdays I take Becky and Simon to the park. They often play football with their friends.
I teach them tricks. For example, when I bring a ball, they throw it for me. When I get their football, they chase me.
Sometimes they get lost in the park. Then they call my name and of course I find them at once.

I like to sit outside in our garden. Sometimes Tabby, the Dixons' cat, comes over the garden wall, but I always bark at her and then she runs away.

On Sundays I usually go out with my people in the car. There are always lots of cars on the road. Sometimes there are dogs in them, too. I bark at them and they bark at me, too. That's brilliant!

We often go out for picnics. I like picnics because there's no table and I can sit in the middle. Oops! Sometimes Simon puts his drink down next to me and it falls over. Silly boy!

In the evening my people often watch TV. Then we play a game. I sit in front of the TV and they throw shoes at me. I pick them up and take them into Becky's bedroom. I like shoes!

At nine o'clock Becky is tired and I take her to bed. She's nice to me, so she can always sleep in my bed.
I've got a very nice bed and I usually go to sleep at once because it's late – and because after my long day I'm dog-tired.

1 True or false?

Correct the false sentences. Example: 1. **That's wrong. Barker** looks after the Burton family.

1. Tabby looks after the Burton family.
2. Barker washes his face every morning.
3. Barker hates muesli.
4. Simon is never late for breakfast.
5. Becky has muesli for lunch.
6. Peggy and Arthur work in their own shop.
7. Tabby always chases Barker.
8. Barker often goes out for picnics with the Burtons.
9. The Burtons watch TV in the morning.
10. They often play a game with shoes.
11. Barker sleeps in Simon's bed.

2 How to write your own story

You can write your own story about a pet.

a) First look at these two texts and say what is different.

Text 1:	**Text 2:**
Robert gets up at quarter to eight every morning. He washes his face. He has breakfast. He goes to school. He can walk. It is not far away.	Robert gets up at quarter to eight every morning and washes his face. After that he has breakfast. Then he goes to school. He can walk because it is not far away.

b) There are more words in Text 2.
They make a text better because they connect sentences.
Make a list of these words: and, ...

c) Now collect ideas for your story. Make lists.

These questions can help you: Who? Where? When? What? Why?
For example, here are some ideas for a story about a cat. Its name is Tommy.

Who?	Where?	When?	What?
Tommy	house	in the morning	to have lunch
his family	garden	on Sundays	to sleep
other pets	car	never	to chase
...	...	after breakfast	friend
		...	funny
			nice
			angry
			...

d) Now write your story down. You can draw pictures for it, too. Look at Barker's story again and use the words from your lists.
You can start like this:

Hello.
I'm Tommy. I'm a black cat, and my people are the Mayers — Johannes and Elke and their children Michaela and Jan. Jan is my favourite pet. Every morning, when I wake him up, I ...

1 Word power: These words go together

1. morning – **evening**, after – …, to hate – …, always – …, early – …, with – …, to start – …, to go to bed – …, to go to sleep – …, to earn – …, to run away – …
2. What can you have? a drink, lunch, …
3. Collect 'fast' words: skates, …
4. Collect 'talking' words: to talk, to ask, …

2 Find the right verb forms

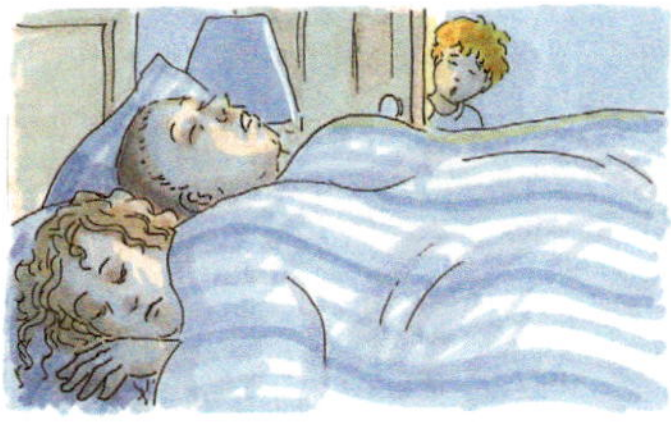

Mark … very early every morning. He … into Mr and Mrs Penrose's room.

At 8 o'clock Mr Penrose … breakfast. Mark … him. He … the table.

At 8.45 Mark … to kindergarten. His father … him there.

Kindergarten … at 12.30. Mr Penrose … Mark and after that they … lunch together. David … lunch at school.

When David and Jenny … home from school, Jenny … her homework and David … the guitar.

David … his homework later, and Jenny … with Mark. Mark … to bed at 6.30.

3 Stars

Name:	Rick Mansfield
How old?	21
From:	Liverpool
Group:	The Underdogs
Instrument:	guitar
Home:	house in London
Married?	No!
Children?	No!
Brothers / sisters?	No!
Favourite colour:	purple
☺:	girls, fast cars, music
☹:	stupid questions

a) Use this information from a magazine and write about Rick Mansfield of *The Underdogs.*

come from • play • have • live • like • hate

Example: Rick Mansfield is 21. He comes from … He …

21 **b)** Now copy the blue words on the left. Then listen to a radio programme about a pop star and write down the information about her.

1 A picnic in Thoresby Park

It is Sunday. The Burtons are at Thoresby Park in Sherwood Forest.

a) Say what is happening, and what they are all doing.

b) Now talk about the picture. Work in pairs.
Example: Is Mr Burton taking the picnic things out of the car?
– No, he isn't. Mrs Burton is doing that. Mr Burton is playing football with Simon.

2 What are they saying?

Finish what these people are saying.
Example: *Becky:* I can't come out on my bike with you now, Sarah. **(do • homework)**
I'm doing my homework.

1. *Mrs Penrose:* David isn't at home. **(go shopping • with • father)**
2. *Mr Dixon:* Sorry, Becky. Sarah and Kim aren't here. **(play • tennis • together)**
3. *Becky:* Oh dear, we can't play outside now! Look! **(rain)**
4. *Robert:* Look, here's our bus! **(come • now)**
5. *David:* Please don't talk to me now, Mark. **(read • book)**
6. *Simon:* Dad's in the kitchen with Mum. **(get • tea ready • together)**
7. *Kim:* Sarah's in the living room, Becky. **(watch • new video)**
8. *Jenny (on the telephone):* I'm with Mark just now. **(play • game • together)**

3 Every day

Write down what they do every day.

Example:
Every day Mr and Mrs Burton get up at …
They …
Every day Simon …

Mr and Mrs Burton	Simon
7.15	8.00
8.45	8.30
6.00	3.40
11.00	9.00

4 At the Penroses' house

1 play / often
2 make / usually
3 set / always
4 listen / sometimes
5 have / often

Say what they are doing – and what they often / sometimes / usually / always do.

Example: You can see Mark here / in this picture. He's playing with his cars.
– He often plays with his cars.

5 Sunday again

Put in the verbs: simple present or present progressive?

1. It's quarter past nine, and Becky ___. She usually ___ at half past seven, but on Sundays she always ___ in bed because there's no school, of course. (get up (2x) • stay)
2. Now it's ten o'clock, and she ___ Barker's breakfast. Her parents ___ breakfast ready for the family. On Sundays her father usually ___ the table. Simon isn't there – he always ___ down for breakfast very late. But wait a minute! Now he ___! (come (2x) • get • make • set)
3. The Burtons often ___ in the car on Sundays. Today they ___ to Sherwood Forest. Now they ___ in the car, and Barker ___ out of the window. He ___, of course! He always ___ when he ___ other dogs. (bark (2x) • go • see • go out • look • sit)
4. It's half past one now and the Burtons ___ their picnic. Barker ___ next to Mrs Burton because she ___ the picnic things out now! Barker ___ picnics! (get • have • love • sit)
5. Now it's eight o'clock in the evening, and the Burtons ___ TV. Barker usually ___ in front of the TV, of course! But now he ___ on the sofa next to Becky. On Sunday evenings he often ___ to sleep on the sofa – after his long day outside! (go • sit (2x) • watch)

unit 4 intro Happy birthday

1 Months and dates

1st	**first**
2nd	**second**
3rd	**third**
4th	fourth
5th	fifth
6th	sixth
7th	seventh
8th	eigh**th**
9th	nin**th**
10th	tenth
11th	eleventh
12th	twel**fth**
13th	thirteenth
14th	fourteenth

15th	fifteenth
16th	sixteenth
17th	seventeenth
18th	eighteenth
19th	nineteenth
20th	twent**ieth**
21st	twenty-**first**
22nd	twenty-**second**
23rd	twenty-**third**
…	
30th	thirt**ieth**
…	
100th	hundredth
…	

Listen to the Calendar Song and sing along. The words are easy!

2 David's birthday list

a) Look at David's birthday list and say the dates of all the birthdays.

Mum	18th January
Jenny	7th February
My birthday	11th May
Becky	24th June
Simon	22nd July
Mark	31st August
Dad	20th September
Sarah	3rd October
Robert	2nd December

Example: Jenny's birthday is on 7th February (say: **the** seventh **of** February).

b) Your turn: Now make a list of all the birthdays in your family and talk about them with your partner.

Example: When is your / your mum's birthday? – It's on …

3 An invitation card

Make an invitation card for your birthday.

G26, 27

4 Birthdays in Britain

In Britain you get lots of cards and presents from your family and other relatives on your birthday. You often have a party in the afternoon. You usually invite all your friends to your home, but sometimes you go to a restaurant or a cinema, or you go swimming or skating. There's lots of food at British birthday parties. There are sweet things like jelly, cakes, ice cream and trifle. And, of course, there's a big birthday cake with your name on it and one candle for each year. At the party you play games. Sometimes your friends give you 'the bumps'. It's an old tradition. They pick you up by your arms and legs and 'bump' you on the floor. One bump for each year. And one for luck. But don't worry – you don't touch the floor, so it doesn't hurt. When you write all your thank you letters to relatives, that hurts much more!

a) Something is wrong with these words. Can you correct them?

1. Here's an **vintoitain** to my **trypa**.
2. We never go to a **tnasuarter**.
3. I like lots of **yljel**, **flirte** and **eci marce**.
4. How many **ladnecs** are on the **kace**?
5. The **spumb** are an old **dottinair**.
6. Don't **rorwy**. They don't **thur** you.
7. This **drac** is from my **silverate** in London.
8. Thank you for the nice **darybith streepn**.

b) Look at the cartoon. Then think of a present from a relative and write your own thank you letter.

5 Make a trifle

You can find the new words in the ***Dictionary*** at the end of the book.

You need: • 1 sponge cake • 200 ml juice or syrup • 500 gm fresh fruit (peaches, raspberries, bananas) • 250 ml custard • 1 packet jelly (green, red or yellow – make a day before) • 250 ml cream.

Take a big glass bowl. Put the sponge cake in and soak it with the juice. Put a layer of fruit and then the custard on top. Now mix the jelly with a fork and put it on the custard. Whip the cream and decorate the jelly with it. – Yummy!

A Jenny's birthday

At the Penroses'. It's two weeks before Jenny's 12th birthday – time to make plans for the special day.

Mr P: Do you usually have a party on your birthday, Jenny?
Jenny: Yes, I do. In Germany we always do something nice on my birthday.
Mrs P: Right. Tell us about it. Do you invite friends to your home?
Jenny: Er – we're quite noisy, so Mum doesn't want to have us in the flat all the time.
Mrs P: Do you go out to a restaurant then?
Jenny: No, we don't. We sometimes go to the cinema. That's great! And after that we all come back to our flat.
Mark: Do your friends give you presents?
Jenny: Yes, they do, Mark. Just like here.
Mark: And do German children have a big birthday cake with candles on it?
Jenny: They usually do.
Mr P: Does your mum make the cake?
Jenny: No, she doesn't. Mum and Dad are too busy. They don't have much time, so Grandma always makes my birthday cake. She lives near us and she makes lovely cakes.
David: Well, this time you can have one of Dad's special birthday cakes!
Jenny: Yummy, yummy!

1 About your birthday

Work with a partner. Ask him/her these questions and write down the answers.
Example: "**Do** you like birthday parties?" → "Yes, I **do**." → Thomas likes birthday parties.
"**Do** you like jelly?" → "No, I **don't**." → Thomas **doesn't** like jelly.

1. Do you like birthday parties?
2. Do you write invitations?
3. Do you go out on your birthday?
4. Do you get presents from your parents?
5. Does your best friend come to your party?
6. Does your dad work on your birthday?
7. Does your mum make good cakes?
8. Does your teacher write you a card?

2 About Jenny

Write sentences about Jenny with the information from the box.
Example: Jenny comes from Germany. She **doesn't** come from England.

1. Jenny	• come from Germany ✓	• come from England ✗
2. She	• live with the Dixons ✗	• live with the Penroses ✓
3. She	• go to school in Munich ✗	• go to school in Nottingham ✓
4. She	• wear school uniform at school ✓	• wear jeans at school ✗
5. She	• write letters to Becky ✗	• write e-mails to Katharina ✓
6. Her mum	• come from Germany ✗	• come from England ✓
7. Her parents	• live in England ✗	• want to come over in May ✓
8. Her dad	• write her e-mails ✓	• call her on the phone ✗
9. Jenny	• love her parents ✓	• like birthdays without them ✗

3 Birthdays in Britain: some questions

Make questions and match them with the right answers.

1. do • British • birthday parties • have • children?
   ➜ Do British children have birthday parties?
2. friends • they • do • invite • to their home?
3. get • they • lots • do • of presents?
4. things • do • sweet • like • they?
5. on • their cakes • do • they • candles • have?
6. them • give • their friends • the bumps • do?
7. write • to their relatives • they • do • thank you letters?

a) Yes, they get cards and presents.
b) Yes, it's a really funny tradition.
c) Yes, that isn't so much fun.
d) Yes, they usually do.
e) Yes, one for each year.
f) Sometimes they do, but sometimes they go out.
g) Yes, they like jelly, trifle, cakes and ice cream.

4 Who does these things?

The names are wrong. Say who does what. Start like this:
1. That isn't Kim. She doesn't go for walks with Barker. It's … . 2. That isn't …

1. Kim? • go for walks

2. Robert? • play

3. Sarah? • read

4. Jenny's mum? • make

5. Jenny? • write texts

6. Mrs Dane? • teach

5 The 'Twenty Questions' game

a) One person thinks of a thing, and the others must guess what it is. They can only ask twenty questions, and the questions must always have 'yes' or 'no' for an answer. Play the game in class. You can ask questions like these:

- Is it big?
- Can you buy it?
- Have you got it with you?
- Do you need it every day?
- Does your teacher use it?

Remember the short answers to these questions:

grammar

Is it …? – Yes, it **is**. / No, it **isn't**.
Can you …? – Yes, you **can**. / No, you **can't**.
Have you got it …? – Yes, I **have**. / No, I **haven't**.
Do you …? – Yes, I **do**. / No, I **don't**.
Does she …? – Yes, she **does**. / No, she **doesn't**.

24 **b)** First listen to this example, then play the game in class.

G28, 29

B A party game

Mark: What are you doing, David?
David: I'm writing a list of games, Mark. For the party.
Mark: Whose party? Oh, – Jenny's party!
David: Shsh! Not so loud. This is a secret.
Mark: What games are on your list?
David: Well, the first game is "Good morning, King Ethelred".
Mark: I don't know that game. How do you play it?
David: Easy. One of the players is the king and the others blindfold him.
Mark: Blindfold him? Why do they do that?
David: So that he can't see them.
Mark: And what do they do then?
David: I'm coming to that! The king sits on a chair in the middle, with the other players in a circle round him. One of them stands up and says "Good morning, King Ethelred" and the king must guess who it is.
Mark: That's easy! Or doesn't he know the other person?
David: Of course he does. Otherwise how does he guess? But the other person says it in a funny voice.
Mark: What, like this? *(shouts)* "Good morning, King Effelwed!"
David: Er – yes, Mark. Just like that.
Mark: What happens if the king guesses wrong?
David: Then it's another player's turn to talk to the king. If the king guesses right, they change places.
Mark: Great! Why don't we play it now?
David: Come on – with just two players? And who wants to play this game now? Mum's at work. Dad's busy.
Mark: I know who.
David: Who do you mean?
Mark: *(shouts)* Jenny! Do you want to play a game with us?
David: Oh, brilliant! So much for my secret!

1 Answer the questions

1. What is David doing?
2. Whose party is it?
3. What is the first game on David's list?
4. Who do the other players blindfold?
5. Why do they blindfold him or her?
6. What does one player do then?
7. What does the king do?
8. What happens if the king guesses wrong?
9. When do players change places?
10. Who wants to play the game with Jenny?

2 Make more questions ... and find the right answers

1. How does	the other players do to the king?	Because the others talk in funny voices.
2. What do	the game start?	He changes places with the other player.
3. Why do	the king do first?	First the players find a king.
4. What does	the game finish?	One of them talks to the king.
5. What do	happens if the king guesses right?	So that he can't see them.
6. Why doesn't	they do that?	You can stop when you want to.
7. What	the others do?	He sits on a chair in the middle.
8. When does	the king always guess who it is?	They blindfold him.

Look at all the questions on this page. Make rules for **how, why, when, what** and **who** questions.

3 Your turn: Where do you live?

You meet a boy or a girl at a party. What questions can you ask them?

Where?	When?	How?	What?
• live • do your homework	• have breakfast • go to bed	• get to school • father/mother get to work	• do after school • watch on TV

Make dialogues with your partner.
Example: "Where do you live?" – "I live in ..."

4 Don't tell Jenny!

The Penroses plan a big party. David tells **Becky** about it. It's **Jenny's** birthday – and the party is a secret, so he doesn't tell **Jenny**. Then **David** writes ten invitation cards. But first he asks his **parents** if he can invite ten children. **Mr and Mrs Penrose** say, "That's OK."

So David invites **Robert, Sarah, Becky, Simon and six others**. Later **Mark** opens **David's** bedroom door when David isn't there. Mark sees the cards. He can't read them, so he asks **Jenny**. So **Jenny** knows about the party now!

Work with your partner. Ask and answer questions about the text.
Use **who** or **whose** for the words in **blue**.

Examples: Who plans a big party? – The Penroses do.
Who does David tell? – He tells Becky.
Whose birthday is it? – It's Jenny's birthday.

5 Sound practice

[ð] – [θ]

"It's the tenth," says Mother.
"The dogs need‿a bath."
"OK," says my brother.
"Put them‿all‿in the bath."
Then‿in get the three.
"There's no room for me!"
says my brother.
"Well,‿I think," says Mother,
"it's your turn next month."

6 Listening: Robert and Jenny

a) Listen to the dialogue and answer these questions.

1. Where are Robert and Jenny?
a in Market Square
b at the supermarket
c in Market Street

2. Why is Jenny happy when the music starts?
a Robert gives her a present.
b She has got an idea.
c It's her favourite song.

3. Why does Robert walk away so fast?
a He has got an idea.
b He must be home for tea.
c Boys are funny.

b) What does Robert do now? Go on with the story. You can make a dialogue and act it out.

G30–32

6 The birthday party

"Is everything ready for the party?" asks Becky.

It is the evening before Jenny's birthday. Becky, Sarah and David are making plans while Jenny is upstairs.

"Oh yes," says David. "Food, drinks, games …"

"We can all bring our best CDs along," says Becky.

"And of course we must give Jenny the bumps!" shouts Sarah. "Oh, – hello, Jenny …"

Sarah stops because suddenly Jenny is there, too.

"What are 'the bumps'?" Jenny asks.

"Oh, er, um …," says Sarah. "Wait and see."

And they all laugh.

Jenny goes out again. She sees Mr Penrose in the hall.

"Uncle Colin, what are 'the bumps'?" she asks.

"The bumps?" he says. "Oh, that's when it's your birthday and people get you by your arms and legs …"

"Oh! And what do they do then?"

"They throw you up in the air and bump you down on the floor."

"What! How many times do they do that?" Jenny asks.

"One bump for each year," he tells her.

"Oh no!" she thinks. "Twelve bumps!"

"And one for luck. Don't you have them in Germany?"

"I don't think so," says Jenny.

■ *Jenny goes to bed. She is excited about her birthday, but she worries about the thirteen bumps. It is a long time before she goes to sleep.*

Now Jenny is standing in the middle of the party. It's a great party and everybody is having fun – except Jenny.

First they play games. Then they listen to music. There are lots of lovely things to eat and drink. There's jelly and ice cream, a big birthday cake and a big trifle, but Jenny isn't hungry. She opens lots of nice presents, but she still isn't happy.

Then she looks around at the other children. They are smiling at her. She can see their teeth. Big white teeth.

"OK, everybody," shouts Robert. "Let's give her the bumps!"

"Oh yes!" the other children cry. Suddenly they are all very big. Robert and Sarah grab Jenny's arms, and Becky and David take her legs. They throw her up in the air and bump her down on the floor.

"One!" they all cry.

"Stop it!" Jenny screams. "Ow! You're hurting me!"

But they don't stop. She shouts and screams, but they go on. "Nine! … Ten! … Eleven! … Twelve! … And one for luck!" they cry. They throw her up in the air, but this time they let go. Jenny flies up, up, up. She hits the ceiling and then comes down, down, down. There's a bowl of trifle under her. It's huge. She flies into it with a big splash.

"Ugh!" cry the others.

There's trifle on the floor, on the walls – and all over David.

"Hey!" shouts David. He's got trifle on his glasses and he can't see where he's going. Crash! He walks all over Jenny's presents.

Now Jenny is angry. She picks up her birthday cake and throws it. It hits David in the face and goes all over Robert, too.

"Yahoo! This is fun," cries Robert. He throws a jelly and it hits Sarah. Now everybody is fighting.

"No!" Jenny shouts. "Stop it!"

Then a hand grabs her and starts to shake her.

"Help!" she cries. "Stop the party. This is terrible!"

■ "Jenny!" The hand is still shaking her. "Wake up, Jenny. You're dreaming!"

Jenny wakes up. The sun is shining into her room and she sees David, Mark, Aunty Pat and Uncle Colin. They are standing next to her bed.

"Good morning, Jenny!" they all cry.

"Happy birthday!"

1 Look at the text

Can you answer these questions?

1. What do the friends want to do to Jenny?
2. How many bumps do people give?
3. Why is Jenny excited?
4. What happens to Jenny at the party?
5. What does David do?
6. What does Jenny throw at David?
7. Why does she want to stop the party?
8. Who does Jenny see when she wakes up?

2 Another ending

Jenny flies up, up, up (line 48).

What happens then?
Write a different ending to the story.

26 3 Listening: A big surprise

a) Listen and answer these questions.

1. Why does David put the radio on?
2. Where does Robert's mum work?
3. What does the person on the phone win?
4. What does Mrs Croft play?

b) Jenny says thank you to Robert for his idea. Write a dialogue.

1 Answer the questions and say why

1. Do you like school?
2. Do you go to bed early?
3. Do you often go to the swimming pool?
4. Does your best friend go to school with you?
5. What do you do at the weekend?
6. When do you watch TV?
7. Who do you invite for your birthday?
8. Who makes your breakfast?

2 Jenny

Put in the right form of the simple present.

dream • not know • they really want • go • not like • be (2x) • think

fly • shake • be (2x) • wake up • grab • bump • hit • fall • see • let go • start

a) Jenny ___ excited. It ___ the evening before her birthday and she can't sleep. She ___ much about 'the bumps', an English birthday tradition, but she ___ the idea. "___ to give me 13 bumps?" she ___. Then she ___ to sleep and ___ about the party.

b) It ___ a terrible party. When the others ___ her, they ___ of her hands and legs. She ___ up, ___ the ceiling and ___ into a big bowl of trifle. Then all the children ___ to fight. After that a hand ___ Jenny and ___ her. She ___ really happy when she ___ and ___ the Penroses.

c) Later Jenny's mum **(phone)** from Germany.
Mum: Hello, Jenny! Happy birthday! **(you like)** your present from me?
Jenny: Oh, yes! Thanks, Mum. **(you know)** about my party?
Mum: Yes, I **(do)**. When **(it start)**?
Jenny: At 4 o'clock this afternoon, I **(think)**.
Mum: Dad **(say)** sorry there's no present from him. But he **(want)** to get you something today. What present **(you want)** from him? What things **(you need)**?
Jenny: I **(not need)** presents. I just **(want)** you and Dad here.
Mum: But, Jenny, we're coming to England in May. **(you not know)** that?
Jenny: Really, Mum? Oh, great!

3 Ask the questions to these answers

1. I'm writing a letter.
2. I live in Sherwood.
3. I usually go to bed at 9.30.
4. My mum? She works in a bookshop.
5. That's my mum's car.
6. I have lunch at school every day.
7. No, I don't go to school by bus.
8. My best friend walks to school with me.
9. My birthday? It's on 25th August.
10. Yes, I do. It's always a big party.
11. My friends – I invite all my friends.
12. My parents give me presents – my friends, too.
13. Yes, I always get a card from my uncle and aunt.
14. No, I don't write thank you letters. I use the telephone.

4 Just for fun

"Only the one present?"

5 Talking about a star

a) Work with a partner. Partner A looks at part A, partner B looks at part B. Ask questions and answer your partner's questions to put in the missing information.

Example: **A** What's his name? – **B** It's David Beckham.

DAVID BECKHAM

A
Name: ?
Birthday: 2nd May
Comes from: ?
Married: yes
Wife's name: Victoria
Children: ?
Children's names: ?
Home: a castle
Job: ?
Club: Manchester United
Shirt number: ?
☺: Italian food, sport on TV, pop music, the sun
☹: ?

B
Name: David Beckham
Birthday: ?
Comes from: Leytonstone
Married: ?
Wife's name: ?
Children: 2
Children's names: Brooklyn, Romeo
Home: ?
Job: play football
Club: ?
Shirt number: 7
☺: ?
☹: country music

b) Now think of another star. You are this person, and your partner must do an interview with you. Write down the information and tell the class about your interview partner later, but don't say the name. They must guess who it is.

6 Word power: A birthday mind map

Make a mind map with birthday words.

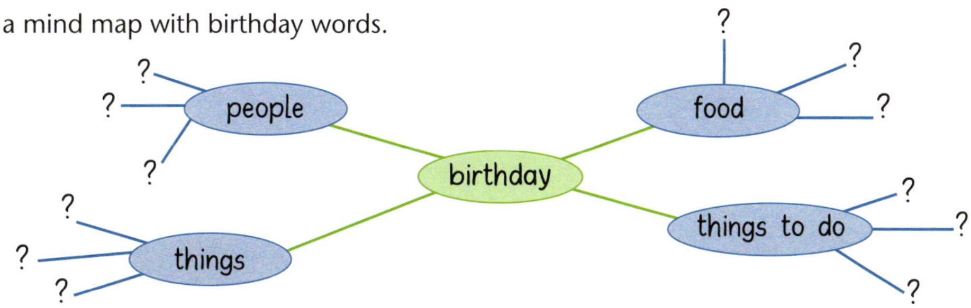

7 Word power: Odd word out

Find the odd word out in each group and put it in the right group.
Match each group with a picture.

1.	2.	3.
lovely	think	bump
noisy	shake	grab
worry	know	hit
busy	want	yummy
hungry	guess	throw
happy	remember	touch

A

B
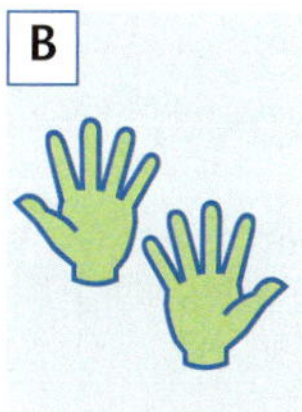

C

3 focus

Focus on the UK

9 1 The people and the pictures

a) First, read the texts about people from different parts of the United Kingdom.

b) Then listen and say which of the pictures on pages 72 and 73 goes with which person and why.

Start like this: I think picture number 1 goes with … because he / she comes from … and the picture shows …

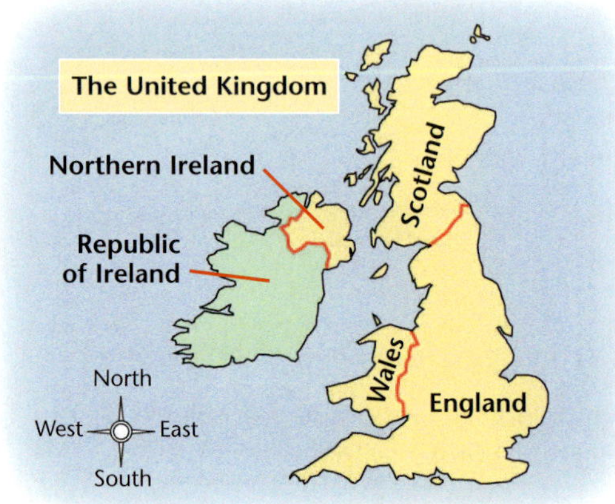

27 2 Listening: Voices

Listen to the voices on the CD. Where are these people and what are they doing? Make a list.

1	2	3	4	5
…	…	…	…	…

2

3

4

5

3 A song: Islandman

32

a) Listen to the song. What words are missing from the text? They are all parts of the body.

[1]span the mighty Tyne [ˈspæn ðə ˌmaɪti ˈtaɪn] – spannen sich über den mächtigen Tyne • [2][sprɔːlz] – breitet sich aus • [3][əˈkrɒs] über • [4][ˈkrʊkɪd] – krumm • [5][ˈeɪntʃnt] – uralt • [6]held apart [ˌheld‿əˈpɑːt] – auseinander gehalten • [7]träumend

Of my body England is the …
The … and the …
My … span the mighty Tyne[1]
London sprawls[2] across[3] my …
Cornwall my crooked[4] ancient[5] …
Wales two … held apart[6]
Scotland is my dreaming[7] …
Ireland is my …

Words: Mike Scott

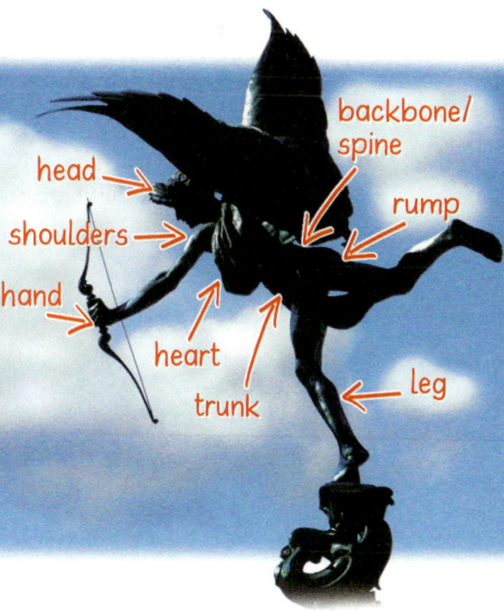

b) Now draw a picture of 'Islandman'.

4 Listening: A UK quiz

33

Listen and find the answers to the quiz with the help of the map in your book.

unit 5 intro

A weekend at the seaside

In England you are never very far from the sea. The Dixons want to spend a weekend at the seaside, so Sarah and Kim are looking at information about places. They think Seahouses in Northumbria is a good place.

1 How to guess new words

a) Look at the information from the Internet on page 75. Talk about the words in **black**. Can you guess what they mean?

tip

- Is the word a noun? An adjective? Or what?
- Does a picture show what the word means?
- Is it like a German word?
- Can the other words in the sentence help?

Example:
- 'Visit' is a verb.
- I can guess what it means from the other words in the sentence.
- I think it's another word for 'go to' a place.
- It must be 'besuchen' in German.

Think for a minute!

b) Look at the Vocabulary on page 183. Are your ideas about the words in **a)** correct?

2 A Seahouses quiz

a) Make a little quiz about Seahouses. Use the information on page 75 and write six questions.

Where ...? How ...? Why ...? What ...? How old ...? ...?

b) Can you answer your partner's questions? Do the quiz without the book!

34 3 Listening: In Seahouses

a) Listen, and put the pictures in the right order. Start: Number one is picture ...

b) Say what is happening in the pictures.

c) What can the people in the pictures say or think? Use your own ideas and write down two or three sentences for each person.

10

Seahouses

Families love to **visit** Seahouses because everybody can find something to see or do there. It is always fun to walk round the old **harbour** and look at all the **boats**, big and **small**.

There is a lovely beach at Seahouses where you can **swim** or play games on the **sand**. The beaches in Northumbria are very long. So they never get too **full**. The **weather** there can be sunny, too!

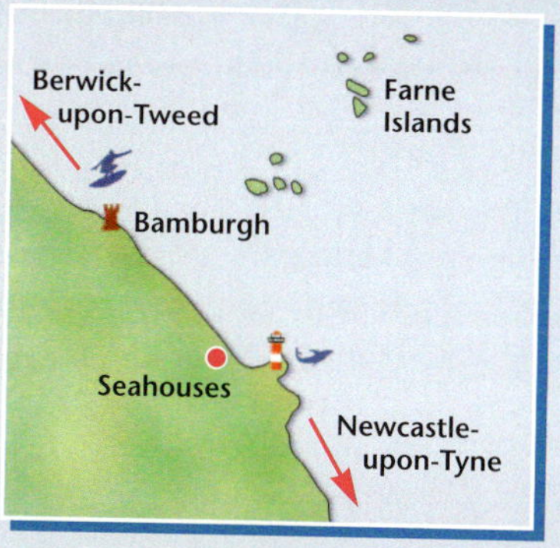

While you are in Seahouses, a **trip** to the Farne Islands is a 'must'. Boats go from the harbour every day. The islands are a great place to see **birds** and **seals**.

The village of Bamburgh is under ten minutes by car from Seahouses. Bamburgh Castle stands on a **rock** next to the sea. The village has an eight-hundred-year-old church, and an **interesting museum**, too.

A On the beach

The Dixons are spending the weekend in Seahouses. On Saturday morning they go to the beach and find a good place.

Kim: Can I have a towel, please? Are the towels in this bag?
Mrs Dixon: Wait, Kim! You mustn't open that bag. That's our picnic. We don't want sand in our sandwiches.
Mr Dixon: There's always sand in sandwiches.
Sarah: Ha ha, that's funny, Dad!
Mrs Dixon: Let's see. The towels must be in this bag. Yes, here you are, Kim. And here's the sunscreen, too.
Kim: Oh, it isn't so hot today. I needn't use sunscreen.
Mrs Dixon: Yes, you must. Maybe you can't feel it with this wind – but the sun is strong.
Sarah: See you all later.
Mr Dixon: Where are you going, Sarah?
Sarah: Into the sea, of course. I can't wait!
Mr Dixon: Listen, you mustn't swim too far from the beach.
Sarah: You needn't worry, Dad. I can swim.
Mr Dixon: The sea isn't like a swimming pool, you know. You must stay near the beach.
Mrs Dixon: Why don't you swim with her?
Mr Dixon: Who? Me? No, thanks. The water in the North Sea is too cold!

1 Words from the text

a) Work with the list on the right. Find examples of the words in the dialogue. What do the words mean? Put them into German.

b) Write your own sentences with the words from **a)**. Show what the words mean with your examples.

English	German
1. can	können
2. can't	...
3. must	...
4. needn't	...
5. mustn't	...

2 Is it OK?

What does Sarah ask?
Find Mrs Dixon's answers.

1. Can I carry the picnic bag?
2. Can I have a drink, please?
3. Can I swim now?
4. Can I phone Becky on your mobile?
5. Can I have my pocket money early?
6. Can I go for a walk alone?
7. Can I play football with those boys?

a) You needn't ask me. You must ask them!
b) No, you mustn't swim after a big lunch.
c) No, sorry. Kim must go with you.
d) Here you are. You mustn't spend it all at once.
e) Of course. You must have lots of drinks in the sun.
f) Oh yes, please! Then I needn't carry so much.
g) Well, OK – but you mustn't talk too long.

3 The Dixons' weekend

Make sentences about the Dixons' weekend. Start: They **must** **needn't** **mustn't**

1. ... worry about Tabby. Their neighbours in Nottingham can look after her.
2. ... find rooms in Seahouses. They don't want to sleep on the beach.
3. ... get up late. They want to have time for everything.
4. ... take the car to the beach. It isn't far from their bed and breakfast place.
5. ... play loud music on the beach. That isn't nice for other people.
6. ... visit Bamburgh Castle on Saturday. The castle is open on Sunday, too.
7. ... buy tickets for the boat. Without tickets they can't go to the Farne Islands.
8. ... go home on Sunday evening. The girls have school again on Monday.

4 A trip to the Farne Islands

Put in the right words: **can** **can't** **must** **needn't** **mustn't**

1. *Sarah:* Come on! The boat starts in a minute. We ___ be late!
2. *Mrs Dixon:* It's OK. We've got time. We ___ run.
3. *Kim:* Look! The islands! We ___ see them already.
4. *Mr Dixon:* Wow! It ___ be great to swim like a seal.
5. *Sarah:* Hey! You're standing in front of me, Kim! I ___ see the seal!
6. *Kim:* Shsh! You ___ be so noisy, Sarah. Look, now the seal is going, you silly girl!
7. *Mr Dixon:* Can I put my bird book in your bag, Janet? Then I ___ carry it in my hand.
8. *Mrs Dixon:* Maybe later, Eddy. But first you ___ give us information about the birds.

13 5 Sound practice

[e]	[æ]	[e] – [æ]
I must **get** a new **pen**	**Ha**ve a **sa**ndwich.	**Te**ll me about your **fa**mily.
He's sitting **ne**xt to his **frie**nd.	I like your **bla**ck **ba**g.	**E**ddy, don't **sta**nd on the **we**t **sa**nd!
They're alr**ea**dy in b**e**d.	Th**a**t m**a**n is **a**ngry.	W**e**ll, th**a**nks for a great week**e**nd.

14 6 A song: Summer holiday[1]

We're all going on a summer holiday,
No more working for a week or two.
Fun and laughter[2] on a summer holiday,
No more worries[3] for me or you
For a week or two.

We're going where the sun shines brightly[4].
We're going where the sea is blue.
We've seen it[5] in the movies[6],
Now let's see if it's true.

Everybody has a summer holiday,
Doing things they always wanted to,
So we're going on a summer holiday
To make our dreams come true[7],
For me and you.

Words: Bruce Welch, Brian Bennett

[1] [ˌsʌmə ˈhɒlədeɪ] Sommerurlaub • [2] [ˈlɑːftə] Gelächter • [3] [ˈwʌriz] Sorgen • [4] [ˈbraɪtli] hell • [5] [ˌwiːv ˈsiːn‿ɪt] Wir haben es gesehen • [6] [ˈmuːviz] Filme • [7] [kʌm ˈtruː] wahr werden

15 B A souvenir of the castle

It is almost the end of the Dixons' weekend in Northumbria.
Sarah and Kim are in the shop at Bamburgh Castle.

Sarah: I want a nice souvenir of the castle.
Kim: Well, there are a lot of souvenirs here. What about a mug?
Sarah: I can't see any mugs.
Kim: There are some mugs over there. At the end of that shelf.
Sarah: Oh, right. No. I don't like them.
Kim: These mouse mats are really nice.
Sarah: Hm. Are there any mats with the castle on them?
Kim: No. There are no mats with pictures of the castle. Only maps of Northumbria.
Sarah: Hey, I like the colour of this bag. Let's see how much it is. Wow, too much!
Kim: Come on, Sarah. Mum and Dad want us back in the car at 5 o'clock.
Sarah: How many minutes have I got?
Kim: Two! – Look, why don't you buy this glass? It's in a nice box, too.
Sarah: No, thanks. But what's that? Oh, it's only some soap. I don't want any soap. – Oh dear, it isn't easy when you haven't got much money.
Kim: But there are so many things here!
Sarah: Maybe I can buy a bar of chocolate.
Kim: And where's your souvenir when you eat the chocolate, silly? – Look at the time. We must go now.
Sarah: No, wait. Here's a tin of sweets, with Bamburgh Castle on the tin. Yes! I can eat the sweets on the way home. And the tin can be my souvenir!

1 Answer the questions

1. Where are Sarah and Kim?
2. What are Kim's ideas for a souvenir?
3. Why doesn't Sarah buy a mouse mat?
4. How much time has Sarah got?
5. Why isn't it easy to find a souvenir?
6. What is Sarah's souvenir?

2 Find the rules

a) Copy the sentences with ***some*** and ***any*** from the dialogue.
Look at the sentences and think. When do we use ***some*** and when do we use ***any***?

b) Go on with the sentences.

1. I can't buy a souvenir. I haven't got	some	soap.
2. I must eat something. Let's buy	any	homework.
3. What can we do today? Have you got		chocolate.
4. I can't wash my hands. There isn't		magazines.
5. Do you want to read? Here are		money.
6. I haven't got time to play. I must do		good ideas?

3 On the shelves

Look at the picture on page 78. Then make sentences with the right words.
Example: There are a lot of sweets.

There	is • isn't • are • aren't	some • a lot of • no • any	sweets • mouse mats • ice cream • CDs • soap • books • biros • posters • mugs • chocolate

4 *much – many*

Put in the right word.

grammar
How **much** time? – How **many** minutes?
How **much** money? – How **many** pence?

1. Good. There aren't ___ people in this shop.
2. Come on. We haven't got ___ time.
3. How ___ chocolate do we want?
4. There are so ___ nice things here!
5. How ___ sweets are in the tin?
6. Don't spend too ___ money!

5 Word power: Can I have this tin of sweets, please?

a) You want to buy these things.
What do you say?
Can I have this ___ of ..., please?

bar box bottle tin

b) You are in the castle café.
Say what you want in English.
(Remember to say 'please'!)

1. zwei Tassen Tee
2. ein Glas Wasser
3. einen großen Teller Sandwiches

1

2

3

4

5

6

6 More information

Put more information in the sentences.
1. The name **of** the village is Bamburgh. 2. Sarah**'s** souvenir ...

1. The name is Bamburgh. **(the village)**
2. The souvenir is a tin. **(Sarah)**
3. The picture is lovely. **(the castle)**
4. The parents are waiting. **(the girls)**
5. The car is in the street. **(the Dixons)**
6. The colour is blue. **(the sky)**
7. The weekend is coming to an end. **(the family)**

grammar
people: 's or s'
- Sarah**'s** souvenir
- the girls**'** room

things: of
- a picture **of** the castle
- the colour **of** those bags

16

7 Sound practice

[v]	[w]	[v] – [w]
Let's **v**isit the **v**illage.	**W**e can **w**alk **w**ithout shoes.	The **w**ind is **v**ery strong.
E**v**erybody lo**v**es the sea.	**Wh**ere are the sand**w**iches?	The **w**eather is lo**v**ely this **w**eek.
A mug o**f** tea, please.	**W**ow! This **w**ater is cold!	**W**ait. I **w**ant a sou**v**enir.

G35–38

17 Grace Darling

The year is 1838. It is the evening of September 6th and the ship *Forfarshire* is in the North Sea, on its way from Hull to Dundee. There are sixty people on the ship, but they can't sleep because a storm is starting. It is raining and the wind is very strong. The ship must fight the big waves, and this means a lot of work for the engines. Too much work. The engines on the *Forfarshire* are old, and suddenly they stop. Now the ship can't go on, and with no engines it can't fight the sea. The waves throw the helpless ship here and there. It is a dark and terrible night, and the people are frightened. They know what can happen to ships in bad storms …

■ Early on September 7th Grace Darling wakes up in the Farne Islands. Grace's home is in the Longstone Lighthouse on one of the islands. Her father William is the lighthouse keeper. Grace wakes up very early this morning because the wind and the sea are so loud. The wind is screaming and shaking the glass in the window. The sea is crashing on the rocks.

Mrs Darling comes into Grace's room. "It's a terrible storm," she tells Grace. Grace gets up from her bed and goes to the window. Outside, the sea is grey and very angry. There are white horses on the huge waves. Suddenly Grace thinks she can see something. "What's that?" she asks her mother. "Look. Out there."
But they can't see what it is because it is too far. So Grace runs and looks through her father's telescope. "Father!" she cries. "There's a wreck on Big Harcar Rock! And I can see some people. They're still alive. We must save them!"

■ Grace grabs some clothes, and a minute later she and her father are already in the lighthouse boat. They start to row to Big Harcar Rock, a mile from the lighthouse. That is a very long way through this terrible sea. The boat is small, and the big waves hit it again and again. It is a dangerous trip, but Grace is strong and helps her father to fight.

"Come on!" she shouts.

"Those people need us! We mustn't give up!"

At last they are almost at the rock, and they can see the name of the ship on the wreck. It is the *Forfarshire*. Some people from the ship are clinging to the rock. When they see the boat they start to scream.

"Help! Please save us!" Only nine men from the *Forfarshire* are still alive, but that is too many for the little lighthouse boat.

"We can't take you all," Mr Darling shouts.

"Make two groups. Some of you must wait until we come back." The men are wet and very cold. But now some of them must wait again while the boat goes back to the lighthouse. They are very frightened because it is so dangerous on the rock. Grace sees how frightened the men are.

"I want to wait with them," she says.

"No!" shouts her father.

"You needn't worry," she says, and jumps from the boat to the rock.

■ While five of the men get into the boat and start the long, slow trip back to the lighthouse, Grace stays on the rock with the others. The storm is still terrible. When some big waves crash on the rock very near them, the men think this is the end. But Grace stays strong. "Don't worry," she tells them. "My father is coming." They wait and wait. Then suddenly, through the rain, they see the little boat with Grace's father and two men in it. Grace waves to her father. He brings the boat near the rock, and Grace helps the men to jump into it. Together with her father Grace rows back through the storm. At last they are at the lighthouse, and all the people are safe.

Today people still talk about brave Grace Darling and her father. You can see their little boat in the Grace Darling Museum in Bamburgh.

1 Because

Finish the sentences with information from the text.

1. The people on the ship can't sleep because ___.
2. The ship can't fight the sea because ___.
3. Grace wakes up very early because ___.
4. Grace and her father row to the rock because ___.
5. Some people must wait again because ___.
6. Grace jumps from the boat because ___.

2 Which words in the text …

1. … tell you about the weather?
2. … give you a picture of the sea?
3. … tell you about Grace?
4. … show you how people feel?

3 Write a dialogue

Go on with **one** of these dialogues.

a) Two men on the Forfarshire in the storm:

1st man: This storm is terrible. I can't sleep.
2nd man: Hey, can you hear the engines?
1st man: No, …

b) The first group gets to the lighthouse:

Mr Darling: Take these men inside.
Mrs Darling: But William! Where's Grace?
Mr Darling: She …

4 Verb forms in the story

A story tells us what people do or what happens. This is the action of the story. But a story can give us a picture of a scene, too.

a) Look at the verbs in the story about Grace Darling. Which tense do we use for actions? Which tense do we use for a picture of a scene?

b) Put the scene in the first picture into words. Find your own verbs.

c) Finish these sentences about the action in the other pictures.
Suddenly they … When the boat is near the rock, they … After that …

d) Go on with the story. Use the right tense for the verbs.

At last they **(get)** back to Longstone and they **(go)** into the lighthouse. Inside, the men from the first group **(sit)** in the kitchen, where Mrs Darling **(look)** after them. When the others suddenly **(walk)** into the room, Mrs Darling **(stop)** what she **(do)**. "At last!" she **(cry)** and **(throw)** her arms round Grace. Outside it **(rain)**, but for Mrs Darling the sun **(shine)** again – because her brave girl **(be)** safe.

G39

1 Pictures with information

What do these pictures tell you? Make sentences with: must mustn't can

Start: 1. You ... ride your bike here. 2. You ... Go on.

2 On the way home

Which word is correct? mustn't needn't

1. *Sarah:* Why are we going back already?
   Mr Dixon: Because we ... get home too late. You've got school tomorrow.
2. *Mr Dixon:* I can look at the map for you.
   Mrs Dixon: You ..., thanks. I know the way.
3. *Sarah:* Mm. These sweets are good.
   Mr Dixon: You ... eat so many sweets! They aren't good for your teeth.
4. *Mr Dixon:* Don't go so fast, Janet!
   Mrs Dixon: You ... worry. I'm a good driver.
5. *Kim:* Ow! You're hurting me, Sarah!
   Mrs Dixon: Quiet, you two! You ... fight all the time.
6. *Mr Dixon:* Have we got any food at home?
   Mrs Dixon: Yes. So we ... stop at the supermarket.

3 Mixed bag

Find words for the numbers.

"My family and I are [1] a week in Seahouses. I love it here [2] there are so [3] things to see and do. My two favourite things are to look [4] the [5] in the harbour and to [6] in the sea. The [7] is sunny today, [8] it's a good day for the beach. We [9] worry about rain because there are [10] clouds in the [11]. When we go [12] the beach this afternoon, I [13] remember to take [14] empty bottle with me. Why? Well, I haven't got [15] money for a souvenir, so my idea is to put [16] sand in a bottle. I think a bottle [17] Seahouses sand is a [18] good souvenir."

4 Watch out

Make sentences with these words. Use: 's s' or of
(Sometimes you must change the order of the words.)

Example: 1. house • Mrs Brown • bed and breakfast place
→ Mrs Brown**'s** house is a bed and breakfast place.

2. the walls • the castle • very old
3. room • the girls • nice and big
4. the name • the café • 'The Lighthouse'
5. towels • everybody • in the bag
6. boat • the Darlings • in the museum
7. the sound • the wind • terrible

revision 3
Unit 4 – Unit 5

1 Different people like different things

Skegness isn't far from Nottingham. The Penroses often go there when the weather is nice.

Work with your partner and ask questions about
- what they like best.
- what they always take to Skegness.
- who likes / does what.

A	What they like best	What they take
Mr Penrose	?	magazines
Mrs Penrose	towns & gardens	?
David	?	tin of sweets
Mark	beach	?
Jenny	?	book

B	What they like best	What they take
Mr Penrose	sea	?
Mrs Penrose	?	sunscreen
David	big swimming pool	?
Mark	?	beach ball
Jenny	shops	?

2 Now – and often

Put in the right forms.

be • go (2x) • love • meet • take

It ___ 4 pm on Tuesday. Becky and Sarah ___ to the park on their bikes. They ___ Barker with them this time. He often ___ with them. He ___ that because he often ___ other dogs!

drive (2x) • fight • go • happen • look • spend

The Dixons often ___ a day at the seaside. Today they ___ to Skegness. Mrs Dixon ___ now. Mr Dixon sometimes ___ , but today he ___ at the map. Sarah and Kim ___ . This often ___ !

get • help • put • set

Mr Penrose usually ___ the table for breakfast. But today David and Mark ___ him. Mark ___ knives and forks on the table, and David ___ the cups and saucers from the shelf.

3 Dialogues

Watch out with the forms.

1. *Jenny:* **(you like)** ice cream, Mark?
   Mark: Yes, I **(love)** it! Let's have some!
2. *Mrs Croft:* Robert! Are you upstairs? What **(you do)**?
   Robert: I **(finish)** my homework. I **(do)** a German exercise for Mr Cooper.
3. *David:* Let's go to the swimming pool.
   Jenny: We can't – look at those clouds. A storm **(start)**. It **(rain)** already, look!
4. *Becky:* Are you busy, Sarah?
   Sarah: Well, yes! I **(read)** a book. It's a true story and it's brilliant.
5. *Sarah:* I can tell you about the story.
   Becky: OK, I **(listen)**.
   Sarah: Well, it's about Grace Darling. Her father **(be)** a lighthouse keeper. One day she **(wake up)** early because the wind and the sea **(be)** so loud, and the sea **(crash)** on the rocks. When she **(look)** through a telescope, she **(see)** a wreck! Then she and her father **(go)** out in a boat and **(row)** to the wreck.
   Becky: And then what **(happen)**?
   Sarah: No idea! I'm only on page 21!

4 Mark has got a cold[1]

Can you find the right words? Examples:

Mark: I've got a cold, Dad. It's terrible! Must I go to kindergarten?
Mr Penrose: Don't worry, Mark. You **needn't** go to kindergarten today.
Mark: Can I play in the garden?
Mr Penrose: No, you've got a bad cold. You **mustn't** go outside, Mark.

needn't **mustn't**	• go to the kindergarten ✔ • go outside ✔ • watch too much TV • take that bottle to bed • help me today • stay in bed all the time • eat too many • finish them

1. *Mark:* Must I stay in bed all day?
   Mr Penrose: Well, no, you ...
2. *Mark:* Can I watch TV?
   Mr Penrose: You can watch 'Play Time' at ten o'clock, but you ...
3. *Mark:* I can't eat all these cornflakes, Dad!
   Mr Penrose: Don't worry, you ...
4. *Mark:* Oh, Dad! I want a drink!
   Mr Penrose: OK – but you ...
5. *Mark:* Is that a new tin of sweets?
   Mr Penrose: Yes, but there's lots of sugar in sweets. You ...
6. *Mark:* Are you OK in the kitchen without me?
   Mr Penrose: Of course, Mark! You ...

[1] cold [kəʊld] – Erkältung

5 Things or people?

Make new sentences – with the right genitive forms. **'s** **s'** **of**

Examples: Bamburgh Castle has got grey walls. (The walls **of** Bamburgh Castle are grey.)
Has Mr Croft got a red car? (Is Mr Croft**'s** car red?)

1. The Dixons have got a house in Sherwood.
2. This village – what's its name? Do you know?
3. I think Mrs Dane is wearing a funny skirt!
4. I like those shoes. I like their colour!
5. Have the children got their beach things in the car?
6. This is our street. Our house is at the end.
7. I hate this music! I really hate the sound.
8. I think the Burtons have got a nice dog.

6 Nine pairs

a) Which words go together? Find the pairs
Example: city centre

b) Now make sentences with the word pairs.
Example: The Dixons live in Nottingham, but they don't live in the city centre.

city • exercise • ice • living • pencil • pocket • school • shop • swimming **+** assistant • bag • book • case • centre • cream • money • pool • room

7 Word power

Can you put the words in the right groups? Write them down. Then think of two or three more words for each group.

1. weekend, ... 2. sea, ... 3. castle, ...
4. cake, ... 5. chair, ... 6. leg, ...

arm • beach • castle ✔ • day • cake ✔ • church • hand • jelly • bed • museum • wave • minute • shop • chair ✔ • weekend ✔ • sandwich • leg ✔ • tooth • rock • trifle • sea ✔ • cupboard • Monday • table

A week on a farm

21 Robert is reading an interesting article in a children's magazine.

FRESH AIR AND FUN

1 How many of us in cities know much about farms? Nethercott House is one of three Farms For City Children. Young people from schools in cities can spend a week there. They help with the work and learn what happens on a farm.

2 This week pupils from Birmingham are at Nethercott, but schools from London, Manchester and Cardiff are regular visitors, too. It isn't a holiday. Work begins at 7.30 am, and doesn't finish until 5 pm. The kids work in three groups. There's always a lot to do!

4 The second group is cleaning the pigsty. Everybody needs their wellies for this job. "Pooh! Pigs make a very strong smell!" says 12-year-old Gemma.

5 The third group's job is to work in the vegetable garden at Nethercott. The same group must feed the turkeys and chickens, and collect the eggs. "I'm scared of the turkeys," Jack, 13, tells us. "When you aren't looking, they can attack you!"

(adapted from: The Funday Times)

Paul Wray spends a day in the country with Farms For City Children at Nethercott House in Devon

3 Today the girls and boys in the first group must fetch the cows from the field. Many of the pupils are surprised how big the animals are! Back in the shed they help to milk the cows, too. They write down how much milk each cow gives.

6 The last job is to bring Bluebell the horse back to the stable before night. After that everybody can have a good dinner and go to sleep … until 7 am the next morning when they must get up and start again!

1 Jobs on the farm

Look through the article again.
How many jobs can you find? Make a list.

- fetch the cows from the field
- milk the …

2 Word power

a) Put the words into two groups:

Country words:	City words:

shop, farm, hill, cinema, field, street, cow, park, green, people, cars, wellies

b) Start a mind map for the country. Use words from **a)** and your own ideas. When you learn more words later in the unit, you can put them in your mind map, too.

3 Your turn: Country and city

Talk about the country and the city.
Say which you like and why.
Examples:

I like the city because you can go to the cinema.

I like the country. The air is fresh.

38 4 Listening: A holiday for the Crofts

Mrs Croft and Robert are making plans.
Listen to what they say.

1. When needn't Mrs Croft work?
2. What does she love at the seaside?
3. Where does Robert want to go?
4. When can Mrs Croft get information?
5. Why must Robert say thank you to Becky?

23 A Robert's postcard from Yorkshire

Monday, July 20

Dear Sarah,
A promise is a promise – so here's a postcard from Yorkshire! The trip here on Saturday was terrible. The roads were full. We stopped and started all the time. But Springfield Farm is great. Yesterday, Jack, a boy on the farm, showed me the animals – some pigs, some cows, and lots and lots of sheep. We stayed in a field and watched how Sam, one of the sheepdogs, worked with the sheep. He was brilliant! (Not like stupid Barker. Do you remember when he chased that rabbit in the park?) Later I helped Jack to feed the chickens. Then I carried all the eggs over to the kitchen. Well, almost all the eggs. I don't know how it happened – but in the farmyard two eggs jumped out of the basket! Bye until the end of the week.
Robert

TO
Sar
11
Sh

1 Information

Find information in the postcard. Say …

1. … why the trip to Yorkshire was terrible.
2. … who showed Robert the animals.
3. … what Robert watched in a field.
4. … what Robert helped Jack to do.
5. … where he carried the eggs.
6. … what happened in the farmyard.

grammar

am / is	**was**	help + **ed**	stay + **ed**
are	**were**	chase + **d**	carry → carr**ied**
		stop + **p** + **ed**	

24 2 Sound practice

[d]	[t]	[ɪd]
Robert stay**ed** on a farm. He lov**ed** it there. And it only rain**ed** on one day.	Robert lik**ed** his new friend Jack. He help**ed** Jack. They work**ed** together.	Jack want**ed** some sheep in a different field. He need**ed** Sam. "Here, boy!" he shout**ed**.

3 Yesterday

collect play milk wash clean

Make sentences about Robert and Jack yesterday.
Start: 1. In the morning they milked the cows. 2. Then they … Go on.

G40–42

4 Thursday in Nottingham

25

This is what Sarah tells Becky.
Find the irregular forms.
Which verbs are they from?
Go on with the list.

Verb	Past form
go	went
get	got
give	
write	
find	

tip
There's a list of irregular forms on page 155. All the other verbs are regular.

You know Robert went to Yorkshire last Saturday? Well, I got a postcard from him yesterday. He gave me a promise, you see. He wrote the postcard on Monday. And I found it when I came home from your house yesterday afternoon. They had a terrible trip to Yorkshire. But the farm is great. Robert told me about the animals, and what he did on Sunday. He saw a brilliant sheepdog. Not like – I mean – he said hello to Barker. Oh yes, and typical Robert! He made an omelette in the farmyard!

5 The Crofts and the Rudds

The Crofts are staying at Springfield Farm with the Rudd family. Put in the past forms.

1. *Mrs Rudd:* Is this your first holiday on a farm?
   Mrs Croft: Yes, it is. It **(be)** Robert's idea.
2. *Robert:* Mm. Nice cake, Mrs Rudd.
   Mrs Rudd: Thank you. I **(make)** it this morning.
3. *Mrs Rudd:* Please clean your room, Jack.
   Jack: Again, Mum? I **(do)** it last week!
4. *Jack:* Do you know where my grandpa is?
   Robert: Well, I **(see)** him in the farmyard after lunch.
5. *Mr Rudd:* Whose is this old shoe?
   Jack: No idea, Dad. Sam **(find)** it.
6. *Mrs Rudd:* The Crofts like it here, Jack. They want to come back next year.
   Jack: I know. Robert **(tell)** me yesterday.

6 Watch out!

Regular or irregular? Make the correct past forms.
Example: 1. People from big cities often **visit** farms.
Last month a family from London visited Springfield Farm.

2. Mr Rudd usually **gets up** very early. Yesterday he ___ at half past four.
3. The Rudds **have** a lot of chickens. When Robert stayed with them, he ___ an egg for breakfast every day.
4. Grandpa Rudd **helps** to do the jobs on the farm. This morning he ___ to milk the cows.
5. On a farm every day **is** a busy day. Yesterday ___ Sunday, but all the Rudds ___ busy.
6. It often **rains** in Yorkshire. But last week it only ___ on one day.
7. When people on the farm don't eat all their food, Mrs Rudd **gives** it to the pigs. Yesterday she ___ the pigs some vegetables.

26 B In the kitchen

Robert comes into the kitchen.

Robert: Oh, you're back again, Jack. I looked in the kitchen ten minutes ago. But you weren't here. Where were you?
Jack: Outside. I wanted to get Lenny.
Robert: Oh, a little lamb! Isn't he sweet! – Why did you want to get him, Jack?
Jack: Because it's time for his milk. Come on, Lenny. Here's your bottle.
Robert: Oh look! He's drinking! Did you make the milk warm for him?
Jack: Yes, I did. But not too hot.
Robert: Can I give Lenny his milk? Please!
Jack: Of course. Just a minute, Lenny.
Robert: Come to me now. That's a good little lamb. – But where's his mother?
Jack: His mother didn't want him.
Robert: Oh, dear! Poor Lenny!
Jack: Well, we weren't surprised. She had three lambs, you see, and she didn't have enough milk. The other two lambs were OK, but Lenny didn't get any milk.
Robert: That wasn't very nice for him.
Jack: No, it wasn't. But I can look after him.
Robert: Look, the bottle is empty now. Was the milk good, Lenny?
Jack: I'm sure it was.
Robert: And did you get enough? No, he didn't! Look, Jack. He wants more.
Jack: Sorry, Lenny. You mustn't have too much. It isn't good for you!

1 Lenny the lamb

Make correct sentences.

1. Jack	a) didn't want Lenny.
2. Robert	b) wasn't too hot.
3. Lenny's mother	c) didn't know where Jack was.
4. Lenny	d) didn't get any milk from his mother.
5. Lenny's milk	e) wasn't in the kitchen ten minutes ago.

2 Questions

Work with a partner. Ask and answer the questions.

1. Was Jack outside ten minutes ago?
2. Did Lenny's mother have four lambs?
3. Were the Rudds surprised when Lenny's mother didn't want him?
4. Were Lenny's brother and sister OK?
5. Did Robert want to feed Lenny, too?
6. Was the milk in the bottle cold?
7. Did Jack give Lenny more milk?

Yes,	she he it they	was. were. did.
No,		wasn't. weren't. didn't.

3 Find the rules

a) Look at the pairs of examples. Which words are different in the past?

b) Find the rules for the past for …
1. negative sentences 2. questions

Present	Past
I don't know much.	I didn't know much.
He doesn't listen.	He didn't listen.
What do they want?	What did they want?
Does she like it?	Did she like it?

4 That isn't right

Start: 1. The Crofts didn't stay on Greenfield Farm. They stayed on Springfield Farm.
2. Robert didn't … He … Go on.

1. The Crofts stayed on Greenfield Farm.
2. Robert wrote a postcard to Jenny.
3. Sarah told David about the postcard.
4. Jack showed Robert the animals on Monday.
5. The two boys watched Sam in the farmyard.
6. Lenny got a bottle of water.

5 Your turn: Sorry!

Work with a partner. Make little dialogues.
Example: Hey! You didn't visit me yesterday. – Sorry. I didn't have time.

Hey! You didn't	visit me yesterday. • phone me last week. • wait for me after school. • say hello on the bus. • give me my comic back. • come to my party. • …
Sorry, I didn't	think of it. • have time. • know your number. • remember. • see you. • …

6 We want to know!

When Robert goes back to Nottingham, his friends want to know about his holiday.
Make questions with ***Did …?***. Then use your own ideas for Robert's answers.
Example: 1. Did you like it on the farm? – Yes, I did. I loved it!

1. you • like it on the farm?
2. the farm • have many animals?
3. you • help with the work?
4. the chickens • give you fresh eggs for breakfast?
5. the pigs • make a terrible smell?
6. you • see any lambs?
7. it • rain a lot in Yorkshire?
8. you • want to come back home?

7 A holiday last year

You want to know about your partner's holiday last year. (It needn't be true.)

a) Make a list of questions.

What? • be • see • like • Why? • do • stay • go • Where? • …

Questions	Answers
Where did you go?	• England
How long were you there?	• two weeks
Where did you stay?	• old castle
Was it sunny?	• …
Did …?	

b) Ask your partner the questions and make notes about the answers.

c) Tell the class about your partner's holiday.

Florian went to England last year.
He was there two weeks.
He stayed in an old castle.

G44–45

1 How to read a story

a) The title

The title of a story can give you ideas. Think about the title 'Problems on Springfield Farm'. Talk about what the problems can be.

Now read the story.

Maybe ...
- a sheep doesn't want ...
- the chickens don't give enough ...
- a ... attacks ...
- a visitor ...
- there's a problem with ...

27 Problems on Springfield Farm

1. "Mary! **We've got a problem!**" Grandpa came into the kitchen, but he didn't sit down. Mrs Rudd saw from his face how worried he was.
"It's one of the sheep," Grandpa went on. "Colin is with her. **She's ready to have her lambs,** but **they aren't coming.** We think there must be two or three in her, but we're not sure. And we don't know how we can help her!"
"Let's phone Alan Smith. He's a good vet," said Mrs Rudd.
She picked up the telephone and made the call.
"What did he say?" Grandpa asked.
"He's coming to the farm right away."

Stop here. Before you go on with the story, look at **b)** on page 94.

2. At that moment Jack and Robert came into the kitchen from the living room.
"Who's coming to the farm?" Jack wanted to know.
Grandpa explained the problem with the sheep.
"I must go out again now," he said.
"No, you're tired. Sit down," said Mrs Rudd. "I can go and help Colin."
"Come on," said Jack to Robert. "Let's go and see what's happening."
They followed Mrs. Rudd over the farmyard and into a shed.

3. Inside the shed there was a lot of noise from the sheep and their new lambs. But one sheep was very quiet. Mr Rudd was with her.
"She's in a bad way. Did you phone the vet?" he asked.
"Yes, I did," answered Mrs Rudd. "He's already on his way."
Ten minutes later they heard the vet's car in the farmyard.
Jack ran out. "Mr Smith! We're in here with the sheep."

4. The vet got his bag from the car and went with Jack into the shed. He examined the sheep. Then he shook his head.
"I'm sorry," he told the Rudds. "She's got two lambs, but they're dead inside her. Well, we can't save the lambs, but we must get them out and save the mother. – Take your friend outside, Jack. He needn't watch this job."
But Robert didn't want to go. "It's OK," he said. "I'm not scared to watch."

■ 5. The vet started to get the lambs out of the sheep. It wasn't nice to watch. Robert felt terrible when he saw the dead lambs. He didn't say a word.

At last the vet finished the job and stood up.

"That's it," he said. "But she's still weak. And of course she hasn't got any lambs now. Without their lambs sheep sometimes die."

"I know, Alan," said Mr Rudd. "But what can we do? We haven't got any new lambs without mothers at the moment."

■ 6. "What about Lenny?" asked Robert. He didn't feel so bad now. "Maybe he can help. His own mother can't feed him."

"It's a good idea, Robert. But Lenny isn't young enough," explained Mrs Rudd. "He's five days old now. If a lamb isn't new, the mother sheep knows it isn't her own lamb. Then she doesn't want it."

"Wait a minute," said Mr Rudd suddenly. "Grandpa did something once. It was many years ago when I was a boy, but maybe we can use the same idea now."

■ 7. "Yes, I know how we can trick the sheep," said Grandpa when Jack fetched him. "Have you got a good knife in your bag, Alan?" The vet gave Grandpa a big knife.

Robert had no idea what Grandpa wanted to do with the knife. But then Grandpa picked up one of the dead lambs.

"Right. We just need the skin," he said.

Suddenly Robert started to feel terrible again. He really didn't want to watch this time. But he didn't need to shut his eyes because Grandpa had a job for him and Jack.

"Go and get Lenny please," he told the two boys.

■ 8. Robert carried Lenny into the shed. Grandpa had the skin of the dead lamb in his hands. He took Lenny from Robert and put the skin round Lenny's little body.

"Why did you do that?" Robert asked.

"Because he needs the right smell for his new mother," was Grandpa's answer.

Grandpa put Lenny next to the sheep.

"Here's your lamb," he said.

Everybody watched and waited.

The sheep looked at Lenny, then touched him with her nose. Lenny looked at the sheep, then he started to drink from her.

"Look! They're happy together!" Robert said with a big smile.

All the Rudds and the vet smiled, too.

"Yes," said Mrs Rudd. "The sad story has a happy ending!"

b) Important ideas

1. Go through the first part of the story again. Look at the words in **blue**. They are the important ideas in the story. You can use them to take notes.

2. Now go on with the story. Take notes. (Don't write too much!)

- a problem
- one of the sheep
- lambs / aren't coming
- phone the vet

c) Headings

Choose one of these headings for each part of the story.

- What the vet says
- What can they do?
- Grandpa's trick
- Inside the shed
- Lenny's new mother
- Robert's idea
- The problem
- The boys want to help

d) Tell the story again

Put in the right information. Don't look at the text. Use your notes from **b)**!

grammar
When we explain what happens in a story, we use the present.

There is a problem with one of 1 on the farm. She is ready to have 2, but they 3. Mrs Rudd phones 4. Jack and Robert follow 5 into 6. When the vet comes, he 7 the sheep. Her lambs are 8. The vet gets the lambs 9. But without their lambs sheep 10. Robert thinks maybe Lenny 11. Grandpa knows how they can 12. He needs the skin of 13. Robert and Jack go and 14. Grandpa puts 15 round 16. This gives Lenny the right 17. Lenny starts to 18. The sad story has a happy 19.

e) The people in the story

Make a list of the people in the story. Then talk about them. Are they important for the story? Why or why not?
Example: Mrs Rudd is important because she phones the vet.

- trick the sheep
- get the dead lambs out of the sheep
- think of Lenny
- remember what Grandpa once did
- phone the vet
- not do much

f) Your turn: What did you think of the story?

Examples: I liked / didn't like it. I thought it was good • silly • interesting • boring • terrible • …

I liked I didn't like	• the ending • Grandpa's trick • it when the vet got the dead lambs out of the sheep • …	because …

39 2 Listening: A telephone call

a) One of the Rudds' neighbours, Tom Potter from Hillside Farm, is phoning the vet. Listen to what the vet says. What do you think Tom Potter says or asks?

b) Work with a partner. One of you is Mrs Rudd. One of you is the vet. Go on with the dialogue from the first part of the story.

Vet: Hello. Alan Smith here.
Mrs Rudd: This is Mary Rudd, Alan. Sorry to phone you in the evening. But …

3 A picture story

a) Talk about the pictures. Say what they show.
Start: 1. Robert and Jack are in the pigsty. They … Sam …

b) Match the groups of words to the pictures. Example: B goes with picture 1.

A: the two boys • stop their work • follow Sam out of the farmyard
B: Robert and Jack • want to feed the pigs • Sam • come into the pigsty • start to bark
C: Jack • fetch • back into the field • Robert • say
D: Jack • start to shut gate • Sam • not happy • bark again
E: Sam • show them a field • lots of cows • the gate • open
F: go • through the gate • see • a cow in the road

c) Tell the story in the past tense. Use words from **b)** – and your own ideas, too, if you want. Find your own title for the story.

Start: Robert and Jack wanted to feed the pigs.
Suddenly Sam came into … and …

tip
Remember! You can connect sentences.
This makes your text better.
Look again at page 58.

35 4 A song: Old MacDonald had a farm

1. Old MacDonald had a farm, E I E I O,
And on his farm he had some chicks, E I E I O.
With a chick-chick here,
And a chick-chick there,
Here a chick, there a chick,
Everywhere a chick-chick.
Old MacDonald had a farm, E I E I O.

2. … some ducks (quack-quack)
3. … some sheep (baa-baa)
4. … a pig (oink-oink)
5. … a cow (moo-moo)

Words: Traditional

1 Word power

Put the words in the right groups:

1. Animals
2. People
3. Places
4. Food and drink
5. Parts of the body

boy • cow • egg • everybody • farmyard • field • hand • head • horse • leg • milk • omelette • pig • shed • sheep • skin • stable • vegetable • vet • visitor

2 From the past to the present

Find the right order for these 'time' words and phrases.

yesterday | in 2000 | a month ago | today | three days ago | two years ago | last week | the day before yesterday | last year

past ➜ present
in 2000 ➜ two years ago ➜ …

3 What did you do?

a) Make six sentences about the past.
Example: Last Saturday I helped at home.

Yesterday On Sunday Last week Last …	I we	help at home • listen to music • phone my grandma • watch TV • have a party • …

b) Now ask a partner six questions.
Example: Did you help at home last Saturday? – No, I didn't.

4 How do you say it?

Which of these past forms have the ending [ɪd]?

asked • corrected • finished • hated • needed • shouted • smiled • started • stayed • visited

5 Last week

Robert's friends tell him about their week. Put in the right forms.

1. *Jenny:* Last Saturday we **(want)** to have a picnic in the country. But the weather **(not be)** good, so we **(go)** to the cinema.
2. *Sarah:* Kim **(make)** me very angry the day before yesterday. She **(tell)** stories about me to Mum and Dad. Of course the stories **(not be)** true. I **(explain)** this to Mum and Dad, but they **(not listen)** to me.
3. *David:* Yesterday we **(play)** football in the park. After our game Mark **(feel)** tired and **(not want)** to walk. So Dad **(carry)** him all the way home!
4. *Becky:* I **(be)** very happy on Saturday. I **(not think)** I **(have)** any money. But when I **(clean)** my room I **(find)** two pounds under my bed!

6 Just for fun

© PUNCH

"Sometimes I think you're not really trying."

7 Tell me more

Read what these people say. Then use the question word and ask a question.
Example: 1. Why did you laugh?

1. I **laughed** in the middle of the English lesson. **(Why?)**
2. I **stayed** on a farm last year. **(How long?)**
3. I **saw** a TV star on holiday. **(Who?)**
4. Look! I **found** this nice little ball. **(Where?)**
5. I **got** up very late this morning. **(When?)**
6. I **learned** something new yesterday. **(What?)**
7. I **was** so worried all last week. **(Why?)**
8. A nice person **gave** me a bar of chocolate! **(Who?)**

8 The postcard

Robert is talking to Sarah after his holiday. Put in the right past forms.

Robert: Hi Sarah. **(you get)** my postcard?
Sarah: Yes, I **(do)**, thanks. I **(like)** the picture on it. **(you stay)** near that place?
Robert: Well, we **(not be)** far from it on Springfield Farm.
Sarah: Becky and I **(look)** at a map and **(find)** the place.
Robert: Becky? Oh – er – **(she see)** my postcard?
Sarah: Well, I **(show)** her the picture.
Robert: And – er – **(she read)** what I **(write)**?
Sarah: No, she **(not do)**. Don't worry, Robert. I **(not think)** it **(be)** a good idea to show her what you **(say)** about Barker!

9 What can you say?

What can you say when these things happen?
Find the right words. Start: 1. You can say "..."

"Wow!" "Ow!" "Pooh!" "Typical!"
"Just a minute." "Oh dear." "Sorry, no idea."

1. You hurt your leg.
2. You hear about a problem.
3. There's a terrible smell.
4. You can't answer a question.
5. Your friend is waiting, but you aren't ready.
6. You are surprised and happy.
7. Your friend does something silly – again!

10 Mixed bag: On the telephone

Robert is phoning Jack from Nottingham. Find a word for every number.

Robert: Hello, Jack. **1** is Robert.
Jack: Oh **2**, Robert. **3** you have a good trip back to Nottingham?
Robert: **4**, we did, thanks. **5** are you?
Jack: Fine. It's good to **6** from you.
Robert: Well, I wanted **7** ask about little Lenny **8** his new mother.
Jack: They're very **9** together. **10** Lenny isn't so little – he's getting quite **11** now!
Robert: And what **12** Sam?
Jack: Oh, poor Sam had a problem with **13** foot two days **14**. But it's OK now.
Robert: Did the **15** come and see him?
Jack: **16**, Grandpa looked after him.
Robert: Well, please **17** hello to everybody from me. And thank **18** for **19** interesting holiday. I had a great time **20** the farm.

Focus on English – a world language

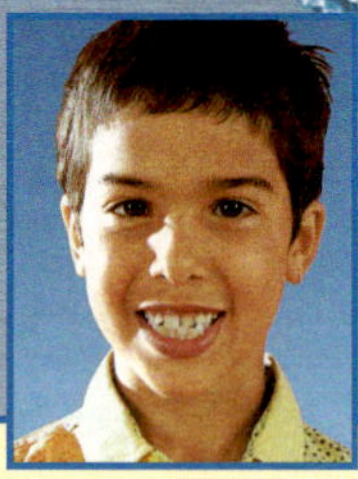

36 People in the USA speak English. But many people there speak other languages, too. **José** lives in San Diego, California. His family is from Mexico. They speak Spanish at home. José goes to a school where the pupils learn English and Spanish.

Noreen lives in Ireland. Her grandmother's first language is Irish. Noreen and her parents' first language is English. Today everybody in Ireland knows English, but children learn Irish at school because people do not want to forget it.

A

B

C

1 The world speaks English

a) Read about English and other languages in the USA, Ireland, Germany, South Africa, India and Australia. Which language picture goes with which country?

b) Work in groups. Use books, magazines and the Internet to find pictures and information about one of the countries on this focus page and make a poster with texts in English.

■ This is **Jörg** from Nürnberg. At home and with his friends he speaks a Franconian dialect. He learns English and French at school. When he is 14, he wants to go to America for a year.

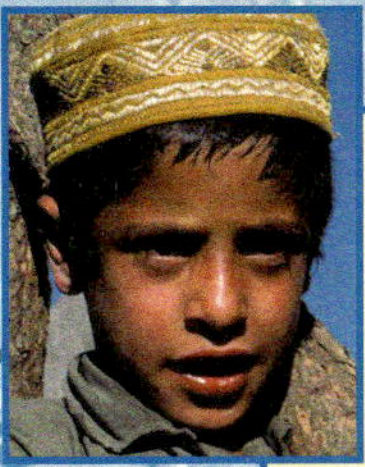

Hanif lives in Delhi, in India. India is a huge country with more than 100 different languages, so many people there can only understand other Indians when they speak English.

■ White people in South Africa usually know only English and Afrikaans, like **Vanessa** from Johannesburg. Black people use African languages like Zulu, for example, and English, too.

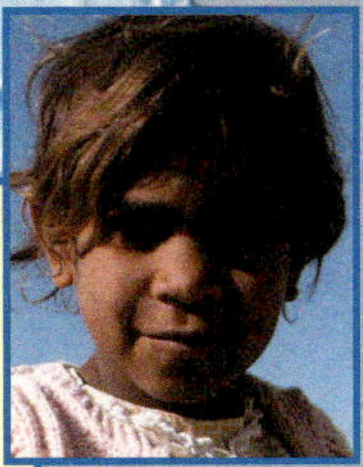

This is **Grace**. She is an Australian Aboriginal. She does not live with her parents, but stays in an Aboriginal community. There she goes to a special Aboriginal school and learns the Aboriginal language. She learns English, too because you need it everywhere in Australia.

D

E

F

2 English in my country

a) Which English words do we use in Germany? Collect examples and make a collage with these words and some pictures.
b) What can you say about English in Germany?

40 3 Listening: Four voices

These four people speak English. Listen and make notes:
a) What are they doing at the moment?
b) Where do they come from?

unit 7 intro

Off to the USA!

1 What do you know?

David is sitting in his room alone. He is looking at a magazine and doing a quiz about the United States of America.

Can you help David? Make groups of four and do the quiz.
Then listen to the CD and check your answers.

What do you know about the USA?
Try this quiz.

1. Why does the American flag have 50 stars? Because the USA has …
- a 50 baseball teams
- b 50 states
- c 50 Indian tribes

2. How far is it from the east coast to the west coast of the USA?
- a 1,500 miles (2,400 km)
- b 2,000 miles (3,500 km)
- c 2,700 miles (4,300 km)

3. Which is the largest state in the USA?
- a Alaska
- b California
- c Washington

4. Which is the largest US city?
- a Denver
- b Los Angeles
- c New York

5. Which of these pop stars isn't American?
- a Jon Bon Jovi
- b Madonna
- c Robbie Williams

6. How many people live in the USA?
- a 80 million
- b 280 million
- c 580 million

7. What can you see in the picture?
- a The Rocky Mountains
- b The Mississippi River
- c The Grand Canyon

2 Listening: Tourist attractions

44

David wants to know more about America. He starts to read about it in a geography book:

'The USA is a huge country with many different landscapes. In the west there are mountains and forests. In the middle there are wide spaces where farmers grow wheat. In the northeast there are large cities like Boston, New York and Philadelphia. The capital of the United States is also in the northeast: it's Washington, D.C. ... '

Oh dear, this is boring. Mum's CD about America is far more interesting.

David puts the CD into his computer and starts to learn about US tourist attractions. Listen to the texts from the CD. Then say which text goes with which picture and name. Where are all these tourist attractions?

Everglades National Park

Niagara Falls

Rodeo

Golden Gate Bridge

Kennedy Space Center

3 A US quiz

Write a short quiz about the USA for the other pupils in your class. You can ask questions about a state, a city, landscapes, national parks, music, stars, tourist attractions or other things. Who can get the most things right?

A David's surprise

One morning early in July, David has a surprise for the others.

David: Hey, you lot. Guess what I'm going to do this summer.

Sarah: Er, let me see. You're going to spend two weeks in Blackpool?

David: No, much better than that!

Robert: One week in Blackpool?

David: No, silly. I'm going to fly to America.

Becky: North or south?

David: North, of course. We're off to the USA at the end of July.

Sarah: Wow, that's fantastic, David!

Robert: Wait. Don't tell me – I think I know. You're going to stay with a rich uncle in Texas, right?

David: Wrong. I haven't got a rich uncle in Texas. But I have got a not very rich aunt in New York, and we're going to stay with her and my cousin.

Becky: Ah! So you've got an American cousin, eh? That's interesting. What's his name?

David: It's Mary-Beth! (laughs)

Becky: Oh, a girl cousin.

Sarah: How long are you going to be in New York?

David: Well, Mum isn't going to stay there. She's going to fly straight on to Denver on business and then pick me up on her way back.

Sarah: What about your dad and Mark? Aren't they going to come with you?

David: No, it's just Mum and me. So I'm going to be in New York without my family. That's going to be brilliant.

Robert: Yes, but you're going to be with your aunt and Mary-Beth! I hope they're OK.

David: So do I.

1 What are they going to do?

Make sentences.

1. David			have a holiday in America.
2. He and his mum	is		fly to New York at the end of July.
3. Mrs Penrose	isn't		stay in New York.
4. She		going to	fly on to Denver on business.
5. David			go to Denver with her.
6. He	are		stay in New York with his aunt and cousin.
7. Mr Penrose and Mark	aren't		come with them.
8. They			stay at home in Nottingham.

2 Listening: Holiday plans

First read the questions. Then listen and make notes.

1. Who is at Nottingham Station?
2. What is David going to send Robert and Becky?
3. What are Sarah's plans for the summer?
4. What is Becky going to do?
5. Why isn't Jenny going to go away?
6. What is Robert going to do?
7. Who is going to stay in Nottingham?

3 At the airport

Say what is going to happen.

4 Your turn

Say what you are going to do …

- after this lesson
- this weekend
- in the holidays
- when you are eighteen

5 A postcard from New York

Put in the correct verbs. Use the simple past (regular or irregular? See page 155).

be | drive | get | meet | play | promise

sleep | talk | take | watch

Hi Robert,
I 1 you a postcard so here it is – from New York! Not bad, eh? We 2 here yesterday. It 3 a long flight (over seven hours) but I 4 a film and 5 a bit. My aunt 6 us at the airport and 7 us back to her apartment. On the first evening Mum and Aunt Meg 8 all the time so I 9 a computer game with Mary-Beth. She's OK but she uses a lot of funny words. Today Aunt Meg 10 us to some of the tourist attractions "downtown" (in the city centre). The skyscrapers here are fantastic. See you when I get back.

David

B You Brits!

David: Hey, this place is brilliant. And you're really good at skating.

Mary-Beth: Yeah. Central Park is great for things like skating, jogging or playing ball games. I really like living in the Big Apple.

David: What? Living in an apple? Ha, ha. Like a worm?

Mary-Beth: We call New York City the Big Apple. Didn't you know that?

David: But I can't see any apple trees around here! – Well, I'm really hungry after all this skating. Do you want some of my cheese and onion crisps?

Mary-Beth: Huh? Crisps? Oh, you mean chips! Sure. Thanks.

David: They aren't chips! Don't you know 'fish and chips'?

Mary-Beth: Yes, it's like burgers and fries. Your chips are our fries.

David: Hm. You Americans like using funny words. What else do you like doing apart from skating?

Mary-Beth: Well, I love surfing the Internet.

David: And what does your mum say?

Mary-Beth: You mean about sitting in front of the screen for too long?

David: Yes.

Mary-Beth: She doesn't mind. She likes using the Internet, too. And you?

David: I like playing the guitar, but I'm not very good at it.

Mary-Beth: Do you like football? If you're interested in seeing a game, we can go and see the Giants on Sunday.

David: Oh yes! But I don't know them. My favourite team is Manchester United.

Mary-Beth: That's soccer, David! I'm talking about football – American football. You Brits!

David: Well, your mum's English, so you're half a Brit.

Mary-Beth: True, actually Brits are quite OK. How about getting an ice cream?

David: Oh yes. Great idea!

1 David and Mary-Beth

Answer these questions.

1. What is the Big Apple?
2. What is Central Park great for?
3. What do David and Mary-Beth like?
4. What are / aren't they good at?
5. Which words have different meanings in British and American English? List these words and meanings (BE – AE – German).

2 Say it in German

1. And you're really good at skating. (l. 2)
2. Well, I'm really hungry after all this skating. (l. 12)
3. What else do you like doing apart from skating? (l. 23)
4. You mean about sitting in front of the screen for too long? (l. 27)
5. She doesn't mind. (l. 30)
6. I like playing the guitar, but I'm not very good at it. (l. 32)
7. If you're interested in seeing a game, … (l. 34)
8. How about getting an ice cream? (l. 46)

3 Gerunds

a) Look at the examples on the right. All the **-ing** forms in the box are gerunds. Can you find out what a gerund is and how it works?

grammar

Skating is fun.	**Football** is fun.
I like **skating**.	I like **football**.
Are you good at **skating**?	Are you good at **football**?
He's interested in **singing**.	He's interested in **music**.
How about **going** for a walk?	How about a **walk**?

b) Collect words that go with gerunds. Use them to make sentences with gerunds.

4 What you can do in New York City

Work with a partner. Use the verbs below and the information on the right to make little dialogues with suggestions and answers.

go • see • watch • visit • look at • get to know • learn • like • love • be interested in

Example:

How about going for a walk in Central Park?

Oh no, I don't like walking. But we can go skating there. …

Central Park: huge park
Empire State Building: highest building in the world until 1954
Rockefeller Center: offices, shops, restaurants, skating
Statue of Liberty: huge statue on an island, view of the city from its head
Broadway: place with a lot of theatres and cinemas
National Museum of the American Indian: information about Indians
Madison Square Garden: big sports and music events
South Street Seaport: museum with ships, fish market, shops, cafés, restaurants

5 Sound practice

42

[θ] a **th**eatre • **th**ree tee**th** • a **th**ousand **th**ings to **th**ink of

[ð] my mo**th**er and fa**th**er • wi**th** **th**em • **th**is wea**th**er • o**th**erwise

[θ] – [ð] My mo**th**er's **th**irty-fif**th** bir**th**day is **th**is mon**th**.

6 Listening: A message for Mary-Beth

50

David is alone at home when Aunt Meg calls. She has got an important message for Mary-Beth.

Listen and make notes. Then use your notes to write a dialogue: David tells Mary-Beth about the call.

G47

43 Dead on the roof?

1. "Hello and welcome to our sightseeing tour of New York City. My name's Frank Pilewski and I'm your pilot today. Sit back and relax. The weather is fantastic this afternoon. We're going to have a great tour."

2. Mary-Beth looked at David. "Are you nervous?" she asked. David smiled. "Nervous? No, I'm not frightened of flying." "Yeah, but flying in a helicopter isn't like being in a plane," she said. A moment later the pilot started the engine and checked his instruments. Then the helicopter took off.

■ 3. Soon David and Mary-Beth were above the skyscrapers. David looked down – and immediately looked up again. He already felt a bit funny. "OK," said the pilot. "This afternoon we're going to see the Hudson River and the island of Manhattan, with Central Park, the Empire State Building, Chinatown and all the rest. But let's start with the Statue of Liberty. There she is. What a beautiful lady!" David gave his camera to Mary-Beth. "Can you take some photos?" he said. "You can see better from where you are." Actually he was a bit frightened when he looked down.

4. "The statue is 46 metres tall and weighs 225 tons," said the pilot. "Can you see the finger? How long is it? What do you think?" Mary-Beth looked at David but his eyes were closed. "One metre," she said. "No. More than one metre," said David suddenly. "I think it's two metres." The pilot laughed. "Not bad, young man!" he said. "It's 2.45 metres. And do you know how the statue got here? Well, it came on a boat from France in 1885. It was a present from the French. Right, now let's fly back to Manhattan."

■ 5. Some time later Mary-Beth grabbed David's arm. "Look!" she said. "There's something on the roof of that skyscraper. It looks like a man. And he's lying on his back!" David looked out of the window. "Yes, I can see him," he said. "What's he doing there?" This was exciting. Suddenly David no longer felt frightened. "And what's that thing next to him? Is it a gun? Do you think he's ... dead? Is he a gangster or something?" "No idea," said Mary-Beth. She talked to the pilot. "There's a man on a roof over there," she said. "Maybe he's dead. Maybe he needs help. We must do something!"

6. The pilot flew in circles round the skyscraper. "The problem is, I can't land on skyscrapers," he

explained. "Well, only in an emergency." Mary-Beth looked at David. "But this is an emergency!"

■ 7. The pilot talked to the police and told them that he was going to land on the roof of the skyscraper.
He went down slowly and landed. Then he turned around and talked to David and Mary-Beth.
"Don't get out. It's too dangerous."
He opened the door and walked towards the man.
But Mary-Beth and David didn't stay in the helicopter. They were too excited. They got out and followed him.

8. The pilot looked at the man. "Is everything OK?" he asked. The man didn't move.
"Looks bad," said the pilot.
Mary-Beth and David stood next to him.
"Hey, wait!" said Mary-Beth. "He's opening his eyes!"
"You're right," said the pilot. "He's not dead."
"And just look at his clothes," said Mary-Beth. "He's a workman, not a gangster."
"And there's his gun," David laughed. "It's an electric drill!"
"Well, it's really hot today," said the pilot.
"I guess he had some work to do up here and just fainted. Come on, let's get him some water from the helicopter. Lucky for him that you two saw him!"

1 Put it right

Correct what is wrong.

1. David, Mary-Beth and Aunt Meg are doing a tour of New York City on a plane.
2. David isn't frightened of flying.
3. David takes some photos of a beautiful lady in Central Park.
4. The Statue of Liberty came on a plane from England in 1985.
5. David sees a man. He's sitting on the roof of a skyscraper.
6. The man has got a gun in his right hand.
7. Mary-Beth doesn't want to land because it's too dangerous.
8. The pilot must land because there's a problem with the helicopter.
9. The police tell the pilot that they are going to land.
10. Mary-Beth and the pilot stay in the helicopter.
11. The man looks at the pilot and moves his legs.
12. The man is wearing gangster's clothes.
13. The man fainted because it's a very cool day.
14. He needs water for his electric drill.

2 Headings

Find a heading for each part of the text. First match the headings on the right with the right parts of the text. Then go on with your own headings.

- The children can't wait
- Taking off
- A dead man on the roof?
- Welcome

3 A newspaper article

a) A journalist arrives with the police and asks a lot of questions. Work with a partner. One of you is the journalist, the other is David or Mary-Beth. Act out the interview. You can start like this:

Journalist: Hello. You were in the helicopter. Who are you? Where are you from?
David: My name is David Penrose. I'm 12. I'm from Nottingham, England.
Journalist: What are you doing here in New York?
David: I'm staying with my aunt and my cousin, Mary-Beth. She's here with me.
Journalist: Why were you in the helicopter? ...

b) You are all journalists now. Find a headline and write a short article about what happened. Here are some tips:

tip

- Every text has a beginning, a middle and an ending.
- Make sure you answer the 'who? – when? – where? – what? – why?' questions (see page 58).
- Don't use sentences from the text.
- Don't forget to connect your sentences.
- Use the past tense. Check all your verb forms.
- Check the word order in your sentences.

Children save workman's life

Yesterday afternoon young David Penrose from Nottingham, UK, and his cousin Mary-Beth Wallace were on a helicopter tour above the roofs of New York City. Suddenly ...

4 Word power

Find the right words.

1. You take photos with a ___.
2. The people in ___ speak French.
3. When your eyes are not open, they are ___.
4. You have ten ___ on your hands.
5. When you do a ___ of a city, you look at all the important things there.
6. If you do something ___, you do not wait.
7. You are ___ when you are excited about something, and can't sleep, for example.
8. When you aren't alive, you're ___.
9. When something is really dangerous for people, there is an ___.
10. A ___ person looks good.
11. When a flight starts, you take off; when it finishes, you ___.
12. A skyscraper is a very tall ___.
13. Your ___ is where you do not have eyes.
14. If you do not walk fast, you walk ___.

47 5 A song: Fly away

I wish[1] that I could[2] fly
Into the sky so very high
Just like a dragonfly[3].

I'd[4] fly above the trees
Over the seas in all degrees[5]
To anywhere I please[6].

Oh I want to get away
I want to fly away.
Yeah yeah yeah ...

Let's go and see the stars
The Milky Way[7] or even
Mars
Where it could just be ours[8].

Let's fade[9] into the sun
Let your spirit[10] fly where we are one
Just for a little[11] fun.

Words: Lenny Kravitz

[1] [wɪʃ] wünschte • [2] könnte • [3] ['drægnflaɪ] Libelle • [4] [aɪd] ich würde • [5] [ɪn‿ɔ:l dɪ'gri:z] etwa: überall • [6] egal, wohin • [7] [ˌmɪlki 'weɪ] Milchstraße • [8] unser • [9] [feɪd] etwa: in etwas aufgehen • [10] ['spɪrɪt] Geist • [11] ein bisschen

1 In the USA

Put the words in the right groups.
Which are the odd words out?
(There are two.)

US state	US city	US tourist attraction
...	...	...

Alaska • Boston • California • Central Park • Denver • Disney World • Heathrow • Los Angeles • Mexico • Niagara Falls • Rocky Mountains • Statue of Liberty • Texas • Washington • Washington, DC

2 Plans

David has got three more days in New York. Talk about his and the others' plans.

	David	Mary-Beth and Aunt Meg	David's mum
Thursday	• buy computer game	• take David to Brooklyn Zoo	• finish business in Denver
Friday	• watch baseball on TV	• make nice dinner for others	• fly back to New York
Saturday	• show mum New York	• clean apartment	• see New York with David
Sunday	• fly to Heathrow	• drive to Kennedy Airport	• fly home

Example: What is David going to do on Thursday? –
He's going to buy a computer game.

3 What I did in New York

Back in Nottingham, David is telling Mark and his dad about his holiday.

Put in the right verb forms. Some are gerunds!

"**(stay)** in New York was brilliant. I really **(like)** **(see)** those skyscrapers for the first time. And **(walk)** through Central Park was fun. Mary-Beth **(take)** me there. She's very good at **(skate)**. She likes **(jog)** and **(swim)**, too. You can **(do)** lots of sports in New York. If you're interested in **(watch)** American football, you can **(go)** to a Giants' game. We **(do)**, and two of Mary-Beth's friends **(come)** with us. And, of course, New York is great for **(shop)**, Dad. But if you don't like **(spend)** lots of money, don't **(go)** to Fifth Avenue. It's too dangerous! If you like **(see)** things from the air, you can **(try)** a helicopter tour. We **(go)** on one and it **(be)** really exciting! Mum? How about **(go)** back to New York next summer – with Mark and Dad this time?"

Start like this: **Staying** in New York was ...

4 Word power: Food and drink

Put all the food and drink words that you know into these groups (some can be in more than one group):

breakfast	lunch	tea	dinner	sweets
...	...	...	...	...

4 revision Unit 6 – Unit 7

1 When?

Finish these sentences with a time phrase. Use a different time phrase for each sentence. Example: Mary-Beth is writing an e-mail **at the moment.**

PAST PRESENT FUTURE

1. Mary-Beth is writing an e-mail ___.
2. Jenny is going to buy a skateboard ___.
3. David went to the cinema ___.
4. Becky and Simon are going to have a party ___.
5. Robert watches The Big Breakfast on TV ___.
6. Barker had a lot of fun in the park ___.

2 Ask a silly question ...

Sometimes you can see what people are going to do. But you still ask them about their plans – and then they give you a silly answer. Look at the pictures and make funny dialogues.

Example: *David:* Are you going to drink some milk?
Mary-Beth: No, I'm going to wash my face in it!

3 Back in New York

Put in the correct forms of the simple past.

Last night David **(have)** a terrible dream. He **(be)** back in New York with Mary-Beth. They **(be)** in a helicopter. First they **(fly)** over the Empire State Building. David **(look)** down and **(feel)** terrible, especially when the pilot **(start)** to land. "No! It's too dangerous," he **(cry)**. He **(not want)** to land there. "OK!" the pilot **(shout)**. But where **(David want)** to land? He **(have)** no idea – maybe at the zoo? "Right!" the pilot **(answer)**. But the pilot's voice **(be)** different now. David **(turn)** his head and **(find)** Mary-Beth in the pilot's place. She **(not smile)**. "Our pilot **(jump)** out," she **(say)**. "I'm your pilot now!" When they **(arrive)** at the Bronx Zoo, they **(land)** in a field and David **(get)** out. Then the helicopter **(take)** off again – without David! He **(look)** around and **(see)** a huge apple with little legs and big teeth. "A Brit! Yummy!" **(cry)** the big apple and **(come)** slowly towards David. David **(want)** to run away, but he **(not can)** move his legs. He **(stand)** there and **(wait)**. The big apple **(show)** its teeth and ... But just then it **(start)** to rain. David **(feel)** water on his face. "Wake up, David!" **(say)** a voice. It **(be)** Mark.

4 Who says what

Finish the sentences with the phrases on the right. Use gerunds.
Example: 1. *David:* I like playing the guitar, but I'm not very good at it.

1. *David:* I like ___, but I'm not very good at it.
2. *Jenny:* ___ is OK, but I still want to go back to Munich.
3. *Becky:* I like ___. He's always so happy!
4. *Kim:* ___ isn't always easy.
5. *Sarah:* ___ is fun!
6. *Simon:* I hate ___.
7. *Mary-Beth:* I love ___.
8. *Robert:* How about ___ to see our old friends, Mum?
9. *Mark:* I don't like ___.

a) have a little sister
b) watch TV without David
c) tidy my room
d) live in the Big Apple
e) play the guitar ✓
f) drive down to London
g) take Barker for a walk
h) live in Nottingham
i) play football with the others

5 Your turn

Talk with a partner about what you like and don't like doing.

Examples: I like ___. What do you like? – Oh, I like ___, too.
Are you interested in ___? – Not really. I don't like ___. I think ___ is more fun.

love • like • be interested in • not like • hate
+
do • meet • ride • play • help • watch • go • tidy • …
+
friends • new people • in the kitchen • (my) things • … on TV • football • homework • music • to other countries • on holiday • poor people • out to eat • …

6 Mixed bag: Two e-mails

Put in the missing words:

a) about • ago • are • beach • brother • did • didn't • drove • flight • funny • is • many • our • sea • stay • Sunday • terrible • went • without

Hi there David,
How 1 you? And how 2 Aunty Pat? And what 3 your dad and your little 4 ? 5 you have a good 6 back to London? After we 7 you to Kennedy Airport on 8 morning, we 9 want to go back to 10 apartment, so we 11 down to Coney Island, a place by the 12 with a nice big 13 , but too 14 people! (It was OK about twenty years 15 , they say, but now it's 16 . That's why we didn't 17 long.
It's 18 , the place is very quiet 19 you two!
See you, Mary-Beth

b) after • at • dream • eat • going • got • happy • had • hated • in • still • stupid • tell • thanks • holiday • while • young

Hi Mary-Beth,
1 for your e-mail. We're all fine. Mark is 2 now that I'm back. He really 3 staying 4 home 5 I was 6 New York! But he's too 7 to fly to America. I mean, he 8 goes to kindergarten! Mum and I 9 back OK. Thanks again for looking 10 me in New York. I 11 a great 12 . Actually, I had a bad 13 last night. I was back in New York and a big apple tried to 14 me! I'm not 15 to 16 you any more because it was too 17 !
Bye for now, David

7 Word groups

51 **a)** Write this list of headings in your exercise book. Listen and put every word into the right group.

people	things	buildings
…	…	…

b) Find the odd word out in each group and make a sentence with it.

1. send • scared • scream • shake • save
2. stable • pigsty • sheep • shed • pupil
3. surfing • swimming • shopping • skiing • skating
4. knives • shoes • goes • apples • chips
5. fresh • hot • faint • fast • dead
6. box • bottle • tin • pair • basket
7. about • ago • towards • out of • apart from
8. always • sometimes • never • often • almost
9. each • my • some • no • now

c) How many words can you find?

1. Things you take to school:
2. Things you can read:
3. How you can feel:
4. What you can do on the beach:
5. Countries:
6. Parts of the body:
7. Clothes:
8. Games:

d) Start a mind map with one of these words: school, birthday, holiday, city, country, UK, USA

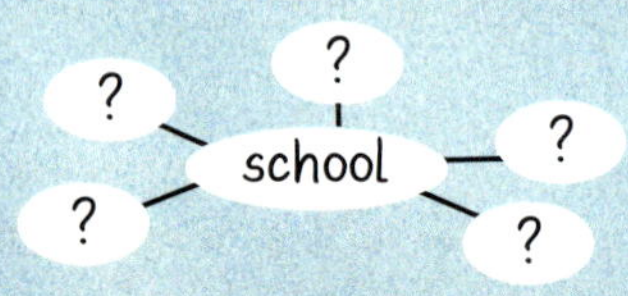

8 Pairs

a) Find word pairs, then make sentences with them.

Example: Barker often **barks at** Tabby.

bark • fall • get • look • pick • sit • turn

after • around • at • down • off • over • up

b) How many words can you make?

Example: **bed**room

? | room • cake • centre • board

c) Some words go together. Find the other word in these pairs:

1. father – mother
2. brother –
3. uncle –
4. knife –
5. cup –
6. eat –
7. day –
8. fish –
9. wake up –
10. above –

9 Find the words

1. Things to wear.
2. All the people.
3. A place where you learn things.
4. Your relatives.
5. At once.
6. To get to a place.
7. Looking at tourist attractions.
8. This vegetable can hurt your eyes!
9. Frightened.
10. Water from the sky.
11. Not dangerous.
12. To say hello or goodbye with your hand.

10 Rhyming[1] words

a) Make pairs. The words in each pair must have the same sound.
Example: day – grey

day • night • please • you • look • red

b) Can you find more words for each group? Make lists.

c) Play a rhyming game with two teams. (Start with a short word! No names, no places!)

Team **A** can start.

that – A
cat – B
flat – A
mat – B
Hm, we can't think of any more words! – A

One point for Team **B**. Now it's Team **B**'s turn to start.

11 A game: I spy[2]

Look at the picture and play with a partner.

You: I spy with my little eye something beginning with 'B'.
Partner: A ball?
You: No.
Partner: A bag?
You: That's right. It's your turn now.

Go on. You can spy things in the classroom, too.

12 Word snakes

Write out the words.
When do you use capital letters[3]?

13 A game: What's the word?

Play this game in class. Can you guess the word before your teacher finishes his or her boat?

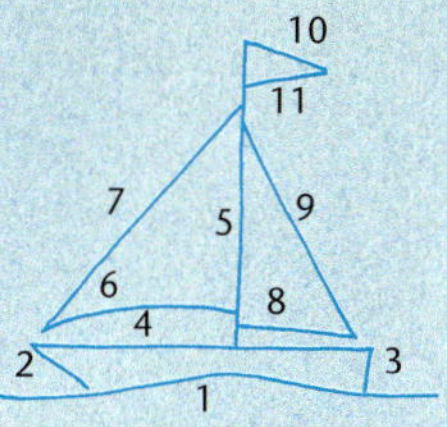

Has it got an 'A' in it?
Yes, it has.

_ A _ _ _ _ _ _

What about an 'E'?
No, it hasn't got an 'E'.

_ A _ _ _ _ _ _

Is there a 'B' in it?
Yes, there is.

B A _ _ _ _ _ _

[1]to rhyme [raɪm] – sich reimen • [2]['aɪ 'spaɪ] – ich sehe was, was du nicht siehst • [3]capital letter – Großbuchstabe

A Christmas time (after Unit 2)

1 Christmas in Britain

It's Christmas Eve, and Mark and Jenny are in Mark and David's room. This is Jenny's first Christmas in England.

Mark: Hey, Jenny, look! Here's my stocking. It's for my presents from Father Christmas.
Jenny: A stocking? Oh, that's a nice idea.
Mark: Here's a mince pie for Father Christmas. He must come a long way – so maybe he's hungry.

It's Christmas Day. Now Mark, David and Jenny have got their presents. They are in the living room.

David: Oh, I'm hungry.
Jenny: What's for dinner?
Mr Penrose: Turkey and then Christmas pudding.
Jenny: Mmm. Great!
Mark: Hey, Jenny, look! Here are the crackers. Let's pull one.
David: No, Mark. We must wait till dinner.
Jenny: What's in the crackers?
Mark: A little present.

It's Boxing Day.

David: Can we go to the park?
Mrs Penrose: No! We've got tickets for a pantomime – Aladdin.
Mark: Oh, great!
Jenny: What's a pantomime?
David: A funny play with silly songs and silly people.
Mrs Penrose: You can only go to pantomimes at Christmas.

48 2 A song: We wish you a Merry Christmas

Traditional

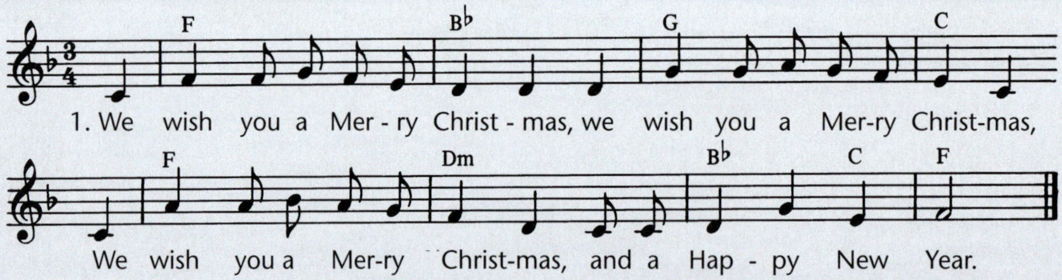

Chorus: Good tidings we bring to you and your kin,
We wish you a Merry Christmas and a Happy New Year.

2. Now bring us some Christmas pudding *(3x)*, and bring us some here.
3. We won't go until we've got some *(3x)*, so bring some right here.
4. For we all like Christmas pudding *(3x)*, so bring some out here.

B Fun page (after Unit 4)

1 Time for a joke

What bird has wings, but cannot fly?

Roast turkey!

Where can you always find money?

In a dictionary.

What is the end of everything?

The letter G.

Mum, can I have a dog for Christmas?

No, you can have turkey like everyone else.

Do you write with your right hand or with your left hand?

Well, I usually write with a pen.

Teacher: Andy, say something beginning with 'I'.
Andy: I is …
Teacher: No, Andy, you must say 'I am'.
Andy: All right, I am the ninth letter of the alphabet.

2 Riddles

Who am I?
My first is in **DOWN**, but not in **BROWN.**
My second is in **THAT**, but not in **THIS.**
My third is in **GIVE**, but not in **GET.**
My fourth is in **I'VE,** but not in **WE'VE.**
My fifth is in **RED,** but not in **BLUE.**

What month am I?
My first is in **JOB**, but not in **WORK.**
My second is in **SUNDAYS,**
but not in **MONDAYS.**
My third is in **NINE,** but not in **EIGHT.**
My fourth is in **THEY,** but not in **YOU.**

3 Questions and answers

How do four elephants get in a car?

Why does the vet go to the library?

Why does the girl's lunch speak German?

Where does Superman buy his T-shirts?

Answers: At the supermarket. • Because the bookworm is ill. • Through the door. • Because it's a hamburger.

4 Cartoons

© PUNCH

"There's a class clown in every school."

© Norman Thelwell

C Poetry page (after Unit 6)

49 1 Some poems

The skateboard

My daddy bought me a skateboard;
he tried it out first at the store.
And that is the reason why Mommy
says Daddy can't walk any more.
Willard R. Espy

Old Mother Hubbard

Old Mother Hubbard
went to the cupboard
to get her poor dog a bone.
But the dog couldn't wait,
so when dinner was late,
he ordered a pizza by phone.
Bruce Lansky

Roses are red

Roses are red.
Violets are blue.
Sugar is sweet.
And so are you.

Poems are texts with a special form. They can have rhymes, a special rhythm (stressed and unstressed syllables in a special order), and sometimes words or letters are repeated. What is special about these poems? Read them aloud, find the rhymes and count the stressed syllables.

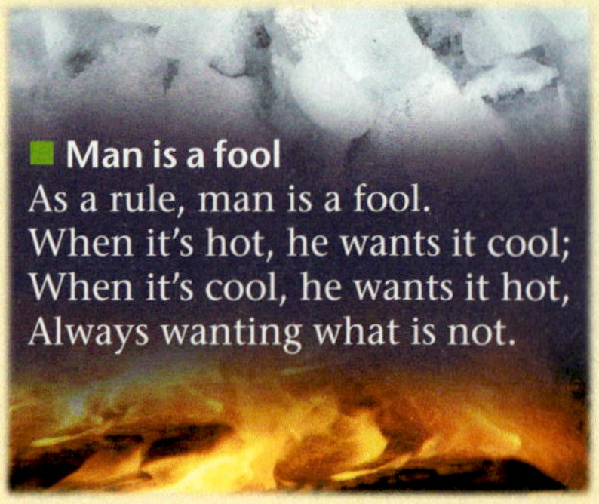

Man is a fool

As a rule, man is a fool.
When it's hot, he wants it cool;
When it's cool, he wants it hot,
Always wanting what is not.

53 2 Anti-smoking poems

Fill in the missing rhyming words.
They all rhyme with a number.

Here lies Sam Shay.
Smoked six packs a day.
He started smoking when he was two.
Now there's nothing he can …

Here lies Sam Shay.
Smoked six packs a day.
He started smoking when he was nine.
Now he isn't feeling …

Here lies Sam Shay.
Smoked six packs a day.
He started smoking when he was three.
Now he's buried beneath a …

Here lies Sam Shay.
Smoked six packs a day.
He started smoking when he was ten.
Now he'll never smoke …
Bruce Lansky

3 Write an eleven word poem

Write a poem like this:

Line 1: one word
Line 2: two words
Line 3: three words
Line 4: four words
Line 5: one word

This is an example:

It's a good idea to start with a colour.

4 More ideas

There are lots of ways to write a poem. Here are some more ideas. Your texts needn't be very long.

a) Take a poem and change some of the words. Here is an example (Roses are red):

Horses are big.
Hamsters are small.
Animals are great.
I like them all.

b) Write a poem with words that start with the same letter.

Becky **B**urton **b**uys a **b**ox
of **b**oring **b**ooks **b**efore her **b**rilliant
brother's **b**irthday.

c) Write a text with words that have the same sound.

I like a nice surprise.
I ride my bike at night.
I think I am all right.

d) Draw pictures with words.

e) Collect rhyming words on the blackboard in class and write a poem with all the words.

f) Do you remember the alphabet rap on page 17? You can write your own rap like this: Read the following line aloud. Stress the numbers, the other syllables are not stressed:

a one and a two and a three and a four

Now you have got the rhythm.
Write a rap to this rhythm.

D The paper bag princess (after Unit 6)

1

Elizabeth was a beautiful princess.
She lived in a castle and had a lot of beautiful princess clothes.
She was going to marry Prince Ronald.

2

One day a dragon smashed her castle, burnt all her clothes, and carried off Prince Ronald. Elizabeth wanted to chase the dragon and get Ronald back. She needed some clothes, but she could only find a paper bag. So she put on the paper bag and followed the dragon. He was easy to follow, because where he went there were a lot of burnt forests and dead horses.

3

Finally, Elizabeth came to a cave with a large door. She banged on the door. The dragon looked out of the door and said, "Well, a princess! I love to eat princesses, but I ate a whole castle today. I am a very busy dragon. Come back tomorrow."
"Wait," shouted Elizabeth. "Is it true that you are the strongest dragon in the world?"
"Yes," said the dragon.

4

"Is it true," said Elizabeth, "that you can burn up ten forests with your breath?"
"Oh, yes," said the dragon, and he took a huge, deep breath and breathed out so much fire that he burnt up fifty forests.
"Fantastic," said Elizabeth, and the dragon took a huge breath again and breathed out so much fire that he burnt up one hundred forests.

5

"Brilliant," said Elizabeth, and the dragon took a huge breath again, but this time nothing came out. The dragon no longer had enough fire to cook a burger.

6

Elizabeth said, "Dragon, is it true that you can fly around the world in just ten seconds?" "Why, yes," said the dragon, and jumped up and flew all the way around the world in ten seconds. He was very tired when he got back, but Elizabeth shouted, "Fantastic, do it again!" So the dragon jumped up and flew around the world in twenty seconds. When he got back, he was too tired to talk, and he lay down and went straight to sleep.

7

Elizabeth whispered, "Hey, dragon." The dragon didn't move. She shouted in his ear, "Hey, dragon!" The dragon was so tired that he didn't move.
Elizabeth walked over the dragon and opened the door to the cave.

8

There was Prince Ronald. He looked at her and said, "Elizabeth, you are a mess! You smell like burnt trees, your hair is dirty and you are wearing an old paper bag. Come back when you look like a real princess."
"Ronald," said Elizabeth, "your clothes are really beautiful and your hair is beautiful, too. You look like a real prince, but you are a bum."
They didn't get married.

E A very cultured bird (after Unit 7)

This story is from a book called 'Superfudge' by Judy Blume. In it an American boy, Peter, tells stories about his family, especially his brother Fudge (really Farley). Peter is in the sixth grade, and Fudge is in the kindergarten class at his school.

One night Mom said, "Fudgie, you're doing so well in school, we would like to give you a little present. What would you like?"
"A bird," Fudge said.
"A bird?" Mom repeated.
"Yes. My very own bird."
"A bird," Dad said.
"I thought, something like a yo-yo," Mom said.
"I have a yo-yo," Fudge told her. "But I don't have a bird."
"Well ...," Mom said.
"And he can sleep in my room, right?" Fudge asked.
"Yes," Dad said.
"In my bed?"
"No," Dad said. "Birds sleep in cages, not beds."
"Birds can't sleep in beds," Mom said.
"Why not?" Fudge asked.
"Because they like to sleep standing up," Mom said.
"They do?" Fudge asked.
"Yes."
"I must try that tonight," Fudge said.

▲▼▲

Grandma came to visit for a few days.
"I'm getting a bird," Fudge told her.
"What kind of bird?" Grandma asked.
"I don't know. What kind of bird am I getting?" he asked me.
"A myna bird," I said. "Myna birds can talk."
"A talking bird?" Fudge asked.
"Yes. You can teach a myna bird to say anything," I added.
"Anything?" Fudge asked.
"Well, almost anything," I told him.
"A talking bird," Fudge said, smiling.
"Fudgie's getting a talking bird."

▲▼▲

"Guess what?" Fudge said.
"What?" Grandma said.
"I saw him ... I saw my myna bird!"
"Where?" I asked.
"At the pet store," Fudge said. "We're bringing him home tomorrow. They had to order a cage. He's all black, with yellow legs and a yellow nose. And he can talk!"
"What can he say?"
"He can say hello, in French."
"In French?" I asked.
"That's right, in French," Mom said. "He's very cultured."
"And I've already named him," Fudge said.
"What did you name him, Fudgie?" Grandma asked.
I expected him to say Pierre or Jacques, as he spoke French.
"Uncle Feather," Fudge said.
"Uncle Feather?" I said.
"Yes, Uncle Feather," Fudge said again.
"Isn't that a good name for a bird?"
"It's uh ... unusual," I said.
"And interesting, right?" Fudge asked.
"Oh, yes ... definitely interesting," I told him.

The next day, Mom, Dad and Fudge went down to the pet store and came back with Uncle Feather, a cage and a cover, a box of food and a book called "Getting to Know Your Myna Bird". "Bonjour ... bonjour ...," Uncle Feather said over and over again.

"That means hello in French," Fudge told me, as if I didn't already know. Dad carried the cage up to Fudgie's room, which was next to my room. All afternoon all I heard was "bonjour ... bonjour" in bird-voice. I banged on the wall of Fudgie's room.

"Can't you teach him to say something else?"

"I'm trying ... I'm trying ...," Fudge shouted.

"I'm trying ... I'm trying ...," Uncle Feather repeated.

The next morning, when I went to see Uncle Feather, he greeted me with, "Bonjour, stupid ... ."

"Isn't he smart?" Fudge asked. "Doesn't he learn fast?"

"Yeah ... he's terrific!" I said.

Grandma looked at Uncle Feather in his cage and said, "And you're a lovely birdie, aren't you?"

"Lovely birdie ... lovely birdie ...," Uncle Feather said.

Grandma laughed. "Oh my, and so smart!"

"So smart ... so smart ... oh my ... so smart ...," Uncle Feather said.

"He likes to eat worms and insects and plants," Fudge said at breakfast. "So I have to go find him some worms."

"Oh, no!" Mom said. "He is very happy with the food we bought for him at the pet store."

"But Uncle Feather needs worms to be happy. You want him to be happy, don't you?"

"I'm sure he can be happy without worms!" Mom said, and pushed her plate aside.

"Let's talk about this later," Dad said. "It's not the best breakfast conversation."

"Worms, worms, worms, worms ...," Fudge sang.

"That's enough, Fudge!" Dad said, but Mom was already in the bathroom and she didn't come back to the table.

After two weeks, Fudge was ready to bring Uncle Feather to school for Show and Tell. And I got special permission from Mr Green to miss half of English and go down to Fudge's classroom in case of problems. Mrs Hildebrandt's kindergarten class sat in a circle on the floor.

Uncle Feather's cage stood in the middle of the circle. When everyone was ready, Fudge pulled the cover off the cage and said, "Presenting ... Uncle Feather!"

"Ooohhh ...," all the kids said.

"What a beautiful bird Farley has," Mrs Hildebrandt said. "Isn't he a beautiful bird, class?"

"Yes," Mrs Hildebrandt's class answered, sounding like robots.

"He speaks French," Fudge said.

"Does he really?" Mrs Hildebrandt asked.

"Yes," Fudge told her.

"Well, isn't that funny," Mrs Hildebrandt said. "So do I!" She went right up to Uncle Feather's cage, bent over, and said, "Parlez-vous français?"

Uncle Feather cocked his head, looked straight at her and said, "Bonjour, stupid!"

translation & mediation

Tipp

Beim Übersetzen ist es meist nicht sinnvoll, jedes Wort einzeln zu übersetzen, weil ein und dieselbe Sache in der einen Sprache manchmal ganz anders ausgedrückt wird als in der anderen. Wenn du also etwas ins Englische übersetzen willst, dann überlege zunächst, wie Becky oder Robert dazu sagen würden.

Wie heißt du?	*What's your name?*
Wie geht's dir?	*How are you?*
Wo kommst du her?	*Where are you from?*

1 Im Pausenhof

Let's start 7

Stell dir vor, du triffst eine englische Gastschülerin im Pausenhof.
Wie könnte ein erstes Gespräch aussehen?

Du: (begrüßt sie, stellst dich vor und fragst, wie sie heißt)
Sally: *My name is Sally.*
Du: (fragst, wo sie herkommt)
Sally: *I'm from Mansfield. That's not very far*[1] *from Nottingham.*
Du: (sagst, wo du herkommst, und fragst, wie alt sie ist)
Sally: *I'm 13. And you?*
Du: (sagst, wie alt du bist)
Sally: *Who's your English teacher?*
Du: (sagst den Namen deines Lehrers / deiner Lehrerin)
Sally: *Is s/he nice?*
Du: (bejahst die Frage)
Sally: *Is that your English book?*
Du: (verneinst und sagst, dass das der Ordner mit deinen Lieblingscomics ist)
Sally: *Oh great! I like comics. Let's read them together.*

[1] far [fɑː] – weit

2 Jennys Fotos

Unit 1 • Language A

Jenny zeigt ihrem Cousin David einige Fotos aus Deutschland. Was sagen die beiden?

Jenny: Schau her, das ist meine Familie: Mein Vater, meine Mutter und unsere Katze.

David: Und wer ist das da?
Jenny: Der Mann und die Frau auf dem Bild sind Onkel Herbert und Tante Susi. Sie haben einen Supermarkt.
David: Wirklich? Und was ist das hier?
Jenny: Das ist unsere Wohnung. Sie liegt nicht im Stadtzentrum. Sie liegt neben einem Park. Wir haben auch einen großen Garten.
David: Wirklich nett. Und was ist das da?
Jenny: Das ist mein Zimmer. Es ist nicht besonders ordentlich.
David: Ich finde, es ist in Ordnung! ... Wow! Du hast ja eine super Stereoanlage!
Jenny: Hast du auch eine Stereoanlage?
David: Nein, nur einen CD-Player. Aber ich habe meinen eigenen Computer!
Jenny: Können wir die neue CD von den *Underdogs* anhören?
David: Warum nicht?

3 Beim Frühstück

Unit 1 • Text

Bereitet diesen Dialog in Dreiergruppen gut vor, um ihn danach mit verteilten Rollen auf Englisch vorzutragen. Schafft ihr es, ohne jedes Wort vorher schriftlich zu übersetzen?

Dad: Wo ist mein Messer? Bist du nicht heute mit dem Tischdecken an der Reihe?
Child: Ja, ich bin dran, aber ich kann die Messer nicht finden.
Mum: Die Messer sind dort drüben!
Child: Und wo sind die Teller?
Mum: Die Teller sind natürlich im Schrank. – Iiiiih!
Dad: Was ist denn los?
Mum: Ein Frosch! Da, unter dem Tisch!
Dad: Ich kann ihn nicht sehen! Wo ist er?
Child: Da, schau, neben dem Schrank, auf dem Regal.
Dad: Wie kommt denn ein Frosch in unsere Küche?
Child: Komm her, kleiner Frosch! Ich bin dein Freund.
Mum: Macht die Tür auf, dann kann er in den Garten!
Dad: Das ist eine ausgezeichnete Idee. Machen wir sie auf!

4 In Nottingham

Unit 2 • Language A

Stell dir vor, du bist unterwegs in Nottingham. Du fragst eine Passantin nach dem Weg.

Du: Entschuldigen Sie bitte, können Sie mir sagen, wo ich die Statue von Robin Hood finde?
Woman: *Of course. It's right in front of the castle.*
Du: Und wie komme ich da hin?
Woman: *You can walk, or take the bus.*
Du: Kann ich im Bus eine Fahrkarte kaufen?
Woman: *Yes, you can buy a Day Rider ticket. It's for all buses in the city for one day.*
Du: Gut. Können Sie mir dann noch den Weg zum *Victoria Shopping Centre* zeigen?
Sally: *Of course. Go down Friar Lane to Old Market Square, go down King Street and turn right into Parliament Street. The Victoria Shopping Centre is on the left.*
Du: Vielen Dank. Auf Wiedersehen.

Vor dem *Victoria Shopping Centre* triffst du Becky.

Du: (begrüßt sie und fragst, was sie gerade macht)
Becky: (sagt, dass sie auf Sarah wartet)
Du: (fragst, wo Sarah ist, ob sie drinnen im Laden ist und ob sie sich ein Buch kauft)
Becky: (verneint und sagt, dass Sarah sich Videos ansieht)
Du: (schlägst vor, zusammen hineinzugehen und einen Zeichentrickfilm anzusehen)
Becky: (bittet dich, noch eine Minute zu warten, sagt, du könntest schon hineingehen, aber sie müsse noch eine SMS schreiben)
Du: (sagst, dass du dann mit ihr wartest)

5 Sie, Sie oder sie?

Unit 2 • Language B

Übersetze die folgenden Sätze.

1. Die Katze ist unter dem Schreibtisch, Mrs Dane. Können Sie sie sehen?
2. Sarah schaut sich zwei Videos an, aber sie kann sie nicht kaufen.
3. Becky ruft ihre Freundin auf dem Handy an, aber sie kann sie nicht hören.
4. David und Robert warten auf Becky. Können sie sie anrufen?
5. Entschuldigung, ich kann Sie nicht hören. Können Sie das wiederholen?
6. Schauen Sie, da ist die Statue! – Wo? Ich kann sie nicht auf dem Stadtplan finden.

6 Wann und wie oft?

Unit 3 • Language A

Übersetze die folgenden Sätze. Achte auf die Wortstellung.

1. Morgens bin ich immer müde.
2. Am Sonntag essen wir normalerweise um 12 Uhr zu Mittag.
3. Wann ist das Schwimmbad mittwochs geöffnet?
4. Meine Eltern sehen abends oft fern.
5. Ich frühstücke sonntags immer im Bett.
6. Wir tragen niemals Schuluniformen.
7. Es ist schon fünf vor neun.
8. Die Lehrerin kommt nie zu spät.
9. In der Theatergruppe treffen wir uns dienstags um Viertel nach vier.
10. Manchmal spielen wir am Samstag Fußball.
11. Am Abend gehen wir spazieren.
12. Robert ist jedes Wochenende bei den Penroses.
13. Die Kinder fahren manchmal mit dem Bus in die Stadtmitte. Sie gehen normalerweise freitags nach der Schule.

7 Ein normaler Schultag

Unit 3 • Language A

Schreibe eine E-Mail an deine(n) englische(n) Brieffreund(in), in der du ihm / ihr über deinen Schulalltag berichtest.

Du wählst die richtige Anrede und bedankst dich zunächst für seine / ihre letzte E-Mail.

Dann schreibst du,
- dass du heute von deinem Schultag erzählst,
- wann du aufstehen musst und wie du zur Schule kommst (zu Fuß, mit dem Bus, mit dem Zug),
- wann bei euch der Unterricht beginnt und wann er endet,
- welches Fach du besonders oder nicht so sehr magst,
- dass du nach der Schule heimgehst und deine Hausaufgaben machst,
- was du in deiner Freizeit unternimmst. (Nenne mehrere Beispiele.)

Du schreibst, dass du keine *assembly* hast und fragst, was das überhaupt ist.

Du fügst hinzu, dass es bei euch an der Schule keine Schuluniform gibt.

Du berichtest noch kurz über deine Wochenenden und schreibst,
- dass du samstags manchmal deiner Mutter beim Einkaufen oder deinem Vater im Garten helfen musst,
- dass du oft deiner Tante in der Küche hilfst (weil du dann gewöhnlich ein Eis als Belohnung bekommst),
- dass du den Sonntag magst, weil du da lange im Bett bleiben kannst.

Du schreibst, dass du jetzt aufhören musst, weil du deine Deutschhausaufgabe fertigmachen musst, und verabschiedest dich mit herzlichen Grüßen.

Tipp

Für schriftliche Übersetzungen

- Lies dir zunächst die ganze Übersetzung in Ruhe durch.
- Notiere dir alle Stellen, bei denen du besonders aufpassen musst.
- Fange an, Satz für Satz zu übersetzen.
- Lasse Wörter oder Sätze, bei denen du unsicher bist, nie aus, sondern entscheide dich für eine vorläufige Übersetzung und markiere die Stelle, damit du später noch einmal gezielt daran arbeiten kannst.
- Achte darauf, dass die Wortstellung im Englischen nicht so frei ist wie im Deutschen.
- Wenn dir ein Wort absolut nicht einfallen will, versuche ein ähnliches zu wählen.
- Wenn du fertig bist, vergleiche deinen Text sorgfältig mit dem Originaltext und hake alle Wörter ab, für die du eine Entsprechung gefunden hast.
- Denke dabei wieder daran, dass nicht jedes Wort in einer Sprache auch genau einem Wort in der anderen Sprache entspricht.

8 Becky und Barker — Unit 3 • Text

Becky erzählt von ihrem Hund Barker. Übersetze ins Englische.

Ich habe ein sehr nettes Haustier, einen Hund. Sein Name ist Barker. Jeden Morgen um halb acht weckt er mich und wäscht mir das Gesicht. Dann frühstücken wir zusammen. Um zehn vor halb neun muss ich zur Schule. Barker gefällt das nicht. Meine Eltern nehmen ihn mit zu ihrem Fahrradgeschäft, aber am Nachmittag sind wir wieder zusammen und ich führe ihn aus. Wir gehen oft in den Park. Robert ist sauer auf Barker, weil Barker Kaninchen jagt. Ich bringe Barker Kunststücke bei: Ich werfe einen kleinen gelben Ball und er bringt ihn zurück. Wenn er die Katze der Dixons auf der Gartenmauer sieht, fängt er sofort an zu bellen. Ich liebe Barker, aber manchmal macht er alberne Sachen: Wenn wir abends fernsehen, setzt er sich immer vor den Fernseher. Mein Vater wirft dann mit Schuhen auf ihn. Barker gefällt dieses Spiel. Er nimmt die Schuhe und trägt sie in mein Zimmer. Ich kann ihm aber nie wirklich böse sein.

9 Alles Gute zum Geburtstag — Unit 4 • Language B

Ein britischer Gastschüler ist zu Besuch bei euch in der Klasse. Stellt Fragen, um herauszufinden, wie man in Großbritannien Geburtstag feiert. Könnt ihr sie auch beantworten?

1. Feiert man in Großbritannien den Geburtstag normalerweise mit einer Party?
2. Wen lädt man ein?
3. Lädt man alle Freunde nach Hause ein?
4. Wo geht man hin?
5. Welche Spiele spielt man bei einem Geburtstagsfest?
6. Was bekommt man zum Geburtstag?
7. Wer gibt einem Karten und Geschenke?
8. Was isst man bei einem Geburtstagsfest?
9. Bekommt man einen Kuchen?
10. Wie viele Kerzen sind auf dem Kuchen?
11. Was sind die *bumps*?
12. Tun sie weh?
13. Wie bedankt man sich für ein Geschenk?
14. Sind Geburtstagsfeiern in Deutschland anders?

10 Ein Wochenende am Meer — Unit 5 • Intro

Du möchtest mit deinen Eltern für ein Wochenende ans Meer fahren, vom 25.–27. August. Ihr wollt ein Zimmer mit Aussicht (Meerblick), Bad und Frühstück. Wie musst du die Felder des Online-Reservierungsformulars ausfüllen, um deine Reservierung vorzunehmen?

Seaview Hotel booking form

Name:		Date of arrival[1]: (DD/MM/YYYY)	
Address:		Date of departure[2]: (DD/MM/YYYY)	
E-mail address:		Number of nights:	
Telephone number:		Number of people:	
Fax number:		Special needs[3]:	
		Submit[4]	Reset

[1] [ə'raɪvl] – Ankunft • [2] [dɪ'pɑːtʃə] – Abreise • [3] [niːdz] – Wünsche, Bedürfnisse • [4] [səb'mɪt] *hier:* absenden

11 Am Strand — Unit 5 • Language A+B

Schaut euch den Dialog gut an und übertragt ihn in Partnerarbeit ins Englische. Schreibt euer Ergebnis auf und tragt es danach mit verteilten Rollen vor.

Kim: Kann ich ein Sandwich haben? Ich habe Hunger.

Sarah: Moment mal, wir haben Sandwiches, aber wir dürfen sie jetzt noch nicht essen. Wir müssen auf Mama und Papa warten.

Kim: Na, dann gib mir mal was zu trinken, bitte.

Sarah: Wir haben keine Getränke.

Kim: Wirklich? Und was ist das hier?

Sarah: Das ist eine Flasche Wasser. OK, die kannst du haben.

Kim: Hey, da ist ja eine Tafel Schokolade! Mmmh!

Sarah: Du darfst nicht die ganze Schokolade aufessen, wir haben nicht viel dabei!

Kim: Aber ich habe Hunger. Willst du auch welche?

Sarah: Nein danke, ich gehe jetzt schwimmen.

Kim: Ja, aber du darfst nicht so weit rausschwimmen!

Sarah: Du brauchst dir keine Sorgen zu machen, ich kann schwimmen! Warum schwimmst du nicht mit?

Kim: Nein danke, das Wasser in der Nordsee ist viel zu kalt.

Sarah: Dann musst du aber Sonnenschutzcreme benutzen.

Kim: Aber heute ist es doch gar nicht so heiß, da brauche ich doch keinen Sonnenschutz!

Sarah: Doch, du musst! Vielleicht kannst du die Sonne bei dem Wind nicht fühlen, aber sie brennt heute sehr heiß!

12 Ein sehr mutiges Mädchen

Unit 5 • Text

Übersetze in Ruhe diesen Text. Achte dabei auf die Verwendung des *simple present* und des *present progressive.*

Grace Darling wacht sehr früh auf, weil der Wind an ihrem Fenster rüttelt und das Meer gegen die Klippen peitscht. Grace steht auf und geht ans Fenster. Das Meer ist grau und stürmisch. Plötzlich sieht sie etwas! Mit dem Fernrohr kann sie auf dem Big Harcar Rock ein gestrandetes Schiff und einige Menschen erkennen. "Wir müssen sie retten", sagt sie zu ihrem Vater, und wenige Minuten später rudern sie in ihrem kleinen Boot hinaus. Es ist ein langer, gefährlicher Weg durch eine fürchterliche See. Als sie schließlich am Wrack ankommen, sehen sie neun Menschen. Diese halten sich am Felsen fest. Die Wellen schlagen heftig gegen die Klippen. Der Wind heult. Die Männer sind völlig durchnässt, unterkühlt und haben Angst. Grace und ihr Vater können aber nicht alle auf einmal mitnehmen. Einige Männer müssen warten, bis Grace und ihr Vater zurückkommen. Grace will mit der zweiten Gruppe warten und springt vom Boot auf die Klippen. So bringt ihr Vater die ersten fünf Männer zum Leuchtturm, und Grace bleibt mit den anderen auf den Klippen zurück. Die Männer haben Angst, aber Grace bleibt stark: "Ihr braucht euch keine Sorgen zu machen, mein Vater kommt wieder!" sagt sie. Sie müssen lange Zeit warten, doch das kleine Boot kommt zurück, und schließlich sind alle in Sicherheit.

Tipp

Im Deutschen macht es meist keinen Unterschied, ob du das Präteritum oder das Perfekt verwendest, wenn du über Vergangenes berichtest. Vor allem süddeutsche Sprecher verwenden häufig das Perfekt.

a) Letzte Woche fuhr Robert nach Yorkshire. Dort arbeitete er auf einem Bauernhof.

b) Letzte Woche ist Robert nach Yorkshire gefahren. Dort hat er auf einem Bauernhof gearbeitet.

Im Englischen musst du sowohl für **a)** als auch für **b)** das *simple past* verwenden (die unregelmäßigen Formen findest du auf S. 155):

Last week Robert went to Yorkshire.
He worked on a farm there.

13 Urlaub auf dem Bauernhof

Unit 6 • Language A+B

Du bist im Urlaub auf einem Bauernhof in Yorkshire. Du schreibst einem englischen Freund eine Karte, die mindestens den folgenden Inhalt haben sollte:

- das Wetter ist gut
- dein neuer Freund, ein Junge auf dem Bauernhof, heißt Jack
- du hast letzte Woche Folgendes erlebt: Arbeit auf dem Bauernhof, Kühe melken, Schweinestall sauber machen, Hühner füttern, Eier einsammeln, Angriff eines Truthahns, Beobachtung des Hütehundes bei der Arbeit
- liebe Grüße

14 Robert und das Schaf — Unit 6 • Text

Du bist mit deiner Mutter und deinem kleinen Bruder zu Gast auf der *Springfield Farm.* Grandpa Rudd erzählt euch vom vorigen Jahr. Du musst dolmetschen, weil dein Bruder noch kein Englisch kann.

Grandpa: *Mrs Croft and Robert were really nice. The boy helped us very much.*
Brother: Was hat er denn gemacht?
Grandpa: *He milked the cows with Jack every day. They fed the chickens and collected the eggs. Sometimes they cleaned out the pigsty, too.*
Brother: Kann ich auch helfen?
Grandpa: *Of course you can. You children have good ideas sometimes. Robert, for example, helped us a lot last year when there was a problem with one of our sheep.*
Brother: Was ist passiert?
Grandpa: *There were two dead lambs inside the sheep, and she couldn't[1] get them out. So we called the vet. He got them out, but he said sheep sometimes die without their lambs. We didn't know what to do.*
Mum: Oh, das ist ja traurig! Und was hat Robert gemacht?
Grandpa: *We had a lamb, Lenny. His mother didn't want him. So we fed him milk from a bottle. Robert remembered him. It was his idea to bring Lenny. But he was too old, so we had to trick the mother sheep.*
Mum: Wie haben Sie das gemacht?
Grandpa: *It's not a very nice trick. I took the skin of one of the dead lambs and put it around Lenny.*
Brother: Wirklich? Warum haben Sie das gemacht?
Grandpa: *Because he needed the right smell. Then it was OK, she looked at him and touched him with her nose. After that he could drink from her.*
Brother: Wow! Das ist ja eine schreckliche Geschichte. Aber sie hatte doch noch einen guten Ausgang.
Grandpa: *Yes. Everybody was happy!*

[1] couldn't [kʊdnt] – konnte nicht

15 Präpositionen — Unit 7

Übersetze die folgenden Sätze. Achte nicht nur auf die Präpositionen.

1. David ist in der Schule.
2. Schau! Beckys Hund bellt Tabby an.
3. Ich wohne in der Pfenniggasse, außerhalb des Stadtzentrums.
4. Mary-Beth bleibt nicht mit David im Hubschrauber.
5. Die Mädchen singen immer im Bus.
6. Jetzt steigen sie aus dem Bus.
7. Fahrt ihr oft mit dem Fahrrad in die Stadt?
8. Sarah ist heute bei den Burtons.
9. Der Laden ist nachmittags von 14 bis 19 Uhr geöffnet, außer am Wochenende.
10. Treffen wir uns doch vor dem Kino!
11. Es ist auf der rechten Seite.
12. Robert interessiert sich fürs Skifahren.
13. Heb den Ball auf und wirf ihn aus dem Fenster!
14. Becky ist dabei, nach oben in ihr Zimmer zu gehen.
15. Meine Freundin aus London steht gerade neben mir.
16. Dreh dich um! Ich will dich anschauen.
17. Alaska ist der größte Staat der USA, und mein Hund ist der beste Hund der Welt.
18. New York ist in der Nähe von Boston.
19. Was ist auf dem Bild zu sehen?
20. Was magst du sonst noch außer Gemüse?
21. Sind die Katzen noch im Garten? Nein, sie sind schon wieder drinnen.
22. Erinnerst du dich an Großvater Jones?

Tipp

Im Deutschen kann man mit dem Präsens Handlungen oder Sachverhalte ausdrücken, die gewohnheitsmäßig oder gerade im Moment oder aber in der Zukunft (Vorhaben, Plan) stattfinden. Im Englischen muss man je nach Situation *simple present, present progressive* oder *going-to future* verwenden.

David schreibt oft E-Mails.
David often writes e-mails.

David schreibt (gerade) E-Mails.
David is writing e-mails.

David schreibt seinen Freunden E-Mails aus New York (wenn er dort angekommen ist).
David is going to write his friends e-mails from New York.

16 Ein Besucher aus Schottland

Unit 7 • Language A+B

Deine Oma möchte deinen schottischen Gastschüler Ian kennen lernen. Du musst dolmetschen, weil sie nicht so gut Englisch kann. Ihr könnt auch einen ähnlichen Dialog erfinden und spielen.

Oma: Wann bist du denn angekommen?
Ian: *I think it was 7 o'clock on Saturday evening.*
Oma: Hattet ihr eine angenehme Reise?
Ian: *Yes, it was interesting to see the different landscapes here in Germany. And we played games on the train almost all the time.*
Oma: Ja, Deutschland ist sehr schön im Sommer. Was machst du denn so, wenn du nicht in der Schule bist?
Ian: *Oh, I like reading, going for a walk with our dog or playing football with my friends. I like surfing the Internet, too.*
Oma: Und was machst du jetzt gerade?
Ian: *I'm reading a holiday magazine. Look! Isn't it great?*
Oma: Ja, das sieht fantastisch aus. Ist das ein Hubschrauber?
Ian: *Yes, it's a helicopter sightseeing tour of Manhattan.*
Oma: Also wirst du nach New York fliegen?
Ian: *Yes, my parents are going to go there on business in October. They're going to take me with them. The USA is a huge country, and there is so much to see, but we're only going to stay in New York City for a week. So I'm not going to see the Kennedy Space Center, Hollywood or the Grand Canyon, but the Statue of Liberty, the skyscrapers, Central Park and Broadway. Maybe we can go and see Niagara Falls, too.*
Oma: Das wird wirklich sehr interessant, da bin ich sicher. Du musst uns unbedingt davon erzählen. Aber hast du keine Angst vor dem Fliegen?
Ian: *No, I love flying. And what about you? Are you going to go away for a holiday?*
Oma: Nein, Opa und ich bleiben daheim. Wir werden etwas im Garten arbeiten. Habt ihr zu Hause auch einen Garten?
Ian: *Well, it's not really a garden, it's very small, but my mum loves it.*
Oma: Wie ist es denn mit der Landschaft in Schottland?
Ian: *It's beautiful. The hills are quite high in the west, and there are many wide open spaces. It's good for walking or skiing.*
Oma: Oh, das ist schön. (Dein Name) geht im Januar nach Schottland. Dann könnt ihr zwei ja zusammen Ski fahren gehen. (Dein Name) ist sehr gut im Skifahren!

Grammar

Wenn man sich im Straßenverkehr nicht an die Regeln hält, dann kracht es. Wenn man sich in einer Sprache nicht an die Regeln hält, dann versteht niemand, was eigentlich los ist. Das kann unter Umständen böse Folgen haben.

Also: wie im Straßenverkehr gibt es auch in einer Sprache Regeln, an die man sich halten muss. Diese Regeln werden Grammatik genannt. Sie sind hier für die englische Sprache zusammengestellt. Sie sollen dir zeigen, wie die englische Sprache richtig benutzt wird.

Jedes Grammatikkapitel hat eine Nummer, z. B. **G1**, **G2**, mit einer ziemlich dicken Überschrift, damit man weiß, worum es geht. Meistens fängt ein Kapitel in der Grammatik mit einer kleinen Einführung an. Dann folgt eine Übersicht mit Beispielen.

Hinter den kleinen blauen Punkten (◗) stehen die Regeln. Die müssen gelernt und natürlich befolgt werden. Zwei Dinge sind wichtig: Die Regeln zeigen,

- wie die Formen gebildet werden und
- wie und wozu man sie benutzt.

An einigen Stellen findest du **!**. Hier stehen Dinge, auf die du ganz besonders achten musst. Schließlich gibt es durch Monny eine Menge nützlicher Lerntipps und Lernhilfen. Die Seitenangabe rechts neben der Überschrift (z. B. ***page 28***) zeigt dir bei jedem Grammatikkapitel, wo es im Buch zum ersten Mal vorkommt.

Der Grammatikteil fasst die Sprachregeln zusammen, die du aus dem Unterricht kennst. Er kann dir auch helfen,

- wenn du Hausaufgaben machst
- wenn du dich auf eine Schulaufgabe vorbereitest
- wenn du etwas nicht ganz verstanden hast
- wenn du etwas wiederholen möchtest
- wenn du ein paar Stunden gefehlt hast.

Auf der gegenüberliegenden Seite findest du eine Liste der grammatischen Begriffe aus diesem Buch. Die Angabe **G**... zeigt, wo du im Grammatikteil zu dem Begriff etwas findest.

Grammatical terms

Englisch	Englisches Beispiel	Deutsch
adjective	Robert is a **good** friend.	Adjektiv / Eigenschaftswort
adverb G23	Barker **often** barks at people.	Adverb / Umstandswort
adverbial phrase		Adverbiale Bestimmung
of place G23	They play **in the park**.	des Ortes
of time G23	They go there **on Saturdays**.	der Zeit
article		Artikel
definite G15	Your book is on **the** table.	bestimmter Artikel
indefinite G16	That's **a** good idea! (**an** idea)	unbestimmter Artikel
auxiliary	**Can** you draw a monster?	Hilfsverb
can G14	I **can** speak English.	
must G33	You **must** use sunscreen.	
mustn't G34	We **mustn't** speak German.	
needn't G34	You **needn't** go to school today.	
to be G1, 7	I **am**, you **are**, he **is** etc.	
connective	**and, or, because, when** etc.	Konjunktion / Bindewort
consonant	**b, f, g, t** etc.	Konsonant / Mitlaut
did / didn't G43, 44, 45	**Did** you watch TV yesterday? No, I **didn't**.	
do / don't G28, 29, 30, 32	**Do** you like it? No, I **don't**.	
does / doesn't G28, 29	**Does** she like tea? No, she **doesn't**.	
genitive		Genitiv (Wessen-Fall)
s-genitive G10	Jenny is **David's** cousin.	
of-genitive G38	a photo **of** a dog.	
gerund G47	I like **playing** football.	Gerundium
going-to future G46	We're **going to** make a cake.	Going-to-Futur
has got / have got G11, 12, 13	Becky **has got** a brother. They **have got** a computer.	
imperative G9	**Give** me your book, please.	Imperativ / Befehlsform
infinitive	**to play**	Infinitiv / Grundform
long forms G1, 2	**I am, he is, is not**	Langformen
negative (form)	I **can't** draw. He is **not** here.	Verneinung
noun G4, G17	**book, girl, cousin**	Nomen (Substantiv) / Hauptwort
object	Jenny buys **a pen**.	Objekt / Satzergänzung
object pronoun G20	**me, him, us**, etc.	Personalpronomen im Objektfall
past tense		Vergangenheit
simple past G40, 41, 42, 43	Everybody **watched** and **waited**.	einfache V. / Präteritum
personal pronoun G1	**he, she, it, we, they** etc.	Personalpronomen / persönliches Fürwort
plural G4, 17	two girls; **children; men**	Plural / Mehrzahl
possessive determiner G3	**my, your, his, her** etc.	Possessivbegleiter / besitzanzeigendes Fürwort
preposition	**in** the park; **on** the table	Präposition / Verhältniswort
present tense G25		Präsens / Gegenwart
simple present G22, 23, 24	I often **go** to school by bike.	einfaches Präsens / einfache Gegenwart
present progressive G18, 19	Look, **he's playing** football.	Verlaufsform des Präsens
question G1, 13, 19, 29	**Are you Rebecca?**	Frage
question word G8, 30	**Who?, What?, Where?** etc.	Fragewort
sentence	**I'm the teacher now.**	Satz
short answers G7, 13, 14, 19, 29	No, **I'm not.** No, **she isn't.**	Kurzantworten
short forms G1, 11	**I'm, he's, isn't**	Kurzformen
singular	**a girl, an animal, one pen**	Singular / Einzahl
subject	**The bike** is in the shop.	Subjekt / Satzgegenstand
this / that, these / those G6	**This** is Simon, and **that's** Becky.	
verb	Can you **draw** a monster?	Verb (Vollverb) / Tätigkeitswort (Zeitwort)
vowel	**a, e, i, o, u**	Vokal / Selbstlaut
word order G23, 29		Wortstellung

let's start

page 8–23

G1 Die Personalpronomen und die Formen von *to be*
The personal pronouns and the forms of *to be*

I, you, he, she, it, we, you, they sind Personalpronomen oder persönliche Fürwörter (auf Deutsch: ich, du, er, sie, es, wir, ihr, sie). ***To be*** ist ein Verb, das in verschiedenen Formen auftritt. Die Form ***to be*** selbst heißt Infinitiv (Grundform).

	Langformen *(long forms)*		Kurzformen *(short forms)*	
Singular	I am	from Nottingham.	I'm	from Nottingham.
	You are	my friend.	You're	my friend.
	He is	eleven.	He's	eleven.
	She is	nice.	She's	nice.
	It is	a nice picture.	It's	a nice picture.
Plural	We are	at Haywood School.	We're	at Haywood School.
	You are	funny monsters.	You're	funny monsters.
	They are	new.	They're	new.

- Die Präsensformen von ***to be*** lauten im Singular (Einzahl) ***am, are, is,*** im Plural (Mehrzahl) ***are.***
- Sie können als Langform oder als Kurzform auftreten. Beim Schreiben verwendet man meist die Langform, beim Sprechen meist die Kurzform. Auch wenn man Gespräche aufschreibt oder an Freunde schreibt, wird die Kurzform verwendet.

- ***I*** wird immer groß geschrieben.
- Für eine männliche Person steht ***he*** (er).
  Für eine weibliche Person steht ***she*** (sie).
- ***You*** kann sowohl **du** als auch **Sie** oder **ihr** heißen:
  *Are **you** Becky?* (Bist **du** ...?)
  *Are **you** Mr Cooper?* (Sind **Sie** ...?)
  *Are **you** new, Sarah and Robert?* (Seid **ihr** ...?)

!

Here's the folder. ... der Ordner.	**It's** **Er ist**	black. schwarz.
This is the school bag. ... die Schultasche.	**It's** **Sie ist**	new. neu.
There's the book. ... das Buch.	**It's** **Es ist**	funny. lustig.
Where's the dog? ... der Hund?	**It's** **Er ist**	in the house. im Haus.
Barker is a dog. Tabby is a cat.	**He's** **She's**	a nice dog. nice, too.

- Im Unterschied zum Deutschen steht für eine Sache immer ***it.***
- Auch für Tiere verwendet man gewöhnlich ***it.***
- Für Tiere, die man gut kennt und beim Eigennamen nennt, verwendet man ***he*** bzw. ***she.***

G2 Die Verneinung von *to be* — The negation of *to be*

Singular	I'm	**not**	English.
	You are	**n't**	eleven.
	He is	**n't**	at Haywood School.
	She is	**n't**	here.
	It is	**n't**	on the desk.
Plural	We are	**n't**	in 7 MD.
	You are	**n't**	my friends.
	They are	**n't**	from Nottingham.

- Man verneint die Formen von ***to be,*** indem man ***not*** hinzufügt: ***I am not, you are not, she is not*** usw.
- In der gesprochenen Sprache zieht man diese Formen zu ***I'm not, aren't*** und ***isn't*** zusammen.
- In der 1. Person Singular (Einzahl) kann ***not*** nicht verkürzt werden.

G3 Die Possessivbegleiter — The possessive determiners

Personal pronouns		Possessive determiners	
I	'm from London.	**My**	name is Robert.
You	're in 7MD, Robert.	**Your**	tutor is Mrs Dane.
He	's eleven.	**His**	friend is twelve.
She	's in my tutor group.	**Her**	name is Becky.
It	's not here.	**Its**	box is on the table.
We	're in 7MD.	**Our**	classroom is over there.
You	're new in Nottingham.	**Your**	tutor is Mr Cooper.
They	're at Haywood School.	**Their**	school is in Nottingham.

- Mit den Possessivbegleitern (besitzanzeigenden Fürwörtern) kann man ausdrücken, zu wem etwas oder jemand gehört.
- ***Your*** kann **dein, euer** oder **Ihr** heißen:
  *I'm **your** German teacher, Robert.* (Ich bin **dein** …)
  *I'm **your** tutor, boys and girls.* (Ich bin **euer** …)
  *Is that **your** biro, Mr Cooper?* (Ist das **Ihr** …)

!

you're → du bist, ihr seid		*You're a nice cat, Tabby.*
your → dein, euer		*Your folder is on the desk, David.*
he's [hi:z] → er ist		*He's from London.*
his [hɪz] → sein		*His friend is from London, too.*
they're → sie sind		*They're late.*
their → ihre		*Their German teacher is new.*
there → dort		*There's a pencil under the chair.*
it's → er / sie / es ist		*It's a nice school.*
its → sein, ihr		*Its box is on the table.*

G4 Die Pluralformen der Nomen   The plural of nouns

Singular (Einzahl)	**Plural** (Mehrzahl)
a book	two books
a dog	three dogs
a pencil case	four pencil cases

- Die Pluralform (Mehrzahl) der meisten englischen Nomen (Hauptwörter) wird gebildet, indem man *-s* an die Singularform anhängt.

Besonderheiten bei der Aussprache

!

[s]	[z]	[ɪz]
two boo**ks** [ks]	three be**ds** [dz]	eight pencil ca**ses** [sɪz]
seven ca**ts** [ts]	ten bir**os** [z]	six exerci**ses** [zɪz]
four tutor grou**ps** [ps]	five frie**nds** [dz]	nine senten**ces** [sɪz]

- Nach den stimmlosen Lauten [p, t, k, f, θ] wird das Plural *-s* stimmlos (scharf) ausgesprochen -[s].
- Nach Vokalen und stimmhaften Konsonanten [b, d, g, l, m, n, ð, v] wird das Plural *-s* stimmhaft (weich) ausgesprochen -[z].
- Nach den Zischlauten [s, z, ʃ, tʃ, ʒ, dʒ] wird die Pluralendung [ɪz] ausgesprochen und *-es* geschrieben.

! Beachte besonders die Aussprache von ***house*** [haʊs] und ***houses*** ['haʊzɪz].

G5 *There is … / There are …*

There is	a new girl in our tutor group.	In unserer Klasse ist ein neues Mädchen.
There's	a monster in my room.	In meinem Zimmer gibt es …
There are	two green folders on the bed.	Da sind zwei grüne …

- Man kann ***there is / there's*** und ***there are*** verwenden, um auf Dinge oder Personen hinzuweisen. Es entspricht dem Deutschen **es gibt … / da sind …**
- Wenn es sich um **eine** Person oder **einen** Gegenstand handelt, wird ***there is (short form: there's)*** verwendet; bei **mehreren** Personen oder Dingen steht ***there are.***

G6 *This / that* *these / those*

- Wenn man zwei Personen oder Dinge vorstellen oder zeigen möchte, sagt man **zuerst *this*, dann *that*.**
- ***This*** wird auch gebraucht, um auf Personen oder Dinge hinzuweisen, die sich **in der Nähe** befinden, ***that*** auf solche, die **weiter entfernt** sind.
- Beim Sprechen verwendet man ***that*** häufig mit der Kurzform ***(that's).*** Es steht auch oft zusammen mit ***over there.***

- ***These*** ist die Pluralform von ***this, those*** die Pluralform von ***that. These*** und ***those*** werden genauso verwendet wie ***this*** und ***that.*** Die Kurzform steht aber nur bei ***that.***
- Die hinweisenden Fürwörter ***this / these*** und ***that / those*** können anstelle eines Nomens oder eines Personalpronomens stehen. Sie heißen dann Demonstrativpronomen. Stehen sie vor einem Nomen, nennt man sie Demonstrativbegleiter. Vergleiche: ***This** is a funny dog.* ***This dog** is funny.*

G7 Fragen und Kurzantworten mit *to be* — Questions and short answers with *to be*

Wie im Deutschen stellt man bei einer Frage mit ***to be*** Subjekt und Verb um, z. B.:

Robert ist aus London.	***Robert is*** *from London.*
Ist Robert aus London?	***Is Robert*** *from London?*

Am I late?	Yes, you are.	No, you aren't.
Are you eleven?	Yes, I am.	No, I'm not.
Is he at Haywood School?	Yes, he is.	No, he isn't.
Is she late?	Yes, she is.	No, she isn't.
Is it under the chair?	Yes, it is.	No, it isn't.
Are we late?	Yes, you are.	No, you aren't.
Are you in 7 MD, Robert and Sarah?	Yes, we are.	No, we aren't.
Are they at Haywood School?	Yes, they are.	No, they aren't.

- ***Yes*** oder ***no*** allein können manchmal etwas unhöflich klingen. Deshalb wird im Englischen häufig mit einem verkürzten Satz geantwortet (mit einer Kurzantwort oder ***short answer***).
- Bei den Ja-Antworten verwendet man immer die Langform von ***to be***.

! Auf die Frage *Is that …?* antwortet man mit *Yes, it is. / No, it isn't.*, auch wenn nach Personen gefragt wird, z. B.: *Is **that** Mrs Burton? – Yes, **it** is.*

G8 Die Fragewörter *where, who, what, how* — The question words *where, who, what, how*

Where	are you, Sarah?	I'm in my room.	**Wo?**
Where	are your exercise books?	They're in my schoolbag.	
Where	's your blue biro?	It's under my desk.	
Where	are you from?	I'm from London.	**Woher?**
Where	are they from?	They're from Nottingham.	
Who	's that?	It's my English teacher.	**Wer?**
Who	's your tutor?	Her name is Mrs Dane.	
What	's in your pencil case?	A pen, a biro, and a ruler.	**Was?**
What	's that in English?	It's a blackboard.	
How	old is Becky?	She's twelve.	**Wie alt?**
How	old is Robert?	He's twelve, too.	

! ***Who*** fragt nach Personen. ***who?*** = wer?
Where fragt nach einem Ort. ***where?*** = wo?

G9 Der Imperativ   The imperative

Mit dem Imperativ (Befehlsform) gibt man jemandem die Anweisung oder den Rat, etwas zu tun. Wenn man jemanden auffordert, etwas nicht zu tun, verwendet man den verneinten Imperativ.

Bring	the comic here, please.
Sit	down and be quiet, please.
Look	at those dogs.
Don't	be silly.
Don't	sing too loud, please.
Don't	write in your books, please.

- Der Imperativ (Befehlsform) lautet wie der Infinitiv ohne ***to***. In einem Befehls- oder Aufforderungssatz stellt man die Befehlsform oft an den Satzanfang.
- Der verneinte Imperativ wird mit ***don't*** und dem Infinitiv ohne ***to*** gebildet.

! Der Imperativ ohne ***please*** klingt im Englischen oft unhöflich. ***Please*** muss deshalb meistens mit verwendet werden. Der Imperativ lautet immer gleich, egal ob eine oder mehrere Personen angesprochen werden: *Don't write in your books, please.*
Schreibe / Schreibt bitte nicht in deine / eure Bücher!

unit 1

G10 Der s-Genitiv   The s-genitive

page 24, 27

Mit dem s-Genitiv drückt man aus, dass jemandem etwas gehört oder zugeordnet ist. Er wird bei Personen und auch bei Tieren verwendet.

Singular	
Sarah**'s** picture is funny.	Sarahs Bild …
Sarah is Kim**'s** sister.	… Kims Schwester.
The cat**'s** bed is over there.	Das Bett der Katze …

- Im Singular hängt man zuerst einen Apostroph *(')* und dann ***s*** an das Nomen. (Vergleiche die unterschiedliche Schreibung im Englischen und im Deutschen!)

Plural
The girl**s'** bikes are new.
The Burton**s'** shop is in Sherwood.

- Bei regelmäßigen Pluralformen mit der Endung ***-s*** hängt man im Genitiv Plural nur einen Apostroph *(')* an. Die Aussprache ändert sich nicht.

The **girl's** bike is new. ←→ The **girls'** bikes are new.

G11 *Have got / has got*

page 28

Langformen *(long forms)*			**Kurzformen** *(short forms)*		
I	**have got**	a new football.	I	**'ve got**	a new football.
You	**have got**	a nice room.	You	**'ve got**	a nice room.
He	**has got**	a sister.	He	**'s got**	a sister.
She	**has got**	a new book.	She	**'s got**	a new book.
We	**have got**	a new English teacher.	We	**'ve got**	a new English teacher.
You	**have got**	two dogs.	You	**'ve got**	two dogs.
They	**have got**	a tree in their garden.	They	**'ve got**	a tree in their garden.

- ***Have got / has got*** heißt im Deutschen **haben** oder **besitzen**:
  Z. B.: *I've got a brother.* – Ich habe einen Bruder.
- In der dritten Person Singular – bei ***he, she*** und ***it*** – verwendet man ***has got.***
- Ebenso wie bei den Formen von ***to be*** benutzt man auch bei ***have got / has got*** die Langformen eher in der geschriebenen Sprache, die Kurzformen ***'ve got / 's got*** eher in der gesprochenen Sprache.

! ***She's** got a nice room.* = ***She has** got a nice room.*
***She's** nice.* = ***She is** nice.*

G12 Die Verneinung von *have got / has got*

The negation of *have got / has got*

page 28

I	**haven't got**	a computer.
You	**haven't got**	a skateboard.
He	**hasn't got**	a cat.
She	**hasn't got**	a stereo in her room.
It	**hasn't got**	a window.
We	**haven't got**	a tree in our garden.
You	**haven't got**	a new tutor.
They	**haven't got**	a new teacher.

- ***Have got / has got*** werden dadurch verneint, dass man ***not*** zwischen ***have / has*** und ***got*** einfügt.
- In der gesprochenen Sprache wird ***not*** in der Regel zu ***n't*** verkürzt und an ***have / has*** angehängt: ***haven't*** bzw. ***hasn't.***

G13 Fragen und Kurzantworten mit *have got / has got*

Questions and short answers with *have got / has got*

page 28

Have you got	a new CD, Becky?	Yes,	**I have.**
Has Robert got	a red biro?	Yes,	**he has.**
Have you got	a dog, Becky and Simon?	Yes,	**we have.**
Have you got	a CD player, Simon?	No,	**I haven't.**
Has Barker got	a football magazine on his bed?	No,	**he hasn't.**
Have the Burtons got	a new house?	No,	**they haven't.**

- Bei Fragen werden ***have*** und ***has*** vor das Subjekt (Satzgegenstand) ***(you, Robert, Barker, the Burtons)*** gestellt.
- Bei den Kurzantworten wird ***got*** einfach weggelassen.
- Genau wie bei den Kurzantworten mit ***to be*** klingen ***Yes, I have*** oder ***No, I haven't*** höflicher als nur ***Yes*** oder ***No.***

G14 Das modale Hilfsverb *can* — The modal auxiliary *can*

page 28

I	**can**	say three words in Italian.		
She	**can**	draw very nice pictures.		
We	**can**	go to the swimming pool.		
Mark	**can't**	write his name.		
You	**can't**	come in. I'm busy.		
	Can	you spell 'brilliant'?	– Yes, I	**can.**
	Can	Robert and Simon come in?	– No, they	**can't.**
	Can't	we listen to it?	– No, you	**can't.**

- Das modale Hilfsverb ***can*** ist in allen Personen gleich und drückt aus, dass jemand etwas tun kann oder darf. Es wird zusammen mit dem Infinitiv ohne ***to*** eines anderen Verbs gebraucht.
  Vergleiche: *He can say three words in Italian.*
  Er kann drei Wörter auf Italienisch (sagen).
- Die verneinte Form von ***can*** [kæn] heißt ***can't*** [kɑːnt]. Manchmal wird beim Schreiben die Langform *(long form)* ***cannot*** ['kænɒt] verwendet. ***Cannot*** ist immer ein Wort.
- Mit ***can*** kann man auch jemanden fragen, ob man etwas tun darf, oder jemanden bitten, etwas zu tun. *Can I come in? – Yes, you can. You can bring the comics here, please.*

! *He **can say** three words in Italian.*
Er **kann** drei Wörter auf Italienisch **(sagen)**.

G15 Der bestimmte Artikel — The definite article

page 28

Während es im Deutschen **der, die** und **das** gibt, verwendet man im Englischen immer ***the*** (also für männliche und weibliche Personen und für Sachen im Singular und im Plural).

the [ðə]	**the** [ði]
the table	the example
the tidy room	the exercise
the unit	the answer
the classroom	the orange folder

- Die Aussprache von ***the*** ist vor Vokalen [ði], ansonsten wird es [ðə] ausgesprochen.

- Das Wort ***unit*** beginnt zwar mit einem geschriebenen Vokal, wird aber ['juːnɪt] ausgesprochen, also ist die Aussprache von ***the*** hier [ðə].

Die **Aussprache** entscheidet – nicht die Schreibung!

G16 Der unbestimmte Artikel — The indefinite article

page 28

a [ə]			an [ən]		
Is that	a	tennis racket?	I've got	an	idea.
Hey, that's	a	great CD.	Oh, that's	an	old CD.
Our teacher has got	a	bike.	Jenny has got	an	English book.

- Der unbestimmte Artikel (deutsch: **ein** oder **eine**) heißt im Englischen ***a*** oder ***an***.
- Vor einem Konsonanten *(tennis, great, bike)* verwendet man ***a*** [ə].
- Vor einem Vokal *(idea, old, English)* verwendet man ***an*** [ən].

! Es heißt *an uncle* [ən‿ˈʌŋkl], aber ***a unit*** [ə ˈju:nɪt]. Vergleiche **G15**. Die Aussprache entscheidet!

G17 Der Plural der Nomen (unregelmäßige Formen)

The plural of nouns (irregular forms)

page 30

- Die Pluralform der meisten englischen Nomen wird gebildet, indem man *-s* an die Singularform anhängt. Vergleiche **G4**.
- Es gibt aber eine Reihe von Nomen, die unregelmäßige Pluralformen haben.

Singular	Plural
a man [mæn]	three **men** [men]
one wo**man** [ˈwʊmən]	two wo**men** [ˈwɪmɪn]
a child [tʃaɪld]	five child**ren** [ˈtʃɪldrən]

! Der s-Genitiv bei diesen unregelmäßigen Pluralformen wird durch Anhängen eines ***'s*** gebildet:

The children's schoolbags are under their chairs.
The women's dogs are nice.
The men's answers are right.

Besonderheiten beim Sprechen und Schreiben

Auch manche Pluralformen, die auf *-s* enden, haben bei Schreibung und Aussprache Besonderheiten:

- Nomen, die im Singular auf *-f* oder *-fe* [-f] enden, haben meistens die Pluralendung ***-ves*** [-vz]. Zur Aussprache vergleiche **G4**.
- Endet ein Nomen auf Konsonant + *y* ***(famil + y)***, so ist die Pluralendung ***-ies***.
- Steht vor dem ***y*** ein Vokal ***(bo + y)***, so bleibt das ***y***.

Singular	Plural
a shel**f** [-f] one kni**fe** [-f]	two shel**ves** [-vz] three kni**ves** [-vz]
one famil**y**	two famil**ies**
one bo**y**	four bo**ys**

unit 2

G18 Die Verlaufsform des Präsens — The present progressive

page 40

The boys and girls are in the classroom.
Mr Cooper is late.

Robert **is looking** at his German book.
Robert schaut sich (gerade) sein Deutschbuch an.
He**'s reading** a new story.
Er liest (gerade) eine neue Geschichte.
Jenny **is checking** his German.
Jenny überprüft (gerade) sein Deutsch.

Sarah **is reading** a comic.
Sarah liest (im Moment) einen Comic.
She**'s looking** at the pictures.
Sie sieht sich (gerade) die Bilder an.

David and Becky **are working** together.
David und Becky arbeiten (gerade) zusammen.
They**'re doing** an exercise together.
Sie machen (gerade) eine Übung zusammen.

- Mit der Verlaufsform des Präsens *(present progressive)* drückt man aus, dass jemand gerade dabei ist, etwas zu tun *(She's reading.)*. Ebenso wird damit ein Vorgang beschrieben, der gerade abläuft und noch nicht zu Ende ist.
- Die Verlaufsform wird mit einer Form von ***to be*** *(am, is, are)* und dem Infinitiv (ohne *to*) des Verbs + ***ing***-Endung gebildet: *Robert is read+**ing**. They are play+**ing** football.*
- Im Deutschen gibt es die Verlaufsform nicht. Die Bedeutung dieser Form wird deshalb oft mit **gerade, im Moment, im Augenblick** oder **jetzt** ausgedrückt:
  *She's **doing** her homework.* = Sie macht gerade ihre Hausaufgaben.

Besonderheiten beim Schreiben

!

make	~~e~~	Becky is **making** a poster.
write	~~e~~	Robert is **writing** the words in his exercise book.
get	+t	Jenny is **getting** things ready for tea.
put	+t	She is **putting** the things on the table.

- Verben mit stummem ***-e*** am Ende verlieren dieses vor der ***ing***-Endung.
- Verben mit einem kurzen Vokal vor dem Endkonsonanten verdoppeln diesen Endkonsonanten.

G19 Fragen und Kurzantworten in der Verlaufsform des Präsens

page 40, 42

Questions and short answers with the present progressive

Are	you	doing	your homework, Simon?	Yes,	I am.	
Are	you	working	together?	Yes,	we are.	
Is	David	playing	a game?	Yes,	he is.	
Is	it	raining?		Yes,	it is.	
Are	you	reading	a comic, Becky?	No,	I'm not.	I'm reading a book.
Are	you	doing	your homework?	No,	we aren't.	We're playing a game.
Is	she	listening	to her new CD?	No,	she isn't.	She's watching TV.
Are	they	playing	football?	No,	they aren't.	They're playing tennis.

- Bei Fragen in der Verlaufsform werden die Langformen von ***to be*** vorangestellt (Vergleiche G7).
- Bei den verneinten Antworten verwendet man meistens die Kurzantworten mit ***to be***. (Vergleiche G7).
- Bei den Ja-Antworten muss immer die Langform von ***to be*** stehen.

G20 Die Objektform der Personalpronomen

page 42

The object case of the personal pronouns

Subjektform	Objektform			
I	Hey Sarah, can you play football with	me	?	mir
	Here you can see	me	with my mother.	mich
you	I can help	you	in the kitchen.	dir
	I can't draw a picture for	you	.	dich
he	What about Mark? – I can tell	him	a story.	ihm
	Maybe I can phone	him	.	ihn
she	Can you help	her	in the kitchen?	ihr
	Sorry, I can't find	her	.	sie
it	Look, here's a frog. Let's play with	it	.	ihm
	Let's put	it	under the tree.	ihn
we	Can you help	us	with our bikes?	uns
	Can you fetch	us	in the car?	
you	Robert! David! Can Mark play with	you	?	euch
	Here's a football for	you	.	
they	The boys are doing their homework. Help	them	, please.	ihnen
	We can't carry	them	all.	sie

- Im **Englischen** gibt es für jedes Personalpronomen nur **eine** Objektform, im **Deutschen** dagegen meist **zwei**.

unit 3

G21 Die Uhrzeit   Telling the time   *page 50–51*

- Für die ersten 30 Minuten wird auf die vorhergehende Stunde Bezug genommen, z. B.

11.00: eleven o'clock		
11.05: five	**past**	eleven
11.15: quarter	**past**	eleven
11.30: half	**past**	eleven

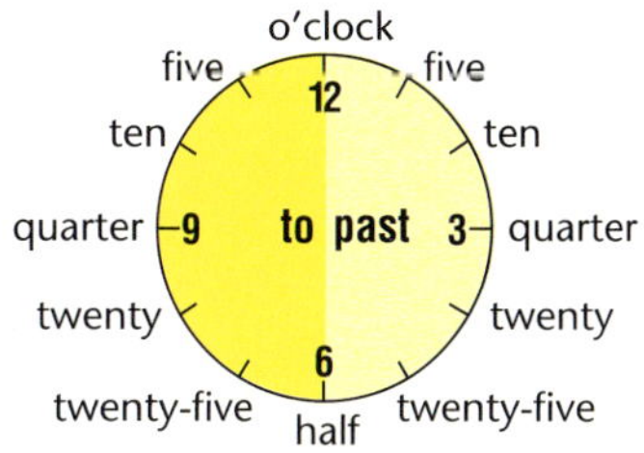

- Bei den restlichen 29 Minuten bezieht man sich auf die folgende Stunde, z. B.

11.45: quarter	**to**	twelve
11.50: ten	**to**	twelve
11.55: five	**to**	twelve
12.00: twelve o'clock		

- Bei Zeitangaben mit Zahlen, die durch fünf teilbar sind, wird das Wort ***minutes*** meist weggelassen. Bei allen anderen Minutenangaben muss es jedoch stehen:
  It's 25 (minutes) past ten. – It's 29 minutes past ten.
- Man kann die Uhrzeit auch ohne ***past*** und ***to*** ausdrücken. In diesem Fall beziehen sich alle Zeitangaben auf die vorhergehende Stunde:

5:09 *five-oh-nine* **5:15** *five fifteen* **5:25** *five twenty-five* **5:30** *five thirty* **5:58** *five fifty-eight*

- Beim Nennen der Tageszeit werden die Zeitangaben **bis** 12 Uhr mittags oft mit dem Zusatz ***am*** versehen. Die Zeitangaben **nach** 12 Uhr mittags erhalten den Zusatz ***pm***.
  *It's 9 **am**.* – Es ist neun Uhr **morgens.**
  *It's 9 **pm**.* – Es ist neun Uhr **abends.**

G22 Die einfache Form der Gegenwart   The simple present   *page 52, 54*

Im Englischen gibt es von jeder Zeitform eine Verlaufsform ***(progressive form,* G18**) und eine einfache Form ***(simple form)***. Die einfache Form der Gegenwart lautet:

I	**play**	football.
You	**play**	the guitar.
David	**plays**	tennis.
And Jenny	**plays**	tennis, too.
Our cat	**plays**	with that old tennis ball.
We	**play**	in the park.
But you	**play**	in the playground.
The girls	**play**	in a team.

- Bei ***I, you, we*** und ***they*** hat das ***simple present*** dieselbe Form wie der Infinitiv.
- Nur in der 3. Person Singular (bei ***he, she*** und ***it***) wird **-*s*** angehängt.

- Das ***simple present*** verwendet man, um auszudrücken, dass etwas häufig oder regelmäßig geschieht oder dass jemand etwas gewohnheitsmäßig tut.
- Das ***simple present*** muss man auch verwenden, wenn man beschreibt, wie jemand mehrere Dinge nacheinander tut (z. B. in einer Erzählung oder einer Zusammenfassung):
  The children talk about their idea. After that they go home and make the posters.
  Then Barker sees the posters and …

G23 Die Wortstellung in Aussagesätzen — Word order in statements — *page 52*

Subjekt	Verb	Objekt
The pupils	wear	school uniform.

- Die Wortstellung im Aussagesatz ist: Subjekt – Verb – Objekt **(S-V-O)**.
- Hierbei bilden Verb und Objekt eine feste Einheit, und man darf keine anderen Satzteile dazwischenstellen.

a) Aussagesätze mit adverbialen Bestimmungen der Zeit und des Ortes

Zeit	S	V	O	Ort	Zeit
	Sarah and Jenny	play	tennis	in the park	every week.
Every week	Sarah and Jenny	play	tennis.		

- Orts- und Zeitangaben stehen in der Regel am Ende des Satzes. Es gilt Ort vor Zeit.
- Wenn man die Zeitangaben stärker betonen will, stellt man sie an den Anfang.

b) Aussagesätze mit Adverbien der Häufigkeit

Subjekt	Adverb	Verb		
Mr and Mrs Croft	**never**	**read**	comics.	Herr und Frau Croft **lesen** **niemals** Comics.
The boys	**always**	**ride**	their bikes.	Die Jungs **fahren** **immer** Fahrrad.
We	**sometimes**	**play**	football after school.	Wir **spielen** **manchmal** Fußball …

- Im Englischen steht das Adverb der Häufigkeit zwischen Subjekt und Verb, im Deutschen meist nach dem Verb.

! *We **are** **usually** at the swimming pool on Fridays.*
*We **can** **always** **go** there after school.*

- Das Adverb der Häufigkeit steht nach dem Verb ***to be*** bzw. zwischen Hilfsverb und Infinitiv.

G24 Das *-s* in der 3. Person Singular — The *-s* in the 3rd person singular — *page 54*

Besonderheiten beim Schreiben und Sprechen

Jenny	**walks**	to school with David.	
She	**helps**	him with his German.	
School	**starts**	at 8.45.	[s]
Jenny	**comes**	home at 3.45.	
Robert	**reads**	comics.	
David	**plays**	the guitar.	[z]
Jenny's school	**finishes**	at 3.30.	
Mr Dixon	**watches**	TV in the evening.	[ɪz]

- Nach stimmlosen Konsonanten wie [k], [p] und [t] wird das *-s* stimmlos [s] gesprochen.
- Nach stimmhaften Konsonanten wie [m] und [d] und nach Vokalen wird das *-s* stimmhaft [z] gesprochen.
- Nach Zischlauten wie [ʃ] und [tʃ] wird *-es* angehängt und [ɪz] gesprochen.

Robert	**flies**	into a big bush.
Jenny	**stays**	in bed on Sundays.
Jenny	**goes**	shopping on Saturdays. [gəʊz]
David	**does**	his homework in the afternoon. [dʌz]

- Verben, die auf *-y* enden: Geht dem *-y* ein Konsonant voraus ***(fly)***, wird die Endung zu ***-ies.*** Steht vor dem *-y* ein Vokal ***(play)***, so bleibt das *-y*, und es wird nur *-s* angehängt.
- An ***go*** und ***do*** wird ***-es*** angehängt. Beachte die unterschiedliche Aussprache!

! Beachte die unregelmäßige Aussprache:
to say [seɪ] – ***he says*** [sez]
to do [du:] – ***she does*** [dʌz]

- Bei der Aussprache und Schreibung der Verben in der 3. Person Singular gelten dieselben Regeln wie bei den Pluralformen der Nomen (vgl. **G4**).

G25 Gegenüberstellung: present progressive – simple present

page 55

! ***Present progressive*** und ***simple present*** dürfen auf keinen Fall verwechselt werden.

We	**'re playing**	football.
I	**'m reading.**	
It	**'s raining.**	
Becky and Sarah	**are doing**	their homework.

- Mit dem ***present progressive*** drückt man aus, dass etwas gerade jetzt geschieht und noch nicht zu Ende ist.

Mit dem ***simple present*** beschreibt man zwei verschiedene Arten von Handlungen, nämlich:

We **never go** to school **on Sundays.**
Jenny **often goes** shopping with Uncle Colin.
She **sometimes makes** breakfast.
The Burtons **take** Barker to the shop **every day.**

Gewohnheitsmäßige Handlungen:

- Mit dem ***simple present*** drückt man aus, dass etwas regelmäßig, oft, manchmal oder nie geschieht. Signalwörter: ***always, often, sometimes, on Sundays, usually, never*** etc.

Robert **shows** his new scooter to David. → **Then** they **go** up to the park.
→ Robert **starts** to ride down the hill. → **Suddenly** he **hits** a stone.
→ Robert **flies into** a big bush.

Aufeinander folgende Handlungen:

- Man verwendet das ***simple present***, um Handlungen zu erzählen, die nacheinander geschehen. Signalwörter:
Then …, after that …, suddenly … .

Gewohnheitsmäßige Handlungen Aufeinander folgende Handlungen →	***simple present***	*Sarah often wears skirts,*
Gerade ablaufende Handlungen Nicht vollendete Handlungen →	***present progressive***	*but today she's wearing jeans.*

unit 4

G26 Die Ordnungszahlen   The ordinal numbers

page 62

1 st **first**	11 th eleventh	21 st twenty-**first**
2 nd **second**	12 th **twelfth**	22 nd twenty-**second**
3 rd **third**	13 th thirteenth	30 th thirt**ieth**
4 th fourth	14 th fourteenth	40 th f**o**rt**ieth**
5 th fi**fth**	15 th fifteenth	50 th fift**ieth**
6 th sixth	16 th sixteenth	60 th six**tieth**
7 th seventh	17 th seventeenth	70 th seven**tieth**
8 th eigh**th**	18 th eighteenth	80 th eigh**tieth**
9 th ni**nth**	19 th nineteenth	90 th nine**tieth**
10 th tenth	20 th twent**ieth**	100 th (one) hundredth

- Wenn man im Deutschen eine Ordnungszahl als Ziffer schreibt, steht ein Punkt nach der Zahl (z. B. am 2. Januar). Im Englischen stehen statt dessen die beiden letzten Buchstaben der ausgeschriebenen Ordnungszahl:
first** = **1st**, **second** = **2nd**, **third** = **3rd**, **fourth** = **4th**, **fifth** = **5th etc.

G27 Das Datum   The date

page 62

Die Schreibung und die Aussprache des Datums unterscheiden sich:

Man schreibt	Man spricht
April 23rd	"April the twenty-third"
oder	**oder**
23rd April	"the twenty-third of April"

- Man kann das Datum auch ganz einfach mit Grundzahlen schreiben: ***April 23*** oder ***23 April***. Aber auch dann sagt man ***"April the twenty-third"*** oder ***"the twenty-third of April"***.

Jahreszahlen

1492	fourteen hundred **and** ninety-two
	oder fourteen ninety-two
1776	seventeen hundred **and** seventy-six
	oder seventeen seventy-six
1900	nineteen hundred
1902	nineteen hundred **and** two
	oder nineteen-oh-two
1945	nineteen hundred **and** forty-five
	oder nineteen forty-five
2000	two thousand
2006	two thousand **and** six
	oder two thousand six

G28 Verneinte Aussagen mit *don't/doesn't*
Negative statements with *don't/doesn't*

page 64

Man verneint eine Aussage mit einer Form von ***to be*** oder mit einem Hilfsverb, indem man ***not*** anhängt (Vergleiche **G2**, **G12**, **G14**):

Becky	**isn't**	at home today.
I	**can't**	play tennis.
They	**haven't**	got a computer.

- Enthält eine Aussage im *simple present* **keine** Form von ***to be*** oder **kein** Hilfsverb, sondern ein Vollverb, so bildet man die Verneinung mit ***don't / doesn't*** + Infinitiv:

Simon	**plays**	football.	(= bejahte Aussage)
He	**doesn't play**	tennis.	(= verneinte Aussage)

! *He plays football.*
He doesn't play tennis.

I	**don't**	like school uniform.	Ich mag keine Schuluniform.
You	**don't**	look happy.	Du siehst nicht glücklich aus.
He	**doesn't**	come from Sherwood.	Er kommt nicht aus Sherwood.
She	**doesn't**	like muesli.	Sie mag kein Müsli.
It	**doesn't**	happen every day.	Es passiert nicht jeden Tag.
We	**don't**	come from London.	Wir kommen nicht aus London.
You	**don't**	like cats.	Ihr mögt keine Katzen.
They	**don't**	live in England.	Sie leben nicht in England.

- ***Not*** wird direkt an ***do / does*** angefügt und meist zu ***-n't*** verkürzt.
- Bei ***he, she, it*** (= 3. Person Singular) wird ***doesn't*** ['dʌznt] verwendet. Das Vollverb steht immer im Infinitiv.

G29 Entscheidungsfragen und Kurzantworten mit *do / does*

page 64

Yes / No questions and short answers with *do / does*

Entscheidungsfragen sind Fragen, die man mit Ja oder Nein beantworten muss. Sie beginnen mit einem Hilfsverb ***(can, must, have / has)*** oder einer Form von ***to be*** (G7, G13, G14).

Can	you play tennis?	– Yes, I can.
Are	you late?	– No, I'm not.
Have	you got a computer?	– Yes, I have.

- Wenn kein solches Hilfsverb (Hv) oder keine Form von ***to be*** vorhanden ist, dann beginnt die Entscheidungsfrage mit ***do / does.***

Entscheidungsfrage				**Kurzantwort**	
Do	I	**look**	OK in this shirt?	Yes, you	**do.**
Do	you	**buy**	magazines?	No, I	**don't.**
Does	he	**like**	tennis?	Yes, he	**does.**
Does	she	**come**	from London?	No, she	**doesn't.**
Does	it	**rain**	here every day?	No, it	**doesn't.**
Do	we	**need**	our books?	Yes, you	**do.**
Do	you	**watch**	TV every evening?	No, we	**don't.**
Do	they	**like**	music?	Yes, they	**do.**

- Bei ***he, she, it*** wird immer die Form ***does*** [dʌz] gebraucht. Das Vollverb steht auch dann immer im Infinitiv.

! *She likes music.*
Does she like music?

- Bei Entscheidungsfragen werden in der Kurzantwort ***do / does*** oder ***don't / doesn't*** benutzt.

HV	S	V	O
	You	like	dogs.
Do	you	like	Barker?
	Jenny	writes	e-mails.
Does	Jenny	write	letters?

- Durch die Formulierung mit ***do / does*** bleibt das englische Satzmuster S-V-O erhalten. Das Vollverb steht bei der Umschreibung mit ***to do*** immer im Infinitiv.

G30 Fragen mit Fragewörtern und *do / does*

Questions with question words and *do / does*

page 66

- Fragen mit Fragewörtern (***what, when, where*** usw.) können mit einer Form von ***to be*** oder mit einem Hilfsverb gebildet werden: ***Where are*** *the children?*
  What can *we do at the Victoria Centre?*
- Sind keine Form von ***to be*** und kein anderes Hilfsverb vorhanden, steht ***do / does*** nach dem Fragewort. Die Wortstellung ist dieselbe wie bei den Entscheidungsfragen (vgl. G29).

	HV	S	V	O	
When	do	you	get	up?	At 8 o'clock.
Where	do	you	live?		I live in Sherwood.
What	do	you	do	after school?	I often play tennis.
How	does	David	get	to school?	He walks there with Jenny.
Why	does	Jenny	live	with the Penroses?	Because she's David's cousin.

G31 Das Fragewort *whose*

The question word *whose*

page 66

Whose book is this?	It's Dad's.
And **whose** magazines are these?	They're Mum's.
And these CDs? **Whose** are they?	They're the girls'.

- ***Whose*** (Wessen ...? / Wem gehört ...?) fragt nach dem Besitzer oder den Besitzern.

! ***Whose*** und ***who's*** kann man leicht verwechseln. ***Whose*** is this? – **Wem gehört** das?
Who's this? – **Wer ist** das?

G32 *Who* und *what* als Subjekt und Objekt

Who **and *what* as subject and object** *page 66*

Subjekt	Who	calls	the school?		Wer ... ?
	Who	helps	Grandpa?		Wer ... ?
	Who	phones	Mr. Penrose?		Wer ... ?
	What	happens	in the park?		Was ... ?
Objekt	Who	do	you	call?	Wen ... ?
	Who	does	Jack	help?	Wem ... ?
	Who	can	you	phone?	Wen ... ?
	What	do	you	see?	Was ... ?

- ***Who*** und ***what*** können Subjekt oder Objekt des Fragesatzes sein.
- Wenn ***who*** oder ***what*** Subjekt des Fragesatzes sind, wird das Hilfsverb ***do*** nicht verwendet.

- Ist ***who*** dagegen Objekt des Fragesatzes, muss man das Hilfsverb ***do*** verwenden, wenn kein anderes Hilfsverb (wie z. B. ***can, must***) vorhanden ist.

unit 5

G33 Das modale Hilfsverb *must* — The modal auxiliary *must* — *page 76*

I	**must**	get my school uniform this afternoon.
He	**must**	be at school at 8.45.
We	**must**	talk about our English homework.
What time	**must**	they be at the airport?
They	**must**	be there at 6 o'clock.

- Das modale Hilfsverb ***must*** ist – genau wie ***can*** – in allen Personen gleich. Es drückt eine Notwendigkeit oder Verpflichtung aus. Es wird zusammen mit dem Infinitiv eines Verbs ohne ***to*** gebraucht.

! Beachte die Wortstellung:
Im Aussagesatz folgt der Infinitiv auf ***must*** und ***can***.

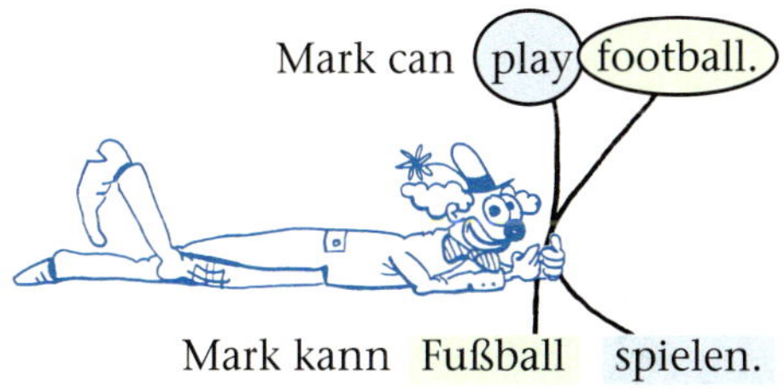

G34 *Mustn't/needn't* — *page 76*

We	**mustn't**	swim after a big lunch.	That's not good for us.
You	**mustn't**	open the bag.	We don't want sand in our sandwiches.
We	**mustn't**	play loud music on the beach.	That isn't nice for other people.

People on the beach	**must**	use sunscreen.	– They	**needn't**	use it after six pm.
I don't feel well.	**Must**	I go to school?	– It's OK, you	**needn't**	go today.
	Must	I stay in bed?	– Well, no, you	**needn't**	stay in bed.

- Während ***mustn't*** ein Verbot ausdrückt, bedeutet ***needn't***, dass man etwas nicht zu tun braucht oder nicht tun muss.
- Die Formen ***mustn't*** und ***needn't*** sind für alle Personen gleich.

! ***Mustn't* darf nicht mit *needn't* verwechselt werden:**

***mustn't:* nicht dürfen**
You ***mustn't*** *swim after a big lunch.*
Ihr **dürft** nach einer großen Mahlzeit **nicht** schwimmen.

***needn't:* nicht brauchen/nicht müssen**
You ***needn't*** *worry. The water's too* ***cold.***
Du **brauchst** dich **nicht** zu sorgen.
Das Wasser ist zu kalt.

G35 *Some* und *any*

page 78

Im Englischen drückt man eine unbestimmte Menge oder Anzahl (im Sinne von **etwas**, **einige** oder **ein paar**) mit ***some*** oder ***any*** aus.

Bejahte Aussagen mit *some*	**Fragen mit *any***	**Verneinte Aussagen mit *not any***
I want to buy ***some*** sweets.	Have we got ***any*** ice cream?	No, there is***n't*** ***any*** ice cream.
Ich möchte (ein paar) Süßigkeiten kaufen.	Haben wir (etwas) Eis?	Nein, es ist kein Eis (mehr) da.
OK, let's get ***some*** ice cream.	Do we want ***any*** drinks?	Yes, we do. There are***n't*** ***any*** in the kitchen.
Gut. Lasst uns (etwas) Eis holen.	Möchten wir (–) Getränke?	Ja. In der Küche sind keine.

- In bejahten Sätzen verwendet man ***some***, in Fragen und verneinten Sätzen meistens ***any***.
- Wenn man etwas anbietet, verwendet man ***some*** auch in Fragen: *Do you want some tea?*
- Im Deutschen bleiben s***ome*** und ***any*** oft unübersetzt: *Do you need any sunscreen?* Brauchst du Sonnenschutz?

G36 *Much* und *many*

page 78

- ***Much*** und ***many*** werden fast ausschließlich in Fragen und verneinten Sätzen gebraucht.

Sorry, but I haven't got **much time**.
How **much ice cream** have we got?
– Not **much**. But we've got **a lot of** water.

- ***Much*** **(= viel)** wird zusammen mit Nomen verwendet, die im Singular stehen und **nicht zählbar** sind.

I haven't got **many T-shirts**.
Have you got **many CDs**?
There aren't **many people** on the beach today.

- ***Many*** **(= viele)** wird mit Nomen verwendet, die im Plural stehen und **zählbar** sind.

- In bejahten Sätzen verwendet man meistens ***a lot of:*** *There are **a lot of** clouds in the sky.*

G37 Mengenangaben mit *of* — Expressions of quantity with *of*

page 78

a	bottle	of	water	eine Flasche Wasser
one	box	of	candles	eine Schachtel Kerzen
two	bars	of	chocolate	zwei Tafeln Schokolade
three	tins	of	dog food	drei Dosen Hundefutter

- Im Englischen werden Mengenangaben mit dem Wort ***of*** gemacht.

G38 Der *of*-Genitiv The *of*-genitive

page 78

C is the third letter	**of**	the alphabet.
Today is the first day	**of**	the week.
Look at the doors	**of**	these houses.
The park is at the end	**of**	the road.
There's a castle in the centre	**of**	Nottingham.

! Vergleiche: Becky**'s** computer the end **of** the road.

- Der Genitiv mit ***of*** drückt eine Art Zuordnung oder Zugehörigkeit zu einer Sache aus.
- Er wird vorwiegend bei Dingen verwendet. Bei Menschen und Tieren dagegen gebraucht man in der Regel den s-Genitiv (Vergleiche **G10**).

G39 Die Verwendung von *simple* und *progressive forms* in Geschichten

page 80

The people on the ship can't sleep because a storm **is starting.** It **is raining.** Suddenly the engines of the Forfarshire **stop.**

At Longstone Lighthouse Grace **wakes** up early. The wind **is screaming** and **shaking** the glass in the windows. The sea **is crashing** on the rocks.

Mrs Darling **comes** into her room. "It's a really terrible storm," she **tells** Grace. Grace **gets** up from her bed and **goes** to the window.

- In vielen Geschichten verwendet man sowohl ***present progressive*** als auch ***simple present.***
- Dabei verwendet man das ***present progressive***, wenn man eine Situation oder Szene als Bild ausmalt.
- Das ***simple present*** benutzt man, um die Abfolge einzelner Handlungsschritte darzustellen.

unit 6

G40 Die einfache Vergangenheit: regelmäßige Formen

page 88

The simple past: regular forms

Das ***simple past*** drückt Ereignisse oder Handlungen aus, die in der Vergangenheit stattgefunden haben und abgeschlossen sind. Deshalb benutzt man es z. B., um Geschichten zu erzählen oder über Erlebnisse zu berichten.

Yesterday	I	**helped**	my father.
On Saturday	Becky	**played**	tennis with David.
Last Friday	it	**rained**	in the afternoon.
Last week	we	**cleaned**	our bikes.
Last night	my parents	**watched**	TV.

- Das ***simple past*** der regelmäßigen Verben wird gebildet, indem man die Endung ***-ed*** an den Infinitiv (ohne ***to***) anhängt: ***help + ed → helped.***
- Die Form des ***simple past*** ist für alle Personen gleich.
- Da das ***simple past*** Vorgänge ausdrückt, die vorbei sind, wird es häufig von Zeitangaben wie z. B. ***last year, yesterday*** usw. begleitet. Solche Signalwörter zeigen, dass das ***simple past*** verwendet werden muss.

G41 Aussprache und Schreibung der einfachen Vergangenheit (regelmäßige Form)

page 88

Bei der Aussprache und beim Schreiben muss man auf folgende Besonderheiten achten:

Beim Sprechen		Beim Schreiben	
st**ayed** [eɪd] sh**owed** [əʊd] clean**ed** [nd]	Nach Vokalen und nach stimmhaften Konsonanten spricht man [d].	to chase – chas**ed** to phone – phon**ed** to save – sav**ed**	Das stumme *-e* am Ende fällt weg.
li**ked** [kt] bum**ped** [pt] laug**hed** [ft]	Nach stimmlosen Konsonanten spricht man [t].	to car**ry** – carr**ied** to t**ry** – tr**ied**	Verben, die auf Konsonanten *+y* enden, erhalten die Endung *-ied*
lan**ded** [dɪd] visi**ted** [tɪd]	Nach [d] oder [t] spricht man [ɪd].	to sto**p** – sto**pped**	Nach kurzem, betontem Vokal wird ein einfacher Endkonsonant verdoppelt.

G42 Das *simple past* von *to be* — The simple past of *to be*

page 88

Were you in London last Sunday?	No, I **wasn't**. I **was** in Nottingham.
Was your grandma with you?	Yes, she **was**. We **were** at the shopping centre.
Was it good?	No, it **wasn't**. There **weren't** many shops open.

- Im ***simple past*** gibt es zwei Verbformen von *to be: I/he/she/it* ***was***
  you/we/they ***were***

G43 Die einfache Vergangenheit: unregelmäßige Formen
The simple past: irregular forms

page 89

Im Englischen gibt es – wie im Deutschen – auch unregelmäßige Verben, z. B.

Infinitiv	simple past	
to have	**had**	Yesterday I **had** breakfast at 8 o'clock.
to go	**went**	After breakfast I **went** to school.
to see	**saw** [sɔː]	On my way I **saw** my friend.
to do	**did**	We **did** five subjects at school.
to get	**got**	At school I **got** a new book.
to give	**gave** [geɪv]	Our teacher **gave** us a lot of homework.
to come	**came** [keɪm]	At 3 o'clock I **came** home.
to say	**said** [sed]	My mother **said**: "Do your homework after tea."

- Während die regelmäßigen Verben im ***simple past*** alle auf *-ed* enden, gibt es für die unregelmäßigen keine Bildungsregeln. Man muss die einzelnen Formen lernen (s. S. 155).
- Auch bei den unregelmäßigen Verben sind die Formen des ***simple past*** für alle Personen gleich. (Ausnahme: ***to be*** – siehe **G42**).

G44 Die Verneinung der einfachen Vergangenheit mit *didn't* *page 90*

Negative sentences in the simple past with *didn't*

Im ***simple present*** verneint man Vollverben mit ***don't*** oder ***doesn't*** (+ Infinitiv des Vollverbs), z. B. *She doesn't like tennis.* Vergleiche **G28**.

Subjekt	didn't	Infinitiv				
I	didn't	play	football.	I	played	tennis.
He	didn't	like	Maths,	but he	liked	his new tutor.
Becky	didn't	do	her homework,	but she	did	a lot of other things.
We	didn't	go	to the supermarket.	We	went	to the cinema.

- Im ***simple past*** verneint man Vollverben mit ***didn't (did not)*** + Infinitiv des Vollverbs. Die Formen sind für alle Personen gleich.

! Nach ***didn't*** steht der **Infinitiv**. Die Zeitform ***simple past*** ist im Hilfsverb ***didn't*** enthalten.

G45 Fragen mit *did/didn't* **Questions with *did/didn't*** *page 90*

Entscheidungsfragen und Fragen mit Fragewörtern (außer Fragen mit ***who*** oder ***what*** als Subjekt, vergleiche **G32**) werden im ***simple present*** mit **do** oder **does** gebildet, z. B.: *Do we need our books? When does David get up?* Vergleiche **G29**, **G30**.

Fragewort	did/ didn't	Subjekt	Verb im Infinitiv		Antwort
	Did	you	watch	TV last night?	Yes, I did.
	Did	the girls	play	tennis yesterday?	No, they didn't.
What	did	Becky	do	yesterday afternoon?	She did her homework.
Where	did	the boys	clean	their bikes?	In the garage.
How	did	Robert	help	his mother?	He made the tea.
Why	didn't	you	swim	with your sister?	Because the North Sea was too cold.

- Im ***simple past*** werden Entscheidungsfragen mit ***did/didn't*** gebildet.
- Auch Fragen mit Fragewörtern bildet man im ***simple past*** mit ***did/didn't***.
- Ausnahme: Fragen mit ***who*** oder ***what*** als Subjekt *(Who made the tea?)*.

! Nach ***did/didn't*** steht der **Infinitiv**. Die Zeitform ist im Hilfsverb ***did/didn't*** schon enthalten.

unit 7

G46 Das *going-to*-Futur — The going-to future

page 102

What are you	**going to do**	this afternoon?	Was hast du … vor?
I'm	**going to make**	a cake.	Ich werde / will …
We're	**going to play**	football.	Wir wollen …
What is Becky	**going to do?**		Was wird Becky machen?
She's	**going to feed**	the dog.	Sie wird / will …
Are you	**going to spend**	your holidays in Scotland?	Habt ihr die Absicht … ?
No, we aren't	**going to have**	a holiday this year.	Nein. Wir werden / wollen …

- ***Going to*** wird verwendet, wenn man über eine beabsichtigte oder geplante (zukünftige) Handlung spricht. Die damit gebildete Zeit nennt man ***going-to future.***
- Mit ***going to*** kann man auch vorhersagen, dass in der Zukunft etwas eintreten wird:
  That's going to be brilliant. Das wird toll werden.
  They're going to be late. Sie werden zu spät kommen.
- Das ***going-to future*** bildet man mit ***am / is / are going to*** + Infinitiv.

G47 Das Gerundium — The gerund

page 104

Das ***gerund*** wird aus einem Verb + ***ing*** gebildet: *read + ing = reading.*
Es kann Subjekt oder Objekt eines Satzes sein.

a) Das Gerundium als Subjekt

Subjekt		
Skating	can be	great.
Swimming	is	my favourite sport.
Playing football	can be	fun.

- Das ***gerund*** hat ähnliche Eigenschaften wie ein Nomen. Deshalb kann es auch Subjekt eines Satzes sein. Es kann auch mit einem weiteren Nomen stehen *(**playing** football).*

b) Das Gerundium als Objekt

	Object		
☺	I	love	**surfing** the Internet.
	What do you	like	**doing** at weekends?
	We	love	**playing** games.
☹	My friend	doesn't like	**running**.
	She	hates	**working** in the garden.
	I	don't like	**playing** the guitar.

- Das ***gerund*** als Objekt steht oft nach Verben der Vorliebe ***(like, love)*** oder der Abneigung ***(not like, hate).***
- Es steht auch nach Ausdrücken wie ***good at, interested in, how about,*** z. B.: ***How about going for a walk?***

! Das ***gerund*** darf nicht mit dem ***present progressive (be + verb + ing)*** verwechselt werden:
*He **is watching** TV.* = Er sieht gerade fern. *He **likes watching** TV.* = Er sieht gern fern.

List of irregular verbs

infinitive	simple past	German
to **be** [bɪ]	**was/were** [wɒz; wɜ:] **U6**, 88	sein
to **beat** [bi:t]	**beat** [bi:t]	besiegen, schlagen
to **bring** [brɪŋ]	**brought** [brɔ:t]	bringen
to **buy** [baɪ]	**bought** [bɔ:t]	kaufen
to **choose** [tʃu:z]	**chose** [tʃəʊz]	(aus)wählen, aussuchen
to **cling** [klɪŋ]	**clung** [klʌŋ]	(sich) festhalten
to **come** [kʌm]	**came** [keɪm] **U6**, 89	kommen
to **do** [du:]	**did** [dɪd] **U6**, 89	tun, machen
to **draw** [drɔ:]	**drew** [dru:]	zeichnen
to **dream** [dri:m]	**dreamed/dreamt** [dri:md; dremt]	träumen
to **drink** [drɪŋk]	**drank** [dræŋk]	trinken
to **drive** [draɪv]	**drove** [drəʊv] **U7**, 103	fahren
to **eat** [i:t]	**ate** [et; eɪt]	essen
to **fall** [fɔ:l]	**fell** [fel]	fallen
to **feed** [fi:d]	**fed** [fed]	füttern
to **feel** [fi:l]	**felt** [felt] **U6**, 93	fühlen
to **fight** [faɪt]	**fought** [fɔ:t]	streiten, kämpfen
to **find** [faɪnd]	**found** [faʊnd] **U6**, 89	finden
to **fly** [flaɪ]	**flew** [flu:] **U7**, 106	fliegen
to **forget** [fə'get]	**forgot** [fə'gɒt]	vergessen
to **get** [get]	**got** [gɒt] **U6**, 89	bekommen, kriegen
to **give** [gɪv]	**gave** [geɪv] **U6**, 89	geben
to **go** [gəʊ]	**went** [went] **U6**, 89	gehen
to **grow** [grəʊ]	**grew** [gru:]	wachsen; anbauen
to **have** [hæv]	**had** [hæd] **U6**, 89	haben
to **hear** [hɪə]	**heard** [hɜ:d] **U6**, 92	hören
to **hit** [hɪt]	**hit** [hɪt]	schlagen; treffen
to **hurt** [hɜ:t]	**hurt** [hɜ:t]	verletzen, weh tun
to **know** [nəʊ]	**knew** [nju:]	wissen; kennen
to **learn** [lɜ:n]	**learned/learnt** [lɜ:nd; lɜ:nt] **U6**, 97	lernen
to **let** [let]	**let** [let]	lassen
to **lie** [laɪ]	**lay** [leɪ]	liegen
to **lose** [lu:z]	**lost** [lɒst]	verlieren
to **make** [meɪk]	**made** [meɪd] **U6**, 89	machen, tun
to **mean** [mi:n]	**meant** [ment]	bedeuten
to **meet** [mi:t]	**met** [met] **U7**, 103	treffen
to **put** [pʊt]	**put** [pʊt] **U6**, 93	stellen, legen, setzen
to **read** [ri:d]	**read** [red]	lesen
to **ride** [raɪd]	**rode** [rəʊd]	fahren; reiten
to **run** [rʌn]	**ran** [ræn] **U6**, 92	rennen, laufen
to **say** [seɪ]	**said** [sed] **U6**, 89	sagen, sprechen
to **see** [si:]	**saw** [sɔ:] **U6**, 89	sehen
to **send** [send]	**sent** [sent]	schicken
to **set** [set]	**set** [set]	setzen, stellen, legen
to **shake** [ʃeɪk]	**shook** [ʃʊk] **U6**, 92	schütteln
to **shine** [ʃaɪn]	**shone** [ʃɒn]	scheinen, glänzen
to **shut** [ʃʌt]	**shut** [ʃʌt]	zumachen, schließen
to **sing** [sɪŋ]	**sang** [sæŋ]	singen
to **sit** [sɪt]	**sat** [sæt]	sitzen
to **sleep** [sli:p]	**slept** [slept] **U7**, 103	schlafen
to **speak** [spi:k]	**spoke** [spəʊk]	sprechen
to **spell** [spel]	**spelt** [spelt]	buchstabieren
to **spend** [spend]	**spent** [spent]	ausgeben; verbringen
to **stand** [stænd]	**stood** [stʊd] **U7**, 107	stehen
to **swim** [swɪm]	**swam** [swæm]	schwimmen
to **take** [teɪk]	**took** [tʊk] **U6**, 93	nehmen
to **teach** [ti:tʃ]	**taught** [tɔ:t]	unterrichten, lehren
to **tell** [tel]	**told** [təʊld] **U6**, 89	sagen, erzählen
to **think** [θɪŋk]	**thought** [θɔ:t]	denken
to **throw** [θrəʊ]	**threw** [θru:]	werfen
to **understand** [ˌʌndə'stænd]	**understood** [ˌʌndə'stʊd]	verstehen
to **wake** [weɪk]	**woke** [wəʊk]	wecken
to **wear** [weə]	**wore** [wɔ:]	tragen
to **win** [wɪn]	**won** [wʌn]	gewinnen, siegen
to **write** [raɪt]	**wrote** [rəʊt] **U6**, 89	schreiben

vocabulary

Aufbau des Vokabulars

Das ***Vocabulary*** hilft dir beim selbstständigen Lernen der neuen Wörter.
In der linken Spalte stehen die englischen Vokabeln in der Reihenfolge, in der sie in der Unit vorkommen. **Halbfett** gedruckte Wörter müssen gelernt werden, mager gedruckte sind zum Verständnis bestimmter Texte notwendig. Wie du die Lautschrift in eckigen Klammern lesen musst, steht unten auf dieser Seite.
In der mittleren Spalte (nur bei **Lernwörtern**) findest du Beispiel- oder Erklärungssätze, Bilder oder Hinweise, die dir beim Lernen helfen. In der rechten Spalte stehen eine oder mehrere deutsche Übersetzungen des englischen Ausdrucks oder eine Erklärung, die dir zeigt, wie ein Ausdruck benutzt wird, wenn es gar keine deutsche Übersetzung gibt.

Tipps zum Vokabellernen findest du in den Kästen zu jeder ***Unit*** und jedem ***Focus.*** Außerdem gibt es noch ***Word games.*** Dies sind kleine Aufgaben, Rätsel und Wortspiele, in denen du die neuen Wörter üben kannst.

Auf das ***Vocabulary*** folgt das ***Dictionary.*** Falls du ein Wort vergessen hast, kannst du einfach in dieser alphabetischen Wortliste nachsehen. Eigennamen findest du am Ende des ***Dictionary***.

Abkürzungen und Zeichen

pl. Plural, Mehrzahl
sg. Singular, Einzahl
↔ ist das Gegenteil von
→ ist verwandt mit
= entspricht
AE = Amerikanisches Englisch
BE = Britisches Englisch

Die **blau** gedruckten Vokabeln sollten bereits aus der Grundschule bekannt sein.
• Wort, das im Deutschen sehr ähnlich ist oder leicht aus bereits bekannten Bestandteilen erschlossen werden kann.
! Bei diesem Zeichen musst du besonders aufpassen.

Lautschrift

Wenn du die Aussprache und Betonung einer Vokabel einmal nachsehen musst, hilft dir die Lautschrift im Vokabular. Sie benutzt einige normale Buchstaben und einige besondere Zeichen. Die Aussprache der einzelnen Zeichen kannst du dir anhand einfacher Wörter merken. Die Betonung wird durch einen Betonungsstrich **vor** der betonten Silbe markiert: [ˈ] zeigt den Hauptakzent des Wortes, [ˌ] den Nebenakzent. Der Bindebogen [‿] zeigt, dass zwei Wörter in der Aussprache miteinander verbunden werden.

Konsonanten		Vokale		Doppellaute	
[ŋ]	morni**ng**	[ɑː]	f**a**ther	[aɪ]	**I**, m**y**
[r]	**r**ed	[ʌ]	b**u**t	[aʊ]	n**ow**, h**ou**se
[s]	thi**s**	[e]	p**e**n	[eə]	th**ere**, p**air**
[z]	i**s**	[ə]	**a** sist**er**	[eɪ]	n**a**me, th**ey**
[ʒ]	televi**s**ion	[ɜː]	g**ir**l	[ɪə]	h**ere**, id**ea**
[dʒ]	pa**ge**	[æ]	fl**a**t	[ɔɪ]	b**oy**
[ʃ]	**sh**e	[ɪ]	**i**t	[əʊ]	hell**o**
[tʃ]	lun**ch**	[i]	happ**y**	[ʊə]	s**ure**
[ð]	**th**e	[iː]	t**ea**cher, sh**e**		
[θ]	**th**anks	[ɒ]	g**o**t		
[v]	**v**ideo	[ɔː]	b**a**ll		
[w]	**w**ow, **o**ne	[ʊ]	b**oo**k		
		[u]	Jan**u**ary		
		[uː]	t**oo**, tw**o**		

Alle anderen Zeichen werden genauso ausgesprochen, wie sie geschrieben werden, z. B. [b], [j], [l] usw.

Mit dem Lernen fängst du an, indem du das Wort, das Beispiel und die deutsche Entsprechung liest. Danach kannst du z. B. die mittlere und die rechte Spalte abdecken und ausprobieren, ob du noch die deutsche Übersetzung zum englischen Wort weißt. Das geht natürlich auch umgekehrt, indem du versuchst, vom deutschen Begriff aus, dich an das englische Wort zu erinnern. Auch das Aufschreiben und das laute Vorsagen der englischen Wörter können dir beim Lernen helfen. Mehr darüber steht in den Lerntipps, die vor jeder Unit im Vokabelverzeichnis zu finden sind.

Let's start! [lets 'stɑ:t]		Lass(t) uns anfangen!
let's [lets] (= let us)		Lass(t) uns
to **let** [let]		lassen
us [ʌs]		wir; uns
• **to start** [stɑ:t]	! Am vorangestellten Wörtchen *to* erkennt man, dass es sich hier um die Grundform (Infinitiv) handelt.	anfangen, starten

1 Hello

Hello! [hə'ləʊ]	 Nomen schreibt man immer klein, so wie hier: *name*.	Hallo!
My name is … [maɪ 'neɪm‿ɪz]		Ich heiße …
my [maɪ]		mein(e)
• **name** [neɪm]		Name
is [ɪz]		ist
I'm [aɪm]		Ich bin
I [aɪ]	! *I* schreibt man immer groß.	ich
eleven [ɪ'levn]		elf
from [frɒm; frəm]	! Wenn man *from* nicht betont, spricht man es [frəm].	aus, von
• **Hi!** [haɪ]		Hi! Hallo!
twelve [twelv]		zwölf
and [ænd; ən(d)]	! Wenn man *and* nicht betont, spricht man es [ənd].	und
new [nju:]		neu
• **in** [ɪn]	I'm new *in* London.	in; rein, herein
the [ðə; ði]	! *The* wird vor Vokalen [ði] gesprochen.	der, die (*auch pl.*), das
• **monster** ['mɒntstə]		Monster
What's your name? [ˌwɒts jə 'neɪm]		Wie heißt du/heißen Sie?
what [wɒt]		was
your [jɔ:; jə]		dein(e); euer/eure; Ihr(e)
How old are you? [haʊ‿'əʊld‿ə ˌju:]	! Achte auf die Verbindungen zwischen den Wörtern!	Wie alt bist du/sind Sie?
how [haʊ]	*How old are you?* – I'm twelve.	wie
old [əʊld]	*old* ↔ new	alt
are [ɑ:; ə]	! Wenn man *are* nicht betont, spricht man es [ə].	bist, sind, seid
you [ju:; jə]	 ‚*You*' kann im Englischen ‚du/ihr/Sie' heißen!	du, ihr, Sie

Where are you from? [ˌweər‿ə jə ˈfrɒm]		Woher kommst du/ kommt ihr/kommen Sie?
Where … from? [ˌweə … ˈfrɒm]		Woher …?
where [weə]	*Where* are you from?	wo; wohin
ten [ten]		zehn

Numbers 1

one [wʌn]	eins	**five** [faɪv]	fünf	**nine** [naɪn]	neun
two [tu:]	zwei	**six** [sɪks]	sechs	**ten** [ten]	zehn
three [θri:]	drei	**seven** [ˈsevn]	sieben	**eleven** [ɪˈlevn]	elf
four [fɔ:]	vier	**eight** [eɪt]	acht	**twelve** [twelv]	zwölf

You and your

you = du, Sie, ihr **your = dein(e), Ihr(e), euer/eure**

Is that **your** friend, Becky?	Ist das **deine** Freundin / **dein** Freund, Becky?
Is that **your** friend, Becky and Robert?	Ist das **eure** Freundin / **euer** Freund, Becky und Robert?
Is that **your** friend, Mr Cooper?	Ist das **Ihre** Freundin / **Ihr** Freund, Herr Cooper?

2 Friends

friend [frend]	Merk dir bei *friend*: im Englischen gibt es oft nur ein Wort für weibliche und männliche Personen.	Freund(in)
Look! [lʊk]	! Dies ist eine Aufforderung. Hier benutzt man die Grundform ohne *to*.	Schau(t)!
to **look** [lʊk]	! Am vorangestellten Wörtchen *to* erkennt man, dass es sich hier um eine Grundform (Infinitiv) handelt.	(aus)sehen; schauen
it's [ɪts] (= it is)	! Siehe G1 auf Seite 132.	es ist
it [ɪt]		es
she's [ʃi:z] (= she is)	This is Becky. *She's* twelve.	sie ist
she [ʃi:]		sie
• **best** [best]		beste(-r/-s)
that [ðæt]		das; jenes
her [hɜ:]		ihr(e); sie; ihr
dog [dɒg]		Hund
yes [jes]		ja
this [ðɪs]		diese(-r/-s)
here [hɪə]	Hello, I'm *here*.	hier
he's [hi:z] (= he is)		er ist
he [hi:]		er
wow! [waʊ]		Wow! Toll!
Woof! [wʊf]		Wau!

	his [hɪz]	! *his* – he's. *His* name is Robert. He's nice.	sein(e)
	you're [jɔ:] (= you are)		du bist; ihr seid; Sie sind
	a(n) [ə; ən]	! Vor Vokalen wird *a* zu *an*.	ein(e)
	nice [naɪs]		nett
	Come on! [kʌm‿'ɒn]	*Come on,* Robert. Let's go.	Komm(t)!
	to come [kʌm]		kommen
	Let's go! [lets 'gəʊ]		Lass(t) uns gehen!
	to go [gəʊ]	Let's *go* to school.	gehen
	Bye! [baɪ]	hello ↔ good*bye*	Tschüss!
	cat [kæt]		Katze
	too [tu:]	Tabby is a nice cat, *too.*	auch
	at [æt; ət]	! Wenn man *at* nicht betont, spricht man es [ət] .	in, auf, bei, an
	school [sku:l]		Schule
	Hey! [heɪ]		He!
	that's [ðæts] (= that is)	*That's* David.	das ist
	tutor group ['tju:tə ˌgru:p]		Klasse (*in einer englischen Schule*)
	tutor ['tju:tə]		Klassenlehrer(in)
	group [gru:p]		Klasse; Gruppe
	Ow! [aʊ]		Autsch!
1	**It's your turn.** ['jɔ: tɜ:n]	 "It's *your turn!*"	Du bist/Sie sind dran.
2	**about** [ə'baʊt]		über; wegen
	to write [raɪt]	*Write* this in your exercise book.	schreiben
	exercise book ['eksəsaɪz ˌbʊk]		Übungsheft
	exercise ['eksəsaɪz]		Übung
	book [bʊk]		Buch; Heft
3	**to make** [meɪk]		machen, tun
	sentences ['sentəntsɪz]	Make *sentences.*	Sätze
	sentence ['sentənts]	This is a *sentence.*	Satz
	example [ɪg'zɑ:mpl]		Beispiel
4	**What's missing?** [ˌwɒts 'mɪsɪŋ]		Was fehlt?
5	**sound practice** ['saʊnd ˌpræktɪs]		*Hör-/Ausspracheübung*
	sound [saʊnd]		Ton, Geräusch
	practice ['præktɪs]		Übung
	to listen (to) ['lɪsn]	! Achtung Aussprache! Das geschriebene *t* wird nicht gesprochen.	zuhören, (an)hören
	to say [seɪ]	*Say* "hello" to Barker.	sagen, sprechen
	number ['nʌmbə]	What's your *number*, Robert?	Zahl, Nummer
	• **telephone** ['telɪfəʊn]		Telefon

Look and let's

Look at that exercise, Jenny.	**Sieh dir** die Aufgabe da an, Jenny.
Look at that exercise, Jenny and Robert.	**Seht euch** die Aufgabe da an, Jenny und Robert.
Look at that exercise, Mr Cooper.	**Sehen Sie** sich die Aufgabe da an, Herr Cooper.
Let's go, Robert.	**Lass uns** gehen, Robert.
Let's go, Mark and David.	**Lasst uns** gehen, Mark und David.
Let's ask Robert, Mr Cooper!	**Lassen Sie** uns Robert fragen, Herr Cooper.

	oh [əʊ]		null
6	• **listening** ['lɪsnɪŋ]		Hören, *hier:* Hörübung

3 David and Robert

	How are you? [ˌhaʊ‿'ɑ: ju:]		Wie geht es dir/euch/Ihnen?
	I'm fine. [aɪm 'faɪn]		Mir geht es gut.
	fine [faɪn]		gut, in Ordnung; schön
	What about you? [ˌwɒt‿əˌbaʊt 'ju:]		Und dir/euch/Ihnen? Und du/ihr/Sie?
	to **be hurt** [bi: 'hɜ:t]		weh tun; verletzt sein
	no [nəʊ]	yes ↔ *no*	nein
	not [nɒt]		nicht
	• **OK** [əʊ'keɪ]		OK
	thanks [θæŋks]		danke
	I like [aɪ 'laɪk]		Ich mag; mir gefällt
	to **like** [laɪk]		mögen, gern haben
	• **skates** [skeɪts]		Inlineskates, Rollschuhe, Schlittschuhe
	they [ðeɪ]		sie (*Plural*)
	aren't [ɑ:nt] (= are not)		sind/bist nicht
	but [bʌt; bət]	! Wenn man *but* nicht betont, spricht man es [bət] .	aber
	they're [ðeə] (= they are)	*They're* nice.	sie sind
	really ['rɪəli]		wirklich
	fast [fɑ:st]		schnell
	great [greɪt]		großartig, toll
	we're [wɪə] (= we are)	*We're* from Nottingham.	wir sind
	we [wi:]		wir
	our ['aʊə]		unser(e)
	house [haʊs]	That's our *house*.	Haus
	over there [ˌəʊvə 'ðeə]	Your things are *over there*.	da drüben
	there [ðeə]	here ↔ *there*	dort
	Welcome! ['welkəm]		Willkommen!
	to [tʊ; tə]	! Wenn man *to* nicht betont, spricht man es [tə] .	*Hier*: in; nach; zu
	isn't [ɪznt] (= is not)	Robert *isn't* here.	ist nicht
	their [ðeə]	! *their* - they're: Die gleiche Aussprache für zwei Wörter.	ihr, ihre *(Plural)*
	girl [gɜ:l]	Becky is a *girl*.	Mädchen
1	to **put in** [pʊt‿'ɪn]		einsetzen
2	**long** [lɒŋ]		lang
	short [ʃɔ:t]	*long* ↔ *short*	kurz
	• **form**, *pl.* **forms** [fɔ:m; fɔ:mz]		Form
	to **be** [bi:]		sein
	am [æm]		bin
3	**boy** [bɔɪ]	*boy* ↔ girl	Junge
4	**role play** ['rəʊl pleɪ]		Rollenspiel
	role [rəʊl]		Rolle
	play [pleɪ]		Spiel, Theaterstück
6	• **song** [sɒŋ]	! Achtung Aussprache! Das *s* muss zischen wie eine 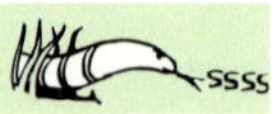	Lied, Song

can [kæn; kən]	! Wenn man *can* nicht betont, spricht man es [kən] aus.	kann, können
to **sing** [sɪŋ]	Let's *sing* a song.	singen
rainbow ['reɪnbəʊ]		Regenbogen
red [red]		rot
yellow ['jeləʊ]		gelb
• **pink** [pɪŋk]		pink, rosa
green [gri:n]		grün
purple ['pɜ:pl]		lila, violett
orange ['ɒrɪndʒ]		orange
blue [blu:]		blau
with [wɪð]		mit
eye [aɪ]		Auge
everything ['evriθɪŋ]	*Everything* is OK.	alles
to **see** [si:]	to see	sehen
• **to sing along** [ˌsɪŋ‿ə'lɒŋ]		mitsingen
me [mi:]	*Sing along* with *me*.	mich; mir
white [waɪt]		weiß
grey [greɪ]		grau
black [blæk]		schwarz
brown [braʊn]		braun
7 **What colour is/are …?** [ˌwɒt 'kʌlər‿ɪz/ɑ:]		Welche Farbe hat/haben …?
colour ['kʌlə]	Red is a nice *colour*.	Farbe
• **monsters** *pl.* ['mɒnstəz]		Monster, Ungeheuer

Short forms

I'm [aɪm]	**he's** [hi:z]	**we're** [wɪə]	**isn't** [ɪznt]	**here's** [hɪəz]	**there's** [ðeəz]
you're [jɔ:]	**she's** [ʃi:z]	**they're** [ðeə]	**aren't** [ɑ:nt]	**where's** [weəz]	**that's** [ðæts]
	it's [ɪts]				

Betont

to [tu:] **at** [æt] **and** [ænd] **from** [frɒm] **for** [fɔ:] **your** [jɔ:]

Unbetont

Welcome **to** the school. [ˌwelkəm tə ðə 'sku:l]	Look **at** the dog. [ˌluk‿ət ðə 'dɒg]	I like Barker **and** Tabby. [aɪ ˌlaɪk ˌbɑ:kər‿ən 'tæbi]
I'm **from** London. [ˌaɪm frəm 'lʌndən]	This is **for** you. [ˌðɪs‿ɪz fə 'ju:]	What's **your** name? [ˌwɒts jə 'neɪm]

4 Robert! Where are your school things?

thing [θɪŋ]	*things*: house – ~~dog~~ – skates – ~~cat~~ – telephone	Sache, Ding
Mum [mʌm]	! *Mum* wird nur als Name groß geschrieben!	Mama
Oh dear! ['əʊ ˌdɪə]		Oje!
school bag ['sku:l bæg]		Schultasche

	bag [bæg]		Tasche
	on [ɒn]		auf
	floor [flɔ:]	The book is on the *floor.*	Fußboden; Stockwerk
	next to ['nekst tə]		neben
	there's [ðeəz] (= there is)		da ist, es gibt
	pencil case ['pentsl ˌkeɪs]	The *pencil case* is green.	Federmäppchen
	pencil ['pentsl]		Bleistift; Buntstift
	folder ['fəʊldə]		Ordner, Mappe
	ruler ['ru:lə]		Lineal
	these [ði:z]		diese (hier)
	football magazine ['fʊtbɔ:l mægəˌzi:n]	Robert likes *football magazines.*	Fußballzeitschrift
	football ['fʊtbɔ:l]		Fußball
	foot, *pl.* **feet** [fʊt; fi:t]	 	Fuß, Füße
	• **ball** [bɔ:l]		Ball
	• **magazine** [mægə'zi:n]		Zeitschrift, Magazin
	maybe ['meɪbi]	Where is she? – *Maybe* at school.	vielleicht
	those [ðəʊz]	These are my books. *Those* are your books.	diese dort, jene
	drawer [drɔ:]		Schublade
	under ['ʌndə]	on ↔ *under*	unter
	• **comic** ['kɒmɪk]		Comic(heft)
	or [ɔ:]		oder
	there are [ðeər‿'ɑ:]	*There are* two comics on the floor.	da sind; es gibt
	desk [desk]		Schreibtisch
	pen [pen]		Füller
	rubber ['rʌbə]	Where is my *rubber*?	Radiergummi
	chair [tʃeə]		Stuhl
	bed [bed]		Bett
	biro ['baɪrəʊ]		Kugelschreiber, Kuli
1	**What's … in English?** [ˌwɒts … ɪn‿'ɪŋglɪʃ]		Was heißt … auf Englisch?
	• **English** ['ɪŋglɪʃ]		englisch; Englisch
2	• **to find** [faɪnd]		finden
	right [raɪt]	**!** *Right* – write: eine Aussprache für zwei verschiedene Wörter.	richtig, korrekt
	• **list** [lɪst]		Liste
4	**teacher** ['ti:tʃə]		Lehrer(in)
5	**game** [geɪm]		Spiel
	• **to play** [pleɪ]		spielen
6	**to draw** [drɔ:]	Let's *draw* a *picture* with our pencils.	zeichnen
	picture ['pɪktʃə]		Bild

There is, there are

There is a magazine on the floor.	Da **liegt** eine Zeitschrift auf dem Boden.
There is a new boy in our tutor group.	In unserer Klasse **gibt es** einen neuen Jungen.
There are five books on the table.	**Da sind** fünf Bücher auf dem Tisch.
There are two tables in the house.	**Es gibt** zwei Tische im Haus.
There are five schools in Nottingham.	**Es gibt** fünf Schulen in Nottingham.

	again [ə'gen]	**again** again again again	wieder
8	**pair** [peə]		Paar
	Goodbye! [gʊd'baɪ]	hello, hi ↔ *goodbye*	Auf Wiedersehen!
	word [wɜːd]		Wort
	easy ['iːzi]		einfach, leicht

5 School!

Wenn man buchstabieren will, z. B. den eigenen Namen, muss man das Alphabet kennen.

a [eɪ]	**e** [iː]	**i** [aɪ]	**m** [em]	**q** [kjuː]	**u** [juː]	
b [biː]	**f** [ef]	**j** [dʒeɪ]	**n** [en]	**r** [ɑː]	**v** [viː]	
c [siː]	**g** [dʒiː]	**k** [keɪ]	**o** [əʊ]	**s** [es]	**w** ['dʌbljuː]	**y** [waɪ]
d [diː]	**h** [eɪtʃ]	**l** [el]	**p** [piː]	**t** [tiː]	**x** [eks]	**z** [zed]

	playground ['pleɪgraʊnd]	There is a *playground* at our school.	Schulhof, Pausenhof
	Yes, he is. [ˌjes hiː‿'ɪz]		Ja, das stimmt.
	silly ['sɪli]		Dummkopf
	to **be good at** ['gʊd‿ət]	Sarah is *good at* football, but she isn't *good at* everything.	gut sein in
	good [gʊd]		gut
	Maths [mæθs]	Robert isn't good at *Maths*.	Mathematik
	No, I'm not. [ˌnəʊ‿aɪm 'nɒt]		Nein, bin ich nicht.
	Ugh! [ɜː]		Igitt!
	Oh yes, you are! [ˌəʊ ˌjes juː‿'ɑː]		Oh doch, das bist du!
	er [ɜː]	"Er?"	äh
	who [huː]	! *Who* heißt **wer**, nicht: wo.	wer
	Mr ['mɪstə]		Herr *(Anrede)*
	German ['dʒɜːmən]		deutsch; Deutsche(r); Deutsch
	brilliant ['brɪljənt]	I like this game. It's *brilliant*.	toll, prima; leuchtend
	very ['veri]	That teacher is *very* nice.	sehr
	Mrs ['mɪsɪz]		Frau *(Anrede)*
1	to **answer** ['ɑːntsə]	! Achtung Aussprache! Bei *answer* ['ɑːntsə] spricht man das *w* nicht.	(be)antworten
	question ['kwestʃn]		Frage
2	to **ask** [ɑːsk]	Can I *ask* you a *question*?	fragen
3	**Watch out!** [wɒtʃ‿'aʊt]		Achtung! Pass(t) auf!
4	**Word power** ['wɜːd ˌpaʊə]		*Besondere Wortschatzübung*
	power ['paʊə]		Kraft, Stärke, Macht
	mind map ['maɪnd mæp]		Wörternetz *(eine Art Schaubild)*
6	• **alphabet** ['ælfəbet]	The ABC is the *alphabet*.	Alphabet
	• **rap** [ræp]		Rap
	every day [ˌevri 'deɪ]		jeden Tag
	every ['evri]		jede(-r/-s)
	day [deɪ]		Tag
	Hear us rap. [ˌhɪər‿ʌs 'ræp]		Hör(t) uns rappen.
	to **spell** [spel]	*Spell* "Mark": M-A-R-K	buchstabieren
	favourite ['feɪvrɪt]	Blue is my *favourite* colour.	Lieblings-
	• **star** [stɑː]		Star; Stern
	double ['dʌbl]		Doppel-, zweimal

6 Pictures in the classroom

	classroom ['klɑ:srʊm]		Klassenzimmer
	class [klɑ:s]	This is my new *class*.	Schulklasse, Klasse
	room [ru:m]		Zimmer; Platz
	its [ɪts]	I like *its* colours.	sein(e); ihr(e)
	like (this/that) [laɪk 'ðɪs/ðæt]		so wie (hier/dort)
	look at ['lʊk‿ət]	Look at that picture.	anschauen
	funny ['fʌni]	Comics can be *funny*.	komisch, lustig
	terrible ['terəbl]	Rap songs are *terrible*.	schrecklich, furchtbar
	Don't laugh! [dəʊnt 'lɑ:f]	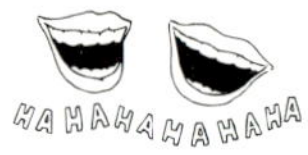	Lach(t) nicht!
	to **laugh** [lɑ:f]		lachen
	too [tu:]		zu
	loud [laʊd]	Don't sing too *loud*.	laut
	Thank you very much! [ˌθæŋk ju: veri 'mʌtʃ]		Vielen Dank! Herzlichen Dank!
	• **so** [səʊ]		so
1	to **match** [mætʃ]		zusammenbringen, zusammenfügen
3	**true** [tru:]	That's *true* – Robert is from London.	wahr
4	**answer** ['ɑ:ntsə]	question ↔ *answer*	Antwort
5	**Simon says** [ˌsaɪmən 'sez]		*Brit. Spiel*
	to **stand (up)** [stænd‿'ʌp]		(auf)stehen
	up [ʌp]		hoch, (hin)auf
	to **sit (down)** [sɪt 'daʊn]	stand up ↔ *sit down*	sich (hin)setzen
	to **shut** [ʃʌt]		zumachen, schließen
	to **open** ['əʊpn]	*Open* your books, please.	öffnen, aufmachen
	to **clap** [klæp]		klatschen
	• **hand** [hænd]	*Clap* your *hands*.	Hand
	to **touch** [tʌtʃ]		berühren; antippen
	nose [nəʊz]	Don't *touch* your *nose*.	Nase
	out [aʊt]		raus, (nach) draußen

7 The lesson

lesson ['lesn]		Unterrichtsstunde, Schulstunde
to **be late** [bi: 'leɪt]	 "You'*re late*."	zu spät sein, zu spät kommen
young [jʌŋ]	*young* ↔ old	jung
quiet ['kwaɪət]		leise
please [pli:z]	*Please* sit down and be *quiet*.	bitte
now [naʊ]		jetzt, nun
ready ['redi]	Robert is *ready* for school *now*.	fertig, bereit
homework ['həʊmwɜ:k]	! Dieses Wort steht immer im Singular.	Hausaufgaben
to **bring** [brɪŋ]	Please don't *bring* comics to school!	bringen
silly ['sɪli]	That's a *silly* game.	dumm, doof, albern
sorry ['sɒri]	Oh, *sorry*!	Tut mir Leid, Entschuldigung

1	• **text** [tekst]	Find the new words in the *text*.	Text; Textnachricht (SMS)
	false [fɔ:ls]	true ↔ *false*	falsch
	to **correct** [kə'rekt]	Can you *correct* my homework, please?	korrigieren, verbessern
2	**morning** ['mɔ:nɪŋ]	School is in the *morning*.	Morgen; Vormittag
	window ['wɪndəʊ]	Can we open the *window*?	Fenster
	blackboard, board ['blækbɔ:d; bɔ:d]	Write your name on the *blackboard*, please.	Tafel
	page [peɪdʒ]	Open your books at *page* 11, please.	Seite
	See you! ['si: ju:]	Bye. *See you* tomorrow!	Bis dann! Bis …
	tomorrow [tə'mɒrəʊ]	*Tomorrow* is Saturday! Great, no school!	morgen
3	• **team** [ti:m]		Gruppe, Team
	No idea! [ˌnəʊ‿aɪ'dɪə]	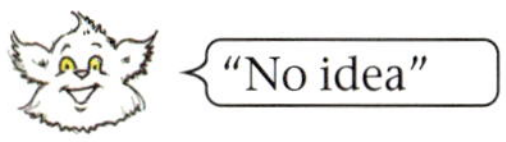	Keine Ahnung!
	no [nəʊ]		kein(e)
	idea [aɪ'dɪə]		Einfall, Idee; Ahnung
	point [pɔɪnt]	That's right. One *point* for your team.	Punkt
4	**Hokey Cokey** [ˌhəʊki 'kəʊki]		*Name eines Tanzes*
	to **put** [pʊt]		setzen, stellen, legen
	left [left]		links; linke(-r/-s)
	• **arm** [ɑ:m]		Arm
	to shake it all about [ˌʃeɪk‿ɪt‿ɔ:l‿ə'baʊt]		ihn *(den Arm)* herumschütteln
	to **do** [du:]	Let's *do* exercise 3.	tun, machen
	to turn around [ˌtɜ:n‿ə'raʊnd]		wenden; umdrehen
	what it's all about [ˌwɒt‿ɪts‿ɔ:l‿ə'baʊt]		worum es geht
	knee [ni:]		Knie
	to bend [bend]		beugen; biegen
	to stretch [stretʃ]		strecken; dehnen
	right [raɪt]	*right* ↔ left	rechts; rechte(-r/-s)
	leg [leg]		Bein
	whole self [ˌhəʊl 'self]		*hier*: ganzer Körper

8 Let's check

	Let's check! [lets 'tʃek]		Lass(t) uns überprüfen!
	to **check** [tʃek]		(über)prüfen; kontrollieren
6	**thirteen** [θɜ:'ti:n]		dreizehn
7	**only** ['əʊnli]	There is *only* one German teacher at our school.	nur; erst; bloß
9	**mixed bag** [ˌmɪkst 'bæg]		buntes Allerlei

focus 1 Focus on families

Das Lernen geht einfacher mit einer Vokabelkartei. Dazu brauchst du einen Karton mit zwei Fächern und Karteikarten aus dünner Pappe oder dickem Papier.
Schreibe das englische Wort auf die eine Seite der Karteikarte.
Füge darunter alles hinzu, was hilft, dir das Wort und seine Verwendung besser zu merken, z. B. Wörter, mit denen das Wort zusammen vorkommt, unregelmäßige Formen, Bilder als Merkhilfen, verwandte Wörter oder Gegensätze. Vergiss nicht einen typischen Beispielsatz. Schreibe dann die deutsche Übersetzung auf die Rückseite. Dann stellst du die Karten vorne in den Karton.
Später überprüfst du, ob du die Übersetzung des Wortes noch weißt, und zwar deutsch – englisch und englisch – deutsch. Zwischendurch mischst du die Karten. Wenn du ein Wort sicher kannst, stellst du die Karte ins hintere Fach.

	focus ['fəʊkəs]		Blickpunkt
	family ['fæmli]	The Burtons are a *family*.	Familie
	tree [tri:]		Baum
	family tree ['fæmli tri:]	You can draw a *family tree*.	Familienstammbaum
	grandpa ['grændpɑ:]	Your father's or your mother's father.	Opa
	grandma ['grændmɑ:]	Your mother's or your father's mother.	Oma
	uncle ['ʌŋkl]	! Alle Familienbezeichnungen werden als Name groß geschrieben, z. B.: *Uncle* Jack, *Grandma* Burton.	Onkel
	aunt [ɑ:nt]	uncle ↔ *aunt*	Tante
	father ['fɑ:ðə]		Vater
	mother ['mʌðə]	*mother* ↔ father	Mutter
	cousin ['kʌzn]	David is Jenny's *cousin* and Jenny is David's *cousin*.	Cousin, Cousine
	sister ['sɪstə]	Becky is Simon's *sister*.	Schwester
	brother ['brʌðə]	*brother* ↔ sister	Bruder
2	• **puzzle** ['pʌzl]	Here's a *puzzle* about the Burtons.	Rätsel; Puzzle
	birthday ['bɜ:θdeɪ]	The best day is my *birthday*.	Geburtstag
	place [pleɪs]		Platz, Stelle, Ort
	table ['teɪbl]	Where's my place at the *table*?	Tisch
	on somebody's right/left [ɒn ˌsʌmbədiz 'raɪt/'left]		zur Rechten/zur Linken von jemandem
	somebody ['sʌmbədi]		jemand
	person ['pɜ:sn]		Person
	to **be married to** [bi: 'mærid tə]	Grandpa *is married to* Grandma.	verheiratet sein mit
4	**parents** ['peərənts]	mother and father = *parents*	Eltern
	tall [tɔ:l]		groß; hoch
	dark [dɑ:k]		dunkel
	• **blonde** [blɒnd]	Her mother is *blonde*.	blond
	sometimes ['sʌmtaɪmz]		manchmal
	Indian ['ɪndiən]		indisch; Inder(in); indianisch; Indianer(in)

of course [əv 'kɔ:s]	Can you play football? – *Of course* I can!	natürlich, selbstverständlich
Italian [ɪ'tæliən]		italienisch; Italiener(in); Italienisch
woman, *pl.* **women** ['wʊmən; 'wɪmɪn]		Frau
child, *pl.* **children** ['tʃaɪld; 'tʃɪldrn]	! Achtung bei der Aussprache von *woman – women* und *child – children.*	Kind
both [bəʊθ]	Robert and David *both* like football.	beide
international [ˌɪntə'næʃnl]	An Indian mother and an Italian father – that's very *international.*	international

unit 1 The Burtons and the Dixons

Du behältst die neuen Wörter besser, wenn du sie dir nur fünf Minuten anschaust, aber dafür nach einer halben Stunde wiederholst und am Ende deiner Hausaufgaben noch einmal fünf Minuten überprüfst.

	unit ['ju:nɪt]	There are seven *units* in this book.	Kapitel; Einheit
	city ['sɪti]	London is a *city.*	Stadt; Großstadt
	centre ['sentə]	Sherwood isn't in the *centre* of Nottingham.	Zentrum
	city centre [ˌsɪti 'sentə]	Becky's house isn't in the *city centre.*	Stadtzentrum, Stadtmitte
	road [rəʊd]	There's a school in our *road.*	Straße
	man, *pl.* **men** [mæn; men]	*man* ↔ woman	Mann
	dad [dæd]	! *Dad* und *Mum* werden nur als Name groß geschrieben.	Papa
1	to **talk** [tɔ:k]	 Achtung: Das *l* wird nicht ausgesprochen.	sprechen, reden
2	**lane** [leɪn]		Gasse; Fahrspur
	forest ['fɒrɪst]		Wald
	swimming pool ['swɪmɪŋ ˌpu:l]	There's a *swimming pool* in Sherwood.	Schwimmbecken; Schwimmbad
	bike [baɪk]		Fahrrad
	shop [ʃɒp]	a bike *shop*, a book*shop*	Geschäft, Laden
	• **supermarket** ['su:pəˌmɑ:kɪt]		Supermarkt
	• **park** [pɑ:k]	Let's play football in the *park.*	Park
3	**inside** [ɪn'saɪd]		innen, drin; nach drinnen
	outside [aʊt'saɪd]	*outside* ↔ *inside*	außen, außerhalb, (nach) draußen
	• **CD** [si:'di:]		CD
	why [waɪ]		warum
	roof [ru:f]	There's a *roof* on every house.	Dach
	wall [wɔ:l]	There's a window in the *wall.*	Wand; Mauer
	door [dɔ:]	That's where you go in.	Tür
	• **garage** ['gærɑ:ʒ]	You can put your bike in the *garage.*	Garage
	garden ['gɑ:dn]		Garten
	bathroom ['bɑ:θrʊm]		Badezimmer

	bath [bɑ:θ]		Bad
	bedroom ['bedrʊm]		Schlafzimmer
	kitchen ['kɪtʃɪn]	Simon and Becky are in the *kitchen*.	Küche
	hall [hɔ:l]		Flur, Diele, Korridor
	living room ['lɪvɪŋ rʊm]		Wohnzimmer
4	• **plan** [plæn]	Draw a *plan* of your house, please.	Plan
	of [ɒv; əv]		von
	(my) own [əʊn]	! Verwende *own* nie ohne *my/your/his/her* etc.: Have you got *your own* room?	eigen(-e/-r/-s)
	flat [flæt]		Wohnung

Language A We're busy

	language ['læŋgwɪdʒ]	English is a *language*.	Sprache
	busy ['bɪzi]	! Achtung Aussprache!	beschäftigt; belebt; voller Menschen
	have got [hæv 'gɒt]		besitzen, haben
	tidy ['taɪdi]	The Burtons' house is very *tidy*.	sauber, ordentlich
	clothes *pl.* [kləʊðz]	! Das englische Wort *clothes* steht immer im Plural: David's *clothes* **are** nice.	Kleider, Kleidung
	empty ['empti]		leer
	bottle ['bɒtl]	Don't put *empty bottles* in your room.	Flasche
	• **skateboard** ['skeɪtbɔ:d]		Skateboard
	• **poster** ['pəʊstə]		Poster
	must [mʌst; məst]	You *must* do your homework.	müssen
	by [baɪ]	A CD *by* the Underdogs.	von
	• **CD player** [ˌsi:'di: ˌpleɪə]	You can play CDs on it.	CD-Spieler
	No, I haven't. [ˌnəʊ‿aɪ 'hævnt]		Nein, hab ich nicht.
	• **stereo** ['steriəʊ]	Have you got a *stereo*?	Stereoanlage
	• **tennis** ['tenɪs]	 This is a ball for *tennis*.	Tennis
	racket ['rækɪt]	You can play tennis with it.	Schläger
	• **computer** [ˌkəm'pju:tə]		Computer
	animal ['ænɪml]		Tier
	horse [hɔ:s]		Pferd
	• **to come in** [kʌm‿'ɪn]	Can I *come in*?	hereinkommen
	already [ɔ:l'redi]	Becky has got the new CD *already*.	schon
	can't [kɑ:nt]	! Achtung Aussprache: can [kæn] – *can't* [kɑ:nt].	nicht können
2	**to use** [ju:z]	Can I *use* your skates?	benutzen, verwenden
5	**to work** [wɜ:k]	*Work* in pairs!	arbeiten

Language B Breakfast at the Dixons' house!

	breakfast ['brekfəst]		Frühstück
	Friday ['fraɪdeɪ]		Freitag
	knife, *pl.* **knives** [naɪf; naɪvz]	! Achte auf die Aussprache: In *knife* wird das *k* nicht gesprochen.	Messer
	to set the table [ˌset ðə 'teɪbl]	*Set the table*, please. Breakfast is ready.	den Tisch decken
	today [tə'deɪ]		heute
	always ['ɔ:lweɪz]		immer, ständig
	lunchbox ['lʌntʃbɒks]	Sarah's *lunchbox* is in her school bag.	Pausenbrotbehälter
	lunch [lʌntʃ]	*Lunch* is at 12.	Essen, Mittagessen
	• **box** [bɒks]	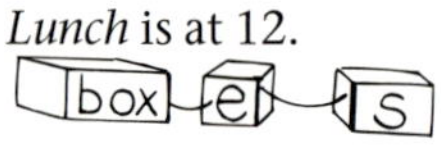	Kiste, Schachtel; Kasten

	shelf, *pl.* **shelves** [ʃelf; ʃelvz]		Regal, Regalbrett
	sure [ʃʊə; ʃɔ:]	Where is the book? – I'm *sure* it's on the shelf.	sicher
	lazy ['leɪzi]		faul
	to fight [faɪt]	Don't *fight* about the new CD, please.	streiten, kämpfen
	to need [ni:d]		brauchen, benötigen
	lock [lɒk]	I need a new *lock* for my bike.	(Fahrrad-)Schloss
	for [fɔ:; fə]	! *For* – four: gleiche Aussprache – verschiedene Schreibweise.	für
	pump [pʌmp]		Pumpe, Luftpumpe
	together [tə'geðə]		zusammen, miteinander
	alone [ə'ləʊn]	together ↔ *alone*	alleine
2	**Find the odd word out!** [ˌɒd wɜ:d‿'aʊt]		Finde das Wort, das nicht in die Gruppe passt! *(Wortschatzübung)*
	odd [ɒd]		seltsam, nicht passend
	• **glass** [glɑ:s]		Glas
	fork [fɔ:k]		Gabel
	spoon [spu:n]		Löffel
	plate [pleɪt]	Put the *plates* on the table, please.	Teller
	bowl [bəʊl]	The *bowl* is next to Kim's lunchbox.	Schale, Schälchen
	cup [kʌp]		Tasse
	saucer ['sɔ:sə]	You put a cup on it.	Untertasse
3	• **plural** ['plʊərl]	Glasses – that's the *plural* form.	Plural, Mehrzahl
	rule [ru:l]	Can you find a *rule* for the plural forms?	Regel
6	**neighbour** ['neɪbə]	 A and B are *neighbours*.	Nachbar(in)

Text The frog

frog [frɒg]	There's a *frog* under the tree.	Frosch
Sunday ['sʌndeɪ]		Sonntag
afternoon [ˌɑ:ftə'nu:n]	this morning – this *afternoon*	Nachmittag
big [bɪg]	**BIG**	groß; dick
to take [teɪk]		(mit)nehmen; bringen
home [həʊm]	Why can't we *take* the dog *home*?	Heim; nach Hause
• **trick** [trɪk]		Trick; Streich
later ['leɪtə]	*Later* the girls are in Becky's room.	später
What's the matter? [ˌwɒts ðə 'mætə]	You look terrible. *What's the matter?*	Was ist los? Was hast du?
little [lɪtl]	Mark is David's *little* brother.	klein
to get [get]	You can *get* a new bike at the bike shop.	(be)kommen
to get into [get‿'ɪntə]	 in  into	in etwas hineingelangen
into ['ɪntu; 'ɪntə]		in, hinein
teatime ['ti:taɪm]	*Teatime* - that's in the afternoon.	Zeit für Nachmittagstee; Abendessen
tea [ti:]	What you have at teatime.	Tee; Abendessen
time [taɪm]	Have you got *time*?	Zeit

	cupboard ['kʌbəd]	! Achtung Aussprache! Nicht: *cup + board*.	Küchenschrank, Schrank
	to call [kɔ:l]		(an)rufen; Bescheid geben

Bringen

Colin, **take** David to school, please.	Colin, **bring** David bitte zur Schule. (= **hinbringen**)
Bring me the ball, Barker.	**Bring** mir den Ball, Barker. (= **herbringen**)

	line [laɪn]	Write a sentence on the *line*.	Zeile; Linie
4	**how many** [haʊ 'meni]	*How many* posters have you got in your room?	wie viele
	many ['meni]		viele
	story ['stɔ:ri]	This *story* is very funny.	Geschichte, Erzählung

Let's check

2	• **fair** [feə]		gerecht, fair
4	**snake** [sneɪk]	There are 18 words in the word *snake*.	Schlange
	• **to mark** [mɑ:k]	*Mark* the short forms, please.	markieren

unit 2 In town

Hast du schon eine Vokabelkartei angelegt? Dann sind die Karten bestimmt schon alle im hinteren Fach. Aber denk daran: Alle paar Wochen solltest du auch diese Karten einmal durchschauen. Wenn du ein Wort nicht mehr kannst, wandert die Karte wieder ins vordere Fach zurück und wird mit den neuen Wörtern wiederholt.

Intro

	town [taʊn]	A little city.	Stadt
	shopping centre ['ʃɒpɪŋ ˌsentə]		Einkaufszentrum
	shopping ['ʃɒpɪŋ]	*Shopping* at a supermarket is fast.	Einkaufen; Einkäufe
	to **go shopping** [ˌgəʊ 'ʃɒpɪŋ]		einkaufen gehen
	• **music** ['mju:zɪk]	! Achtung Aussprache! ['mju:zɪk]	Musik
	• **bookshop** ['bʊkʃɒp]	Our *bookshop* has got books and CDs, but they haven't got magazines.	Buchhandlung
	to **spend** ['spend]	! *To spend* heißt nicht ‚spenden'!	ausgeben; verbringen
	lots of ['lɒts‿əv]	There are *lots of* shops in Nottingham.	viel(e)
	money ['mʌni]		Geld
	by (bus) [baɪ]	Go *by bus*.	mit (dem Bus), per
	bus [bʌs]	! Vorsicht bei der Pluralform: *buses* [-sɪz]!	Bus
	• **ticket** ['tɪkɪt]	You must get a *ticket*, then you can get on a train.	Ticket, Fahrschein, Eintrittskarte
	• **all** [ɔ:l]	*All* children from 5 to 16 go to school.	alle(s); ganz
	• **market** ['mɑ:kɪt]	A *market* is like a supermarket, but it's outside.	Markt

	square [skweə]		Platz
	people ['pi:pl]	! *People* wird oft als Pluralform von *person* verwendet!	Leute, Menschen
	car [kɑ:]	Mrs Penrose has got a German *car.*	Auto
	• **statue** ['stætʃu:]	Oh look, that's not a *statue*, it's a man!	Statue, Standbild
	in front of [ɪn 'frʌnt‿əv]	The garden is *in front of* the house.	vor, davor
	castle ['kɑ:sl]	! Achtung! Das *t* in *castle* wird nicht gesprochen.	Schloss; Burg
2	**poem** ['pəʊɪm]		Gedicht
	train [treɪn]		Zug
	airport ['eəpɔ:t]		Flughafen
	plane [pleɪn]		Flugzeug
	• **taxi** ['tæksi]	You can go by *taxi*, by plane, by car, by train, by bus and by bike.	Taxi
3	**to tell (somebody)** [tel]	I'm Robert. *Tell* me your name, please.	(jemandem) sagen, mitteilen
	way [weɪ]	Can you tell me the *way* to the cinema, please?	Weg; Art und Weise
	to read [ri:d]	Can I *read* your comic, please?	lesen
	• **dialogue** ['daɪəlɒg]	Let's read the *dialogue* with Robert and Simon on page 28 again.	Dialog, Gespräch
	phrase [freɪz]	*Good* is a word, *be good at* is a *phrase*.	Redewendung, Ausdruck
	Excuse me! [ɪk'skju:z mi]		Entschuldigung! Entschuldigen Sie!
	• **information** [ˌɪnfə'meɪʃn]	! I've got lots of *information* about Nottingham. Niemals: ~~informations~~; ~~an information~~.	Information(en)
	down [daʊn]	up ↔ *down*	entlang; herunter, hinunter, nach unten
	row [rəʊ]		Sträßchen; Reihe
	far [fɑ:]		weit
	to turn [tɜ:n]	*Turn* left!	einbiegen, abbiegen; drehen, wenden
	street [stri:t]	King Street and Smithy Row are *streets* in the city centre.	Straße
	map [mæp]	Look at the *map* in your book.	Stadtplan, Landkarte
	• **partner** ['pɑ:tnə]	Let's play a game. You're my *partner.*	Partner(in)
	cinema ['sɪnəmə]		Kino

Sie

she	This is Becky. **She** is nice.	Das ist Becky. **Sie** ist nett.
her	Is this Sarah's book? – Ask **her**!	Ist das Sarahs Buch? – Frag **sie** doch.
they	There are Robert and Becky. **They** are my friends.	Hier sind Robert und Becky. **Sie** sind meine Freunde.
them	Here come Sarah and Jenny. Ask **them**!	Da kommen Sarah und Jenny. Frag **sie**!
it	This is a cup. **It's** red.	Dies ist eine Tasse. **Sie** ist rot.
you	Excuse me, can **you** help me, please?	Entschuldigung, können **Sie** mir bitte helfen?
!	Bring me the book, please!	Bringen **Sie** mir bitte das Buch.

	church [tʃɜ:tʃ]	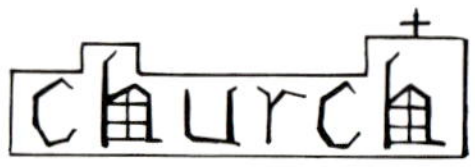	Kirche
4	**them** [ðem; ðəm]	There are Becky and Barker. Let's play with *them*.	sie; ihnen
5	**village** ['vɪlɪdʒ]	a village  a town 	Dorf

Language A Shopping

	media ['mi:diə]	Books, e-mails and the cinema are all *media*.	Medien
	pocket ['pɒkɪt]	Sarah has got 50p in her *pocket*.	Hosen- oder Jackentasche
	• **pocket money** ['pɒkɪt ˌmʌni]	You can buy things with your *pocket money*.	Taschengeld
	to **buy** [baɪ]	You can *buy* things at a shop.	kaufen
	• **video** ['vɪdiəʊ]	I've got "Robin Hood" on *video*.	Video
	• **guitar** [gɪ'tɑ:]	Play the guitar; play a guitar; David can play the *guitar*.	Gitarre
	to **watch** [wɒtʃ]		beobachten, (sich) ansehen
	• **cartoon** [kɑ:'tu:n]		Cartoon; Zeichentrickfilm
	• **TV** [ti:'vi:]	*Television*.	Fernsehen; Fernseher
	television ['telɪvɪʒn]	You can see football and cartoons on *television*.	Fernsehen; Fernseher
	to **watch TV** [ˌwɒtʃ ti:'vi:]		fernsehen
	to **wait (for)** [weɪt]		warten (auf)
	just [dʒʌst]		gerade; nur
	• **minute** ['mɪnɪt]	I'm not ready, wait a *minute*, please.	Minute
4	**different** ['dɪfrnt]		anders, verschieden

Language B Can you fetch us, Mum?

	to **fetch** [fetʃ]	To go and get.	(ab)holen
	to **hear** [hɪə]	Can you *hear* me?	hören
	to **sit** [sɪt]	David, don't *sit* at the computer all day!	sitzen
	• **café** ['kæfeɪ]	Let's have tea in a *café* today.	Café
	to **rain** [reɪn]	Oh dear, it's *raining*! 	regnen
	to **get wet** [get 'wet]		nass werden
	wet [wet]		nass
	mobile ['məʊbaɪl]	! Ein Handy heißt auf Englisch nicht *handy*, sondern *mobile*!	Handy, Mobiltelefon
	engaged [ɪŋ'geɪdʒd]	! *Engaged* heißt nicht ‚engagiert'.	besetzt, belegt
	all the time [ˌɔ:l ðə 'taɪm]	Kim, be quiet, don't sing *all the time*!	die ganze Zeit
	• **to phone** [fəʊn]	telephone → *to phone*	telefonieren
	• **boyfriend** ['bɔɪfrend]	Robert is a friend, but he isn't Becky's *boyfriend*.	Freund
	to **carry** ['kæri]	Can you *carry* this box for me, please?	tragen
	him [hɪm]		ihm; ihn
	• **e-mail** ['i:meɪl]		E-mail

	rain [reɪn]	to rain → the *rain*	Regen
	• **to stop** [stɒp]	to start ↔ *to stop*	aufhören; anhalten
	sun [sʌn]	The *sun* is out, so it's nice in the garden.	Sonne
2	**grammar** ['græmə]	Rules for a language.	Grammatik
5	to help [help]	Can I *help* you? – Yes, you can.	helfen
7	**last** [lɑ:st]	Z is the *last* letter in the alphabet.	letzte(-r/-s)
	letter ['letə]	 The alphabet has got 26 *letters*. You can write *letters*, too.	Buchstabe; Brief

His and her

Robert puts **his** hands in **his** pockets.	Robert steckt **die** Hände in **die** Tasche.
Mark has got a pencil in **his** hand.	Mark hat einen Stift in **der** Hand.
Mrs Croft has got a computer on **her** desk, and a radio in **her** car.	Frau Croft hat einen Computer auf **dem** Schreibtisch und ein Radio **im** Auto.

Text The race

	race [reɪs]	Can we watch the bike *race* on TV, Mum?	Wettlauf, Rennen
	driver ['draɪvə]	A *driver* can drive a car, a bus or a taxi.	Fahrer(in)
	Here you are! [ˌhɪə ju:‿'ɑ:]		Hier bitte! Bitteschön!
	• sunny ['sʌni]	sun → *sunny*	sonnig
	to **get on (the bus)** [get‿'ɒn]		einsteigen (in den Bus)
	to **lose** [lu:z]	Here's a new pencil. Don't *lose* it!	verlieren
	stupid ['stju:pɪd]	silly	dumm, blöd
	twenty ['twenti]		zwanzig
	to **get off (the bus)** [get‿'ɒf]	*to get off* ↔ to get on	aussteigen (aus dem Bus)
	other ['ʌðə]	Different. Is there only your family in your house, or are there *other* people there, too?	anders; andere(-r/-s)
	to **walk** [wɔ:k]		gehen, laufen
	then [ðen]	Sing a song, *then* play a game.	dann
	to **have a race** [ˌhæv‿ə 'reɪs]	Come on, let's *have a race* on our bikes.	ein Rennen veranstalten
	to **be on** [ɒn]	The race *is on*.	im Gange sein, laufen
	to **run** [rʌn]	Look, the bus is coming. *Run*!	rennen, laufen
	towards [tə'wɔ:dz]		auf zu, darauf zu
	which [wɪtʃ]		welche(-r/-s)
	• **champion** ['tʃæmpiən]		Gewinner; Champion
	to shine [ʃaɪn]	It isn't raining, the sun is *shining*.	scheinen; glänzen
	cloud [klaʊd]		Wolke
	sky [skaɪ]		Himmel
	Oops! [u:ps]		Hoppla!, Huch!
	poor [pɔ:; pʊə]	It's raining. *Poor* Tabby is very wet.	arm
	past [pɑ:st]		vorbei, vorüber
	to **win** [wɪn]	To be number one in a race.	gewinnen, siegen
	Huh? [hʌ; hə]	What?	Was? Hä?
2	to go on [gəʊ‿'ɒn]	Start on page 44 and *go on* with the text on page 45.	weitermachen, weiterführen
3	**each** [i:tʃ]		jede(-r/-s)

4	**fun** [fʌn]		Freude, Spaß
	Made in Britain [ˌmeɪd‿ɪn 'brɪtn]		Hergestellt in Großbritannien

Numbers 2

ten [ten]	zehn	**twenty** ['twenti]	zwanzig
eleven [ɪ'levn]	elf	**twenty-one** [ˌtwenti'wʌn]	einundzwanzig
twelve [twelv]	zwölf	**thirty** ['θɜ:ti]	dreißig
thirteen [θɜ:'ti:n]	dreizehn	**forty** ['fɔ:ti]	vierzig
fourteen [fɔ:'ti:n]	vierzehn	**fifty** ['fɪfti]	fünfzig
fifteen [fɪf'ti:n]	fünfzehn	**sixty** ['sɪksti]	sechzig
sixteen [sɪks'ti:n]	sechzehn	**seventy** ['sevnti]	siebzig
seventeen [ˌsevn'ti:n]	siebzehn	**eighty** ['eɪti]	achtzig
eighteen [eɪ'ti:n]	achtzehn	**ninety** ['naɪnti]	neunzig
nineteen [naɪn'ti:n]	neunzehn	**a hundred** [ə'hʌndrəd]	hundert

focus 2 Focus on numbers

Wörter lernen sich einfacher und schneller, wenn man sie sich päckchenweise vornimmt. Am besten lernt man nur 10–15 Wörter in einem Päckchen.

Vorsicht! Nimm dir nicht zu viel auf einmal vor! Schwere Pakete kannst du auch nicht heben.

1	**wrong** [rɒŋ]	right ↔ *wrong*	falsch
	budgie ['bʌdʒi]		Wellensittich
	•**hamster** ['hæmstə]		Hamster
	rabbit ['ræbɪt]		Kaninchen
	•**pony** ['pəʊni]	A little horse.	Pony
4	•**plus** [plʌs]	There are twenty-three in our class *plus* our teacher.	plus
	•**minus** ['maɪnəs]	Twenty-three *minus* 11 girls: so there are twelve boys.	minus; weniger
5	•**British** ['brɪtɪʃ]	The Leinerts are German, and the Crofts are *British*.	britisch
	penny, *pl.* **pence** [peni; pents]	1p is one *penny*. 5p is five *pence*.	Pence (*brit. Währungseinheit*)
	pound [paʊnd]	 Das Zeichen ‚£' steht immer vor der Zahl, wird beim Sprechen aber nach der Zahl genannt.	Pfund (*brit. Währungseinheit*)
6	**shop assistant** ['ʃɒp‿əˌsɪstnt]		Verkäufer(in)
	customer ['kʌstəmə]	A *customer* buys things in a shop.	Kunde, Kundin
	a pair of [ə 'peər‿əv]	Two together: *a pair* of socks; or clothes with two legs: *a pair of* jeans.	ein Paar
	•**jeans** *pl.* [dʒi:nz]	David has got a new pair of blue *jeans*.	Jeans

size [saɪz]	These jeans are the wrong *size*.	Größe, Kleidergröße
How much is/are …? [ˌhaʊ 'mʌtʃ‿ɪz/ɑː]	I need a new pair of jeans. *How much are they?*	Wie viel kostet/kosten …?
to **try (on)** [traɪ‿'ɒn]	You can't just buy those shoes, you must *try* them *on*.	(an)probieren; versuchen
sir [sɜː]		mein Herr *(Anrede)*
• **uniform** ['juːnɪfɔːm]	Jenny has got a *uniform* for school.	Uniform
skirt [skɜːt]	Sarah's new *skirt* is very nice.	Rock
trousers *pl.* ['traʊzəz]	! Die englischen Wörter *trousers* und *jeans* stehen immer im Plural.	Hose
madam ['mædəm]		Gnädige Frau *(Anrede)*
special offer [ˌspeʃl‿'ɒfə]	*Special offer* today: Jeans only £15.	Sonderangebot
special ['speʃl]	It's a *special* day for Robert today, it's his birthday.	besonders, speziell
offer ['ɒfə]		Angebot
• **anorak** ['ænəræk]		Anorak
• **sock** [sɒk]	Sarah has got blue *socks*.	Socke
shoe [ʃuː]		Schuh
• **sweatshirt** ['swetʃɜːt]	 Eine kleine Eselsbrücke: *shirt* – Hemd, *skirt* – Rock.	Sweatshirt
shirt [ʃɜːt]		Hemd
dress [dres]		Kleid

unit 3 Free time

Lerne Vokabeln in Ruhe zu Hause, möglichst immer am gleichen Arbeitsplatz. Versuche einen Arbeitsplatz zu finden, an dem du immer ohne Störung arbeiten kannst.

An deinem Arbeitsplatz solltest du auch zu Beginn der Arbeit alles zur Hand haben: Schreibzeug, Hefte, Bücher, Karteikasten usw..

Intro

free [friː]	There's no school on Saturday. It's a *free* day.	frei
Monday ['mʌndeɪ]	! Siehe *Days of the week*.	Montag
evening ['iːvnɪŋ]	*evening* ↔ morning	Abend
o'clock [ə'klɒk]	! Achte auf die Schreibung: It's six *o'clock*!	Uhr *(Zeitangabe bei vollen Stunden)*
after ['ɑːftə]	*After* school the children go home.	nach
to **go for a walk** [ˌgəʊ fər‿ə 'wɔːk]	It's nice today. Let's *go for a walk*.	spazieren gehen
walk [wɔːk]		Spaziergang
to **ride** [raɪd]	You can *ride* a bike or a horse.	fahren; reiten
to **have dinner** [hæv 'dɪnə]	The Dixons *have dinner* at 7 o'clock.	zu Abend essen
dinner ['dɪnə]		Abendessen
• **theatre** ['θɪətə]		Theater

3	**week** [wi:k]	There are seven days in a *week*.	Woche
	bad [bæd]		schlecht
	because [bɪ'kɒz]	I can't see you *because* it's too dark.	weil
4	**weekend** ['wi:kend]	Saturday and Sunday. Have you got lots of homework for the *weekend?*	Wochenende
	• **end** [end]		Ende, Schluss
	• **zoo** [zu:]	There are lots of animals in a *zoo*.	Zoo, Tierpark
	when [wen]	At what time? *When* can you come to my house this evening?	wann; als; wenn
	open ['əʊpn]	The shop is *open*. Let's go in.	offen; geöffnet
	to [tʊ; tə]	The last lesson is from 2.45 *to* 3.30.	bis
	to **meet** [mi:t]	Let's *meet* after school and play a game.	(sich) treffen
	usually ['ju:ʒli]		normalerweise, gewöhnlich
	half past (two) ['hɑ:f pɑ:st]	! In English it is *half past* two, auf Deutsch sagt man halb drei dazu.	halb (drei)
	early ['ɜ:li]	We can't meet at six o'clock. It's too *early*.	früh
	quarter past/to ['kwɔ:tə pɑ:st/tə]		Viertel nach/vor
	What time …? [wɒt 'taɪm]		Um wie viel Uhr …?
	opening hours ['əʊpnɪŋ‿aʊəz]	*Opening hours:* 10 am to 8 pm.	Öffnungszeiten
	am [ˌeɪ'em]		vormittags (*Uhrzeit*)
	pm [ˌpi:'em]		nachmittags (*Uhrzeit*)

Days of the week

Monday	['mʌndeɪ]	Montag	**Thursday**	['θɜ:zdeɪ]	Donnerstag	**Sunday**	['sʌndeɪ]	Sonntag
Tuesday	['tju:zdeɪ]	Dienstag	**Friday**	['fraɪdeɪ]	Freitag			
Wednesday	['wenzdeɪ]	Mittwoch	**Saturday**	['sætədeɪ]	Samstag			

Language A Jenny's day

dear [dɪə]		lieb
boring ['bɔ:rɪŋ]	School can be *boring*.	langweilig
without [wɪ'ðaʊt]	You can't write *without* a pen.	ohne
for example [fər‿ɪg'zɑ:mpl]		zum Beispiel
to **wear** [weə]	Sarah is *wearing* a pink dress.	anhaben, tragen
never ['nevə]		nie, niemals
to **get up** [get‿'ʌp]	To get out of bed.	aufstehen
before [bɪ'fɔ:]	*before* ↔ after	vor; bevor
Assembly [ə'sembli]	A lot of British schools have *Assembly* in the morning.	Versammlung; Morgenappell
pupil ['pju:pl]	David is a *pupil* at Haywood School.	Schüler(in)
to **finish** ['fɪnɪʃ]	to start ↔ *to finish*	fertig machen; aufhören
subject ['sʌbdʒɪkt]	English and Maths are school *subjects*.	Schulfach; Thema
to **hate** [heɪt]	I *hate* football. It's a stupid game.	hassen, nicht mögen
often ['ɒfn]	I *often* go to school by bike.	oft
ice cream [aɪs 'kri:m]		Eis, Eiscreme
ice [aɪs]		Eis
cream [kri:m]	You can buy *cream* at the supermarket.	Creme; Sahne

	until [ʌn'tɪl; n'tɪl]	We can stay in bed *until* 10.	bis
	to **stay** [steɪ]	To be at a place for a time. Please *stay* here until I fetch you.	bleiben
	to **love** [lʌv]		lieben, gern mögen
	love [lʌv]	At the end of a letter or e-mail you can write *'Love, …'* and your name.	Liebe; Herzliche Grüße *(am Briefende)*
7	**some** [sʌm]	Not all. *Some* children wear an anorak, some pupils wear a sweatshirt.	einige; etwas
	• **match** [mætʃ]	A game (of football / …). Can we watch the *match* this evening?	Wettkampf; Spiel; Match
	at home [ət 'həʊm]		zu Hause

Language B In the park

	scooter ['sku:tə]	Little Mark can't ride a bike, but he can ride a *scooter*.	Roller
	to **show** [ʃəʊ]	Please *show* me your homework.	zeigen
	hill [hɪl]	 ←hill	Hügel
	off [ɒf]		von … weg/ab/herunter
	to **wave** [weɪv]		winken; schwenken
	to **cry** [kraɪ]	"Please help me!" *cries* little Mark.	schreien, rufen; weinen
	to **happen** ['hæpn]	It's dark in here – what's *happening*?	geschehen, passieren
	suddenly ['sʌdnli]	It's very dark, but *suddenly* the sun comes out and it's sunny.	plötzlich, auf einmal
	something ['sʌmθɪŋ]		etwas
	small [smɔ:l]	A pony is a *small* horse.	klein
1	to **chase** [tʃeɪs]	Hey! Your dog is *chasing* my cat! Stop it!	verfolgen, jagen
	to **shout** [ʃaʊt]	I can't hear you; can you *shout*?	schreien, rufen
	late [leɪt]	Oh, I'm *late*!	spät
	to **hit** [hɪt]	David's scooter *hits* a stone.	schlagen; treffen; *hier*: gegen etwas fahren
	stone [stəʊn]	Is that an animal on the floor? Oh, no, it's a *stone*.	Stein
	to **fly** [flaɪ]		fliegen
	• **bush** [bʊʃ]	A little tree. There are some *bushes* in the Burtons' garden.	Busch, Strauch
	out of ['aʊt‿əv]	Take a pencil *out of* your pencil case, please.	aus … heraus
	to **pick up** [pɪk‿'ʌp]	There's a pen on the floor, please *pick* it *up*.	aufheben; abholen
	angry ['æŋgri]	The teacher is *angry* with the children. They are late again.	verärgert, böse
2	to **rush** [rʌʃ]		sich beeilen
5	**present** ['preznt]		Gegenwart, Präsens

Text Barker's story

	to **look after** [lʊk‿'ɑ:ftə]	David *looks after* Mark when his dad isn't there.	aufpassen auf; hüten
	• **job** [dʒɒb]	What's your *job*? – I'm a teacher.	Arbeitsstelle, Job

	pet [pet]	Barker is a *pet*.	Haustier; Liebling
	to **wake (somebody) up** [weɪk‿ˈʌp]	It's 7.30. Mark, can you *wake* David *up*, please?	(jemanden) aufwecken; aufwachen
	• **to wash** [wɒʃ]		(sich) waschen; spülen
	face [feɪs]	Your eyes and nose are on your *face*.	Gesicht
	• **muesli** [ˈmjuːzli]		Müsli
	Yuk! [jʌk]	*Yuk*, what's wrong with this *muesli*?	Igitt!
	to **earn** [ɜːn]	Mrs Penrose has got a good job and *earns* a lot of money.	verdienen
	so (that) [ˈsəʊ ðət]		damit; so dass
	• **to teach** [tiːtʃ]	to *teach* → teacher	unterrichten, lehren
	to **throw** [θrəʊ]	Come on Mark, *throw* the ball!	werfen
	to **get lost** [get ˈlɒst]	Mark, please stay in the garden, then you can't *get lost*.	verloren gehen, sich verirren
	at once [ət ˈwʌnts]		sofort, plötzlich
	to **bark (at)** [bɑːk]	Dogs *bark*: in English they say "Woof!".	(an)bellen
	away [əˈweɪ]		weg (von)
	• **picnic** [ˈpɪknɪk]		Picknick
	middle [ˈmɪdl]	Centre.	Mitte; Mittel-
	drink [drɪŋk]		Getränk
	• **to fall (over)** [fɔːl‿ˈəʊvə]	Mark can't ride a scooter, he often *falls over*.	(hin)fallen; umfallen
	tired [ˈtaɪəd]	I don't want to watch TV. I'm *tired*.	müde
	to **sleep** [sliːp]	You *sleep* in your bedroom.	schlafen
	to **go to sleep** [gəʊ tə ˈsliːp]	You're tired, *go to sleep* now.	einschlafen
	dog-tired [ˌdɒg ˈtaɪəd]		hundemüde
2	**first** [fɜːst]	*first* ↔ last	erste(-r/-s); zuerst
	How to write … [ˌhaʊ tə ˈraɪt]		Wie man … schreibt.
	better [ˈbetə]		besser
	to **connect (to)** [kəˈnekt]	! You can *connect* two words to make other words: *school* and *bag* make *school bag*.	verbinden (mit)
	to **collect** [kəˈlekt]	Jenny *collects* posters.	sammeln

At

Is Robert **at home**?	Ist Robert **zu Hause**?
Sorry, he's **at school**.	Tut mir Leid, aber er ist **in der Schule**.
Simon is **at** Robert's house.	Simon ist **bei** Robert.
! Let's **go home** together.	Lass uns zusammen **nach Hause** gehen.

Let's check

2	• **kindergarten** [ˈkɪndəgɑːtn]		Kindergarten
3	• **instrument** [ˈɪntstrəmənt]	The guitar is an *instrument*.	Instrument
	to live [lɪv]	David and Mark *live* in Nottingham.	wohnen, leben
	to **copy** [ˈkɒpi]	To write again. *Copy* these words into your exercise book.	abschreiben, kopieren
	• **pop star** [ˈpɒp stɑː]		Popstar

unit 4 Happy birthday

Schreibe die englischen Wörter, die du lernen willst, auf kleine Zettel. Auf die Rückseite jedes Zettels schreibst du in einer anderen Farbe die deutsche Bedeutung. (Wenn du eine Kartei führst, kannst du auch die Karteikarten nehmen.) Breite die Karten mit der deutschen Bedeutung nach oben aus. Wenn du den englischen Begriff nennen kannst, darfst du die Karte einsammeln. Wenn du beim Überprüfen feststellst, dass deine Antwort nicht richtig war, musst du die Karte wieder hinlegen. Das Spiel geht natürlich auch umgekehrt.

Vokabeln lernen kannst du auch spielend, allein oder mit Freunden aus deiner Klasse.

Intro

	Happy birthday! [ˌhæpi 'bɜ:θdeɪ]		Herzlichen Glückwunsch zum Geburtstag!
	happy ['hæpi]	Today is my birthday. I'm so *happy*.	glücklich, froh
1	**month** [mʌnθ]		Monat
	date [deɪt]	What's the *date* today?	Datum
	• **calendar** ['kæləndə]	You can find all the dates in a *calendar*.	Kalender
3	**invitation** [ˌɪnvɪ'teɪʃn]		Einladung
	• **card** [kɑ:d]	This is a birthday *card* for Jenny.	Karte
4	**you** [ju:; jə]		man
	present ['preznt]	These are Jenny's birthday *presents*.	Geschenk
	relative ['relətɪv]	Jenny is David's *relative*, she's his cousin.	Verwandte(r)
	• **party** ['pɑ:ti]	It's my birthday, I'm having a *party*.	Party, Feier
	to **invite** [ɪn'vaɪt]	to *invite* → invitation	einladen
	• **restaurant** ['restərənt]		Restaurant, Gaststätte
	swimming ['swɪmɪŋ]	I like *swimming*. 	Schwimmen
	• **skating** ['skeɪtɪŋ]		Inlineskate/Schlittschuh fahren
	food [fu:d]	This is my lunchbox, but there's no *food* in it.	Essen, Nahrung; Lebensmittel
	sweet [swi:t]	Children like *sweet* food.	süß
	jelly ['dʒeli]	Mark likes *jelly* and ice cream together.	Wackelpudding, Gelee
	cake [keɪk]		Kuchen
	trifle ['traɪfl]		*englischer Nachtisch*
	candle ['kændl]		Kerze
	year [jɪə]	365 days. At school: Are you in *Year* 7?	Jahr; Jahrgang
	to **give** [gɪv]	You *give* presents to people on their birthday.	geben; schenken
	to **give somebody the bumps** [ˌgɪv ðə 'bʌmps]	People *give you the bumps* on your birthday.	jemanden hochwerfen und wieder auffangen
	• **tradition** [trə'dɪʃn]		Tradition
	to **bump** [bʌmp]	David is hurt: he often *bumps* his arm on the cupboard in the kitchen.	(an)stoßen
	luck [lʌk]		Glück

to **worry** ['wʌri]		(sich) Sorgen machen
• **thank you letter** ['θæŋk ju: ˌletə]	I must write a *thank you letter* to my aunt for the nice birthday present.	Dankschreiben
much [mʌtʃ]	Thank you very *much* for the book.	viel
more [mɔ:]		mehr
dictionary ['dɪkʃnri]		Wörterbuch

Numbers 3

first [fɜ:st]	erste(-r/-s)	**eleventh** [ɪ'levnθ]	elfte(-r/-s)
second ['seknd]	zweite(-r/-s)	**twelfth** [twelfθ]	zwölfte(-r/-s)
third [θɜ:d]	dritte(-r/-s)	**thirteenth** [θɜ:'ti:nθ]	dreizehnte(-r/-s)
fourth [fɔ:θ]	vierte(-r/-s)	**fourteenth** [fɔ:'ti:nθ]	vierzehnte(-r/-s)
fifth [fɪfθ]	fünfte(-r/-s)	**fifteenth** [fɪf'ti:nθ]	fünfzehnte(-r/-s)
sixth [sɪksθ]	sechste(-r/-s)	**sixteenth** [sɪk'sti:nθ]	sechzehnte(-r/-s)
seventh ['sevnθ]	siebte(-r/-s)	**seventeenth** [ˌsevn'ti:nθ]	siebzehnte(-r/-s)
eighth [eɪtθ]	achte(-r/-s)	**eighteenth** [eɪ'ti:nθ]	achtzehnte(-r/-s)
ninth [naɪnθ]	neunte(-r/-s)	**nineteenth** [naɪn'ti:nθ]	neunzehnte(-r/-s)
tenth [tenθ]	zehnte(-r/-s)	**twentieth** ['twentiɪθ]	zwanzigste(-r/-s)

The months

January ['dʒænjuri]	Januar	**July** [dʒʊ'laɪ]	Juli
February ['februri]	Februar	**August** ['ɔ:gəst]	August
March [mɑ:tʃ]	März	**September** [sep'tembə]	September
April ['eɪprl]	April	**October** [ɒk'təʊbə]	Oktober
May [meɪ]	Mai	**November** [nəʊ'vembə]	November
June [dʒu:n]	Juni	**December** [dɪ'sembə]	Dezember

Language A Jenny's birthday

quite [kwaɪt]	David isn't very tired. He's *quite* tired.	ziemlich; ganz, völlig
noisy ['nɔɪzi]	Loud. I can't hear you, it's so *noisy* in here.	laut
so [səʊ]		also, deshalb
to **want (to)** ['wɒnt tə]	I *want to* listen to a CD, but I can't.	wollen, mögen
back [bæk]	Come *back* here, Barker!	zurück
near [nɪə]	Sarah lives *near* David.	nahe, in der Nähe von
lovely ['lʌvli]	Thank you, that's a *lovely* present.	schön, hübsch; herrlich
well [wel]		gut
time [taɪm]	This *time* my birthday is on a Friday.	Mal
yummy ['jʌmi]	This trifle is *yummy*!	lecker
to **think (of)** ['θɪŋk‿əv]		denken (an)
to **guess** [ges]	I've no idea what it is. – Well, *guess!*	raten, vermuten
in class [ɪn 'klɑ:s]	Play the game *in class*.	in/vor der Klasse
to **remember** [rɪ'membə]	I must *remember* Mum's birthday.	sich erinnern (an); sich merken

Language B A party game

whose [hu:z]	*Whose* CD is this? – It's Kim's.	wessen
Shsh! [ʃ]	Quiet! *Shsh*! I can't hear the music.	Pssst!
secret ['si:krət]	Don't tell the others, it's a *secret*.	Geheimnis
King Ethelred [kɪŋ 'eθlred]		*brit. Spiel*
king [kɪŋ]	! *King* wird als Teil eines Titels immer groß geschrieben.	König
to **know** [nəʊ]	! Achtung Aussprache! Bei Wörtern mit *kn* wird das *k* nicht ausgesprochen.	wissen; kennen
• **player** ['pleɪə]	to play → *player*	Spieler, Mitspieler
to blindfold ['blaɪndfəʊld]		die Augen verbinden
circle ['sɜ:kl]	Stand in the middle of the *circle*.	Kreis
round [raʊnd]	The children run *round* the statue.	um ... herum
otherwise ['ʌðəwaɪz]	Let's buy that music magazine. We can't get the special CD *otherwise*.	sonst
voice [vɔɪs]	Make a funny sound with your *voice*.	Stimme
if [ɪf]		wenn, falls; ob
another [ə'nʌðə]	the same ↔ *another*	noch ein(e); ein(e) andere(-r/-s)
to **change** [tʃeɪndʒ]	*Change* places with your partner.	tauschen, wechseln; (sich) ändern
• **work** [wɜ:k]	to work → at *work*. Mr Burton's at *work*, he's in the bike shop.	Arbeit
who [hu:]		wer, wen
to **mean** [mi:n]	What does 'kindergarten' *mean*?	bedeuten; meinen
5 **next** [nekst]		nächste(-r/-s)
6 to **act something out** [ˌækt sʌmθɪŋ‿'aʊt]	In a theatre people *act out* dialogues.	etwas durchspielen

Text The birthday party

while [waɪl]		während
upstairs [ʌp'steəz]	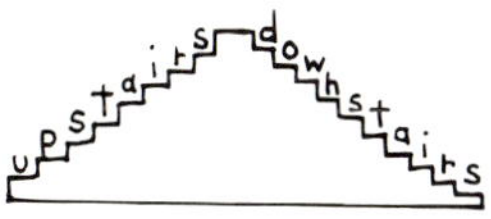	(nach) oben, im Obergeschoss
air [eə]		Luft
excited [ɪk'saɪtɪd]		aufgeregt
everybody ['evribɒdi]	All the people.	jeder; alle
except [ɪk'sept]	Everybody's here, *except* Jenny.	außer
to **eat** [i:t]	*Eat* your breakfast, it's time for school!	essen
• **hungry** ['hʌŋgri]		hungrig
still [stɪl]		noch, immer noch
around [ə'raʊnd]		herum, umher
to **smile** [smaɪl]		lächeln
tooth, *pl.* **teeth** [tu:θ; ti:θ]		Zahn, Zähne
to **grab** [græb]		greifen; schnappen
to **scream** [skri:m]	Don't *scream* so loud.	schreien, kreischen
ceiling ['si:lɪŋ]	A room has a floor and a *ceiling*.	(Zimmer-)Decke
huge [hju:dʒ]	Very big.	riesig, gewaltig
splash [splæʃ]		Spritzer, Planscher
glasses *pl.* ['glɑ:sɪz]		Brille
crash! [kræʃ]	to crash → *crash* 	Krach! Bumm!; Zusammenstoß
to **shake** [ʃeɪk]		schütteln

to **dream** [driːm]		träumen
2 •**ending** [ˈendɪŋ]		Ende, Schluss (*einer Geschichte*)
3 **surprise** [səˈpraɪz]	 "Surprise!"	Überraschung
•**radio** [ˈreɪdiəʊ]		Radio

Let's check

5 •**interview** [ˈɪntəvjuː]	Interview; Befragung

1 Wie viele Wörter kannst du finden, in denen das „s" wie eine Schlange zischt? Schaue das Vokabular bis Ende Unit 4 durch. Die Lautschrift [s] hilft. Zeichne eine oder mehrere Schlangen und schreibe die Wörter hinein. Sprich die Wörter wie eine Schlange aus: ssssay!

2 Es gibt zwei verschiedene Aussprachemöglichkeiten für *the.* Sprich die folgenden Wörter richtig aus. Dann schreibe sie in eine Tabelle mit zwei Spalten in dein Schulheft.

the [ðe]	**the** [ði]
the school	the animal

the school **the animal** **the colour** **the afternoon** **the idea** **the word** **the example** **the window** **the exercise** **the song** **the bike**

3 Was kannst du machen? Ergänze die Listen. Du kannst auch ein Poster mit Bildern herstellen.

Games and things to do	
in the garden / in the playground	**in the house / in the classroom**
play football	write a story, draw a picture

focus 3 Focus on the UK

Das Aufschreiben der Wörter für deine Lernkartei oder in dein Vokabelheft hilft dir schon, die Schreibweise zu behalten. Besonders schwierige Wörter kannst du auf einen Haftzettel schreiben, dabei die Buchstaben, die du sonst immer falsch schreibst, in einer stärkeren Farbe hervorheben. Diese Zettel heftest du z. B. in der Nähe deines Arbeitsplatzes oder am Bett an. So prägen sie sich gut ein.

Es führt kein Weg daran vorbei: Die Schreibweise der Wörter prägt sich am besten durch Schreiben ein.

UK [juːˈkeɪ]	Short for the *United Kingdom.*	Vereinigtes Königreich von Großbritannien und Nordirland

	United Kingdom [juːˌnaɪtɪd ˈkɪŋdəm]	The *UK* is Great Britain (England, Scotland and Wales) and Northern Ireland.	Vereinigtes Königreich von Großbritannien und Nordirland
	that [ðæt; thət]	I know *that* Scotland is in the UK.	dass
	bagpipes [ˈbægpaɪps]	A Scottish instrument.	Dudelsack
	• **whisky** [ˈwɪski]	The best *whisky* is from Scotland.	Whisky
	skiing [ˈskiːɪŋ]	You can go *skiing* in Scotland, too.	Ski fahren
	capital [ˈkæpɪtl]	London is the *capital* of England.	Hauptstadt
	port [pɔːt]	Cuxhaven and Duisburg are big *ports*.	Hafen
	part [pɑːt]	Not all. *Parts* of the book are very good, but the ending isn't.	Teil
	• **rest** [rest]		Rest
	• **rugby** [ˈrʌgbi]		Rugby
	especially [ɪˈspeʃli]	Becky likes animals, *especially* horses.	besonders, vor allem
	to **beat** [biːt]	We're winning, come on, we can *beat* the other team!	besiegen; schlagen
	view [vjuː]	What you can see. You can get a lovely *view* from that hill.	Aussicht, Sicht
	wheel [wiːl]	A bike has got two *wheels*.	Rad
	by [baɪ]	Next to.	bei; an
	river [ˈrɪvə]	The Rhein and the Isar are *rivers*.	Fluss
	beach [biːtʃ]	Mark is playing on the *beach*. He's making a castle.	Strand
	• **surfing** [ˈsɜːfɪŋ]	Cornwall is a good place for *surfing*.	Wellenreiten, Surfen
	country [ˈkʌntri]	! Achtung Aussprache!	Land; ländliche Gegend, Landschaft
1	**north** [nɔːθ]	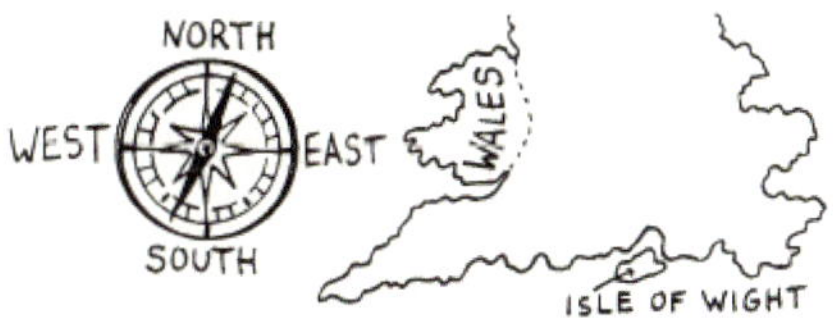	Norden
	• **west** [west]		Westen
	east [iːst]		Osten
	south [saʊθ]		Süden
3	**island** [ˈaɪlənd]		Insel
	body [ˈbɒdi]		Körper
	head [hed]		Kopf
	shoulder [ˈʃəʊldə]	I can't use my left arm. My *shoulder* hurts.	Schulter
	heart [hɑːt]	Look, there's a *heart* on this card.	Herz
	trunk [trʌŋk]		Rumpf
	backbone [ˈbækbəʊn]		Rückgrat
	spine [spaɪn]		Wirbelsäule
	rump [rʌmp]		Hinterteil
4	• quiz [kwɪz]		Quiz, Rätsel

unit 5 A weekend at the seaside

Dass man nicht alles behält, ist doch normal. Dagegen hilft Wiederholung. Nimm dir zusammen mit Freunden Vokabeln aus einer früheren Unit vor. Ihr könnt sie euch gegenseitig ganz durcheinander abfragen oder ein Spiel damit machen.

Intro

	seaside ['si:saɪd]	It's nice to spend a week at the *seaside*.	Küste, Meeresküste
	at the seaside [ət ðə 'si:saɪd]		am Meer
	sea [si:]	! The *sea* = **die** See, nicht: der See.	Meer
1	• **Internet** ['ɪntənet]	Becky can write e-mails and get into the *Internet* on her computer.	Internet
	• **tip** [tɪp]		Tipp
	to visit ['vɪsɪt]		besuchen; besichtigen
	harbour ['hɑ:bə]	The weather is bad, so the boats are staying in the *harbour*.	Hafen
	boat [bəʊt]		Boot, Schiff
	• **to swim** [swɪm]	You can *swim* in the sea.	schwimmen
	• **sand** [sænd]	You can make houses and castles with *sand* on the beach.	Sand
	full [fʊl]	*full* ↔ empty	voll
	weather ['weðə]	The *weather* is sunny today. 	Wetter
	• **trip** [trɪp]	The Burtons are going on a *trip* to London today.	Trip, Reise, Ausflug
	bird [bɜ:d]	*Birds* sit in trees and fly in the air.	Vogel
	seal [si:l]	The *seals* at the zoo get their food at 3 o'clock: you can watch them.	Seehund
	rock [rɒk]	A *rock* is a big stone.	Fels, Stein
	eight-hundred-year-old [ˌeɪt hʌndrəd 'jɪər‿əʊld]	! You can also write: 800-year-old.	achthundert Jahre alt
	interesting ['ɪntrestɪŋ]	You can see old and *interesting* things in a museum.	interessant
	• **museum** [mju:'zi:əm]	*Museums* are interesting.	Museum
	• **correct** [kə'rekt]	to correct → *correct*	richtig, korrekt
3	**bed and breakfast** [ˌbed‿n 'brekfəst]		Zimmer mit Frühstück

Language A On the beach

towel ['taʊəl]		Handtuch
mustn't ['mʌsnt]	! You must. – Du musst. You *mustn't*. – Du darfst nicht.	nicht dürfen
• **sandwich** ['sændwɪdʒ]		Sandwich, belegtes Brot

sunscreen ['sʌnskri:n]		Sonnencreme
hot [hɒt]	The sun is *hot*.	heiß
needn't ['ni:dnt]	It's OK, I've got everything for lunch. You *needn't* go to the supermarket.	nicht brauchen, nicht müssen
to **feel** [fi:l]	I *feel* hot. – Yes, it's sunny!	(sich) fühlen
• **wind** ['wɪnd]	The weather isn't very nice today, there's *wind* and rain.	Wind
strong [strɒŋ]		stark
water ['wɔ:tə]	Rain is *water* from the sky.	Wasser
cold [kəʊld]	hot ↔ *cold*	kalt

Language B A souvenir of the castle

• **souvenir** [ˌsu:vn'ɪə]	My friend has got a little Robin Hood statue as a *souvenir* of Nottingham.	Souvenir, Andenken
almost ['ɔ:lməʊst]	Not quite.	fast, beinahe
a lot of [ə 'lɒt‿əv]	Lots of. I've got *a lot of* friends.	viele, eine Menge
mug [mʌg]	A *mug* is like a big cup.	Becher; Krug
mouse mat ['maʊs mæt]	Becky's computer is grey, but her *mouse mat* is blue and orange.	Mauspad
mouse, *pl.* **mice** [maʊs; maɪs]		Maus
any ['enɪ]	I can't see *any* birds. = I can see no birds.	irgendein(-e/-er); irgendwelche
soap [səʊp]	Wash your hands with *soap* and water.	Seife
bar [bɑ:]	Mrs Dixon is buying two *bars* of soap and a *bar* of chocolate.	Tafel; Riegel; Stück; Stange
• **chocolate** ['tʃɒklət]	*Chocolate* is brown and sweet.	Schokolade
tin [tɪn]	A *tin* of dog food for Barker.	Dose, Büchse
• **sweets** *pl.* [swi:ts]	sweet → *sweets*	Süßigkeiten, Bonbons

Mengenangaben

some water	etwas Wasser	**a bottle** of water	eine Flasche Wasser
some pencils	einige Stifte	**a bar of** chocolate	eine Tafel Schokolade
no soap	keine Seife	**a lot of** cakes/soap	viel(e) …
How many … ?	Wie viele … ?	**How much** … ?	Wie viel … ?

Text Grace Darling

ship [ʃɪp]	A *ship* is a big boat.	Schiff
• **storm** [stɔ:m]	Strong wind and rain. In a *storm* small boats stay in the harbour.	Sturm
wave [weɪv]	In a storm at sea there are big *waves*.	Welle
engine ['endʒɪn]	Almost all cars have the *engine* in front of the driver.	Motor
helpless ['helpləs]	If you can't walk, you are *helpless*.	hilflos
night [naɪt]	day ↔ *night*	Nacht

to **be frightened (of)** ['fraɪtnd]	Some people are *frightened of* big dogs.	Angst haben (vor)
lighthouse ['laɪthaʊs]	You can see a *lighthouse* in the dark.	Leuchtturm
keeper ['ki:pə]	A *keeper* looks after a lighthouse or the animals in a zoo.	Wärter, Aufseher
to **crash** [kræʃ]		aufschlagen, gegen etwas krachen
white horses [waɪt 'hɔ:sɪz]	The wind is strong, and the waves have *white horses* on them.	*hier*: Schaumkronen
through [θru:]	You can see *through* a window.	durch
• **telescope** ['telɪskəʊp]	Look at that bird on the lighthouse – you can see it through the *telescope*.	Teleskop; Fernrohr
wreck [rek]	! Achtung Aussprache: *wreck, write, wrong*.	Wrack
to **be alive** [ə'laɪv]	My grandpa's father is still *alive*. He's 96.	lebendig sein; leben
to **save** [seɪv]		retten, bergen
to **row** [rəʊ]	You can *row* a small boat, but not a big ship.	rudern
mile [maɪl]	1609 metres.	Meile *(brit. Längenmaß)*
again and again [ə'gen‿ənd‿ə'gen]		immer wieder
dangerous ['deɪndʒrəs]	Don't go so fast – it's *dangerous*.	gefährlich
to **give up** [gɪv‿'ʌp]	To stop. I can't play this game, I *give up*.	aufgeben
at last [ət 'lɑ:st]	David is in a shop: he looks at all the shoes, and *at last* a shop assistant says, "Can I help you?"	endlich
to **cling (to)** ['klɪŋ]	A boy is in the water. "Hey, just grab the boat and *cling to* it!"	sich festhalten (an), sich festklammern (an)
• **help** [help]	*Help!* I'm in the water and I can't swim!	Hilfe, Rettung
to **jump** [dʒʌmp]		springen
slow [sləʊ]	*slow* ↔ fast	langsam
safe [seɪf]	*safe* ↔ dangerous; *safe* [f] → to save [v]	sicher
brave [breɪv]	If you do something dangerous, that's silly, or *brave*.	tapfer, mutig
4 • **action** ['ækʃn]	What happens, what people do.	Aktion, Handlung
• **scene** [si:n]	This is a very quiet *scene* in the play, nothing is happening.	Szene; Schauplatz
tense [tens]	Simple present and present progressive are *tenses*.	Zeit, Zeitform (*grammatisch*)

unit 6 A week on a farm

Manchmal hilft es beim Wiederholen, Wörter in eine ganz neue Reihenfolge zu bringen. Du könntest z. B. die Wörter deines Lernpäckchens in alphabetischer Reihenfolge oder nach Wortgruppen zusammenstellen. Wenn du einen Karteikasten angelegt hast, kannst du die Wörter aus dem hinteren Fach jetzt alphabetisch ordnen. Dazu musst du nicht nur auf den ersten, sondern auch auf die folgenden Buchstaben achten. Beispiel: Unter „s" kommt das Wort *shop* vor *soap,* weil das *h* im Alphabet vor dem *o* kommt.

Intro

• **farm** [fɑ:m]	Food comes from *farms* in the country.	Farm, Bauernhof
• **article** ['ɑ:tɪkl]	Becky is writing an *article* for the school magazine.	Artikel (*in der Zeitung, etc.*)
fresh [freʃ]	Can you make some *fresh* tea, please?	frisch
to **learn**, **learnt** [lɜ:n; lɜ:nt]	Some children *learn* German at school.	lernen
regular ['regjələ]	Robert and his mother go on a *regular* trip to the theatre every month.	regelmäßig; gleichmäßig
• **visitor** ['vɪsɪtə]	to visit → *visitor*	Besucher
holiday ['hɒlədeɪ]	There's no school today, it's a *holiday*.	Urlaub, Feiertag
kid [kɪd]	Child. Hey, *kids*. Let's go to the zoo.	Kind; Kitz
cow [kaʊ]		Kuh
field [fi:ld]	Part of a farm.	Feld; Acker
• **to be surprised** [sə'praɪzd]	surprise → *surprised*	überrascht sein
shed [ʃed]	The cows stay in a *shed* at night.	Schuppen, Stall
to **milk** [mɪlk]	On the farm they *milk* the cows in the morning and in the evening.	melken
• **milk** [mɪlk]	to milk → the *milk*	Milch
to **clean** [kli:n]	Petra, please *clean* the board.	säubern, reinigen
pigsty ['pɪgstaɪ]	Cows live in a cowshed, pigs live in a *pigsty*.	Schweinestall
pig [pɪg]		Schwein
welly ['weli]	Don't go into that field in your shoes, it's too wet. Where are your *wellies*?	Gummistiefel
Pooh! [pu:]		Pfui! Bäh!
smell [smel]	Pooh, what a terrible *smell*!	Geruch, Gestank
vegetable ['vedʒtəbl]	The Burtons eat lots of *vegetables* from their garden.	Gemüse
the same [seɪm]	"We've got *the same* T-shirts!" 	derselbe (die-/das-)
to **feed**, **fed** [fi:d; fed]		füttern
turkey ['tɜ:ki]	A big farm bird.	Truthahn, Pute
chicken ['tʃɪkɪn]	A farm bird.	Huhn, Hähnchen
egg [eg]		Ei
to **be scared** [bi: 'skeəd]	 	Angst haben, erschrocken sein
to **attack** [ə'tæk]	Let's play "Robin Hood". We can *attack* Nottingham Castle.	angreifen
stable ['steɪbl]		Stall

Language A Robert's postcard from Yorkshire

• **postcard** ['pəʊstkɑ:d]	Jenny is writing a *postcard* to her parents.	Postkarte
• **post** [pəʊst]	Is there a letter for me in the *post* today?	Post
promise ['prɒmɪs]		Versprechen
yesterday ['jestədeɪ]	*yesterday* – today – tomorrow 	gestern
sheep, *pl.* **sheep** [ʃi:p]		Schaf
• **sheepdog** ['ʃi:pdɒg]	*Sheepdogs* work with sheep.	Hütehund; Schäferhund
over ['əʊvə]	Petra, please take these books *over* to Oliver by the window.	hinüber, über

	farmyard ['fɑ:mjɑ:d]	Part of a farm.	Hof (*auf einem Bauernhof*)
	yard [jɑ:d]	We haven't got a garden, but we've got a *yard* with a shed.	Hof
	basket ['bɑ:skɪt]		Korb, Körbchen
4	**irregular** [ɪ'regjələ]	*irregular* ↔ regular	unregelmäßig
	past [pɑ:st]	'Today' is now, 'yesterday' is *past*.	Vergangenheit
	typical (of) ['tɪpɪkl]	The Haywood uniform is *typical of* many schools in Britain.	typisch (für)
	• **omelette** ['ɒmlət]	Mum, how many eggs do I need for an *omelette*?	Omelett

Language B In the kitchen

	ago [ə'gəʊ]	Robert came to Nottingham from London about ten months *ago*.	vor (*zeitlich*)
	lamb [læm]	! Achtung Aussprache! Das *b* wird nicht ausgesprochen.	Lamm, Lämmchen
	• **to drink, drank** [drɪŋk; dræŋk]	a drink → *to drink*	trinken
	• **warm** [wɔ:m]		warm
3	**enough** [ɪ'nʌf]	Have we got *enough* milk for breakfast?	genug, genügend
	• **negative** ['negətɪv]	'Isn't' is a *negative* form of 'to be'.	negativ, verneint
5	to **say hello** [seɪ hə'ləʊ]	to *say hello* ↔ to say goodbye	Hallo sagen, sich begrüßen
7	**notes** [nəʊts]	Listen to the text and write things down: make/take *notes*.	Notizen, Anmerkungen

Text Problems on Springfield Farm

	• **problem** ['prɒbləm]	"I've got a problem."	Problem, Schwierigkeit
1	• **title** ['taɪtl]	The *title* of this story is "Problems on Springfield Farm".	Titel, Überschrift
	• **to be worried** ['wʌrid]	to worry → *worried*	besorgt, beunruhigt
	vet [vet]	A *vet* looks after animals when there is something wrong with them.	Tierarzt, Tierärztin
	• **call** [kɔ:l]	Can I use your phone please? I must make a *call*.	Anruf
	right away [raɪt‿ə'weɪ]	At once, now.	sofort, gleich
	• **moment** ['məʊmənt]	! Achtung Betonung!	Moment, Augenblick
	to **explain** [ɪk'spleɪn]	To say what something is about.	erklären, erläutern
	to **follow** ['fɒləʊ]	To go after. The lamb is *following* the mother sheep into the shed.	hinterher gehen; (be)folgen
	• **noise** [nɔɪz]	noisy → *noise*	Geräusch, Lärm
	to **be in a bad way** [ɪn‿ə 'bæd ˌweɪ]	A car hit our cat, and now she*'s in a bad way:* we must take her to the vet.	in schlechter Verfassung sein
	to **examine** [ɪg'zæmɪn]	To look at. *Examine* your answers, can you find anything wrong?	untersuchen, kontrollieren
	dead [ded]	*dead* ↔ alive	tot
	weak [wi:k]	*weak* ↔ strong	schwach
	to **die** [daɪ]	Robert has only got one grandpa. His other grandpa *died* four years ago.	sterben

	once [wʌnts]	At a time in the past.	einmal; einst
	•**to trick** [trɪk]	a trick → to *trick*	austricksen, täuschen
	skin [skɪn]	When the weather is sunny, my *skin* goes brown.	Haut, Fell
	•**smile** [smaɪl]	to smile → *a smile*	Lächeln
	sad [sæd]	*sad* ↔ happy.	traurig, schmerzlich
	important [ɪm'pɔ:tnt]	This letter is *important*, David. You must take it to school tomorrow.	wichtig; einflussreich
	to **choose, chose** [tʃu:z; tʃəʊz]	Which colour pen do you want? You can *choose*.	(aus)wählen
	heading ['hedɪŋ]	Title. The article has got a title, and each part of it has got a *heading*.	Überschrift
3	**gate** [geɪt]	When you go out of the garden, please shut the *gate*.	Tor, Pforte
4	**chick** [tʃɪk]	Small chicken. Little *chicks* come out of eggs.	Küken
	everywhere ['evriweə]	In all places.	überall
	duck [dʌk]	*Ducks* are birds, and they can swim.	Ente

Let's check

2	**the day before yesterday** [ðə ˌdeɪ bɪfɔ: 'jestədeɪ]	Today is Sunday, so *the day before yesterday* was Friday.	vorgestern

Zeit- und Häufigkeitsadverbien

always	immer	**first**	zuerst
never	niemals	**after that**	danach
usually	gewöhnlich	**the next day**	am nächsten Tag
often	oft	**then**	dann
at once	sofort	**at last**	endlich
sometimes	manchmal	**the day before yesterday**	vorgestern

1 Schreibe die folgenden Wörter auf Karten:
big – right – busy – white – short – old – new – black – long – lazy – small – wrong
Lege alle Karten mit der Schrift nach unten. Versuche Gegensatzpaare zu finden. Wenn du ein Paar gefunden hast, darfst du die beiden Karten behalten.
Wenn du mit Freunden spielst, kannst du das Spiel erweitern: Man darf das Kartenpaar erst dann behalten, wenn man mit den beiden Wörtern Sätze gebildet hat, z. B.:
*I've got a **small** hamster. – He lives in a **big** house.*
Du findest noch mehr Gegensatzpaare im Vokabular.

2 Denke an das Wort *day*. Wie viele andere Wörter kennst du, die etwas mit *day* zu tun haben? Mach ein Wörternetz in dein Schulheft:

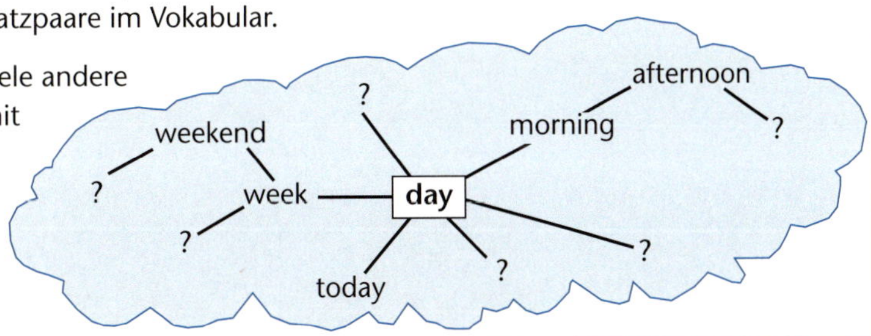

focus 4 Focus on English – a world language

Du behältst Vokabeln besonders gut, wenn du sie zusätzlich vor dem Einschlafen noch einmal ansiehst.

world [wɜːld]	America is in a different part of the *world* from us.	Erde, Welt
to **speak**, **spoke** [spiːk; spəʊk]	To talk. Can I *speak* to Sarah, please?	sprechen
• **Spanish** [ˈspænɪʃ]	Of Spain. In Spain people speak *Spanish*.	spanisch; Spanisch
• **Irish** [ˈaɪrɪʃ]	Of Ireland. There are lots of nice *Irish* songs.	irisch; Irisch
to **forget**, **forgot** [fəˈget; fəˈgɒt]	to *forget* ↔ to remember	vergessen
Franconian [fræŋˈkəʊniən]		fränkisch
• dialect [ˈdaɪəlekt]		Dialekt
French [frentʃ]	Of France. Jenny is learning *French* at school now.	französisch; Französisch
than [ðæn; ðən]	Her English is better *than* her French.	als *(bei Vergleichen)*
to **understand**, **understood** [ˌʌndəˈstænd; ˌʌndəˈstʊd]	Sorry, I can't *understand* you. I don't speak French.	verstehen
• Afrikaans [ˌæfrɪˈkɑːns]		Afrikaans (*Sprache in Südafrika*)
• **African** [ˈæfrɪkən]	Of Africa. Mali, Ghana and South Africa are all *African* countries.	afrikanisch, Afrikaner/-in
Zulu [ˈzuːluː]		Zulu
Aboriginal [ˌæbəˈrɪdʒnl]		Ureinwohner/-in Australiens
• **Australian** [ˈɒstreɪliən]	Of Australia.	australisch
community [kəˈmjuːnəti]	We don't live in a big city, our village is just a small *community*.	Gemeinde; Gemeinschaft
2 • **collage** [kɒˈlɑːʒ]	Let's put lots of different pictures together and make a *collage*.	Collage

Kein, keine

Sarah **can't** speak German.	Sarah kann **kein** Deutsch (sprechen).
No idea.	**Keine** Ahnung.
It's a flat, **not** a house.	Es ist eine Wohnung, **kein** Haus.
Mark **hasn't got** a bike.	Mark hat **kein** Fahrrad.

unit 7 Off to the USA!

Eine Spielmöglichkeit ist die Vokabelkette, die du allein oder mit Freunden spielen kannst. Einer nennt ein Wort. Der nächste muss ein zweites Wort finden, das mit dem letzten Buchstaben des ersten Wortes anfängt. Schau dir Monnys Vokabelkette an.

beach – hour – rock – knife – egg – game

Intro

	Off to the USA! [ˌɒf tə ðə ˌju:esˈeɪ]		Auf in die USA!
	off to [ˈɒf tə]		auf nach
	the **USA** [ˌju:esˈeɪ]	*The United States of America.*	USA
	state [steɪt]	Country or part of a country.	Staat, Land
1	• **American** [əˈmerɪkən]	Of America. *American* football is different from the football game here.	amerikanisch; Amerikaner/-in
	• **flag** [flæg]	The colours of the American *flag* are red, white and blue.	Flagge
	• **baseball** [ˈbeɪsbɔ:l]	An American ball game.	Baseball
	tribe [traɪb]	Group of families. Do you know the names of any American Indian *tribes*?	Stamm
	coast [kəʊst]	Where the country meets the sea.	Küste
	largest [ˈlɑ:dʒɪst]		(der, die, das) größte
	US [ju:ˈes]		Vereinigte Staaten; US-amerikanisch
	mountain [ˈmaʊntɪn]		Berg
2	• **tourist** [ˈtʊərɪst]	Person on holiday.	Tourist
	• **attraction** [əˈtrækʃn]	The Kennedy Space Center is a big tourist *attraction*.	Attraktion, Sehenswürdigkeit
	• **geography** [dʒiˈɒgrəfi]	In *geography* lessons we learn about different countries.	Geographie, Erdkunde
	landscape [ˈlændskeɪp]	A view of the country.	Landschaft
	wide [waɪd]	This table is too *wide*, we can't get it through the door.	groß; breit; weit
	space [speɪs]	There is a lot of *space* in a castle, but there isn't in a shed.	Raum; Weltraum
	• **farmer** [ˈfɑ:mə]		Farmer, Landwirt(in)
	to grow [grəʊ]	We *grow* vegetables in our garden.	anbauen; wachsen
	wheat [wi:t]		Weizen
	also [ˈɔ:lsəʊ]	I like you, too. = I *also* like you.	auch
	far more interesting [ˌfɑ: mɔ:rˈɪntrəstɪŋ]		weitaus interessanter
	• **national park** [ˌnæʃnl ˈpɑ:k]	A special area in the country.	Nationalpark, Naturpark
	• **national** [ˈnæʃnl]	Of a country.	national, landesweit
	• **falls** *(pl.)* [fɔ:lz]	Where a river falls a long way down over rocks you get *falls* or a 'waterfall'.	Wasserfall
	• **rodeo** [rəʊˈdeɪəʊ; ˈrəʊdiəʊ]	You can see lots of horses at a *rodeo*.	Rodeo
	bridge [brɪdʒ]	A *bridge* goes over a river.	Brücke

Language A David's surprise

	you lot ['ju: ˌlɒt]	You people.	ihr alle
	summer ['sʌmə]	The months of June, July and August.	Sommer
	•**fantastic** [fæn'tæstɪk]	Surfing is *fantastic.*	fantastisch, großartig
	rich [rɪtʃ]	With lots of money. Are the Singhs really *rich*?	reich
	to **fly on** [flaɪ‿'ɒn]		weiterfliegen
	straight [streɪt]		gerade, geradewegs
	on business [ɒn 'bɪznɪs]	To go there *on business.*	geschäftlich
	•**business** ['bɪznɪs]	Work. Mr Singh has got his own *business.*	Geschäft; Branche
	to **hope** [həʊp]		hoffen
2	**station** ['steɪʃn]	Look, the train is coming into the *station* now.	Haltestelle, Bahnhof
	•to **send** [send]	I can't explain everything now, but I can *send* you an e-mail.	schicken
3	**fish and chips** [ˌfɪʃ‿n‿'tʃɪps]		Fisch und Pommes frites
5	**flight** [flaɪt]	to fly → a *flight*	Flug
	•**apartment** *(AE)* [ə'pɑ:tmənt]	= flat *(BE)*	Apartment, Wohnung
	downtown *(AE)* [ˌdaʊn'taʊn]	= in the city centre *(BE)*	im Stadtzentrum
	skyscraper ['skaɪskreɪpə]	New *skyscrapers* often have more than 100 floors.	Wolkenkratzer

Language B You Brits!

	Brit [brɪt]		*umgangsspr.*: Engländer
	•**jogging** ['dʒɒgɪŋ]		Jogging
	apple ['æpl]	Have you got an *apple* tree in your garden?	Apfel
	worm [wɜ:m]		Wurm
	cheese [tʃi:z]	We make *cheese* from milk.	Käse
	onion ['ʌnjən]		Zwiebel
	crisp *(BE)* [krɪsp]	= chip *(AE)*	Kartoffelchip
	•**chip** *(AE)* [tʃɪp]	= crisp *(BE)*	Kartoffelchip
	chips *pl. (BE)* [tʃɪps]	= fries *(AE)*	Pommes frites
	•**burger** ['bɜ:gə]	Do you want a *burger* for lunch?	Hamburger
	fries *pl. (AE)* [fraɪz]	= chips *(BE)*	Pommes frites
	else [els]	I've got all the shopping on Mum's list, do we need anything *else*?	andere(-r/-s)
	apart from [ə'pɑ:t frəm]	Except for.	außer, abgesehen von
	screen [skri:n]	TVs and computers have a *screen.*	Bildschirm
	to **mind** [maɪnd]	I don't *mind.* = Es macht mir nichts aus.	etwas dagegen haben
	to **be interested in** [bi‿'ɪntrəstɪd‿ɪn]	Mrs Penrose is *interested in* computers.	interessiert sein an, sich interessieren für
	soccer *(AE)* ['sɒkə]	= football *(BE)*	Fußball
	actually ['æktʃuəli]	! *Actually* heißt nicht ‚aktuell'!	eigentlich; tatsächlich
	How about …? ['haʊ‿ə‿baʊt]	*How about* Mr Penrose, is he in New York, too?	Wie ist es mit …?
3	**gerund** ['dʒernd]	An -ing form. You can use a *gerund* as the subject of a sentence.	Gerundium
4	**below** [bɪ'ləʊ]	Under. The TV magazine is on the shelf *below* the TV. Look, down there!	unterhalb, unten

suggestion [sə'dʒestʃn]	Can I make a *suggestion*? Let's go home.	Vorschlag, Anregung
building ['bɪldɪŋ]	Skyscrapers, sheds and houses are *buildings*.	Gebäude
highest ['haɪɪst]		(der, die, das) höchste; größte
office ['ɒfɪs]		Büro
• **sport** [spɔ:t]		Sport
event [ɪ'vent]	A happening. What important *events* can you remember from last year?	Ereignis
6 **message** ['mesɪdʒ]	Hello, can I leave a *message* for Robert?	Nachricht
• **helicopter** ['helɪˌkɒptə]	You can't fly from London to New York in a *helicopter*.	Helikopter, Hubschrauber
sightseeing ['saɪtsi:ɪŋ]	Looking at tourist attractions.	Besichtigungstour

Gefühle ausdrücken

Great!	Prima! Toll!	**That's terrible!**	Das ist furchtbar!
I like it.	Das finde ich gut.	**Typical!**	Typisch!
Of course!	Natürlich!	**I don't like that.**	Das mag ich nicht.
Never mind.	Macht nichts.	**Ugh!**	Igitt!
I don't mind.	Das ist mir egal.	**No, thank you!**	Nein danke!
Very funny!	Sehr witzig!	**Oh dear!**	Oje!
Don't laugh!	Lach nicht!	**Sorry.**	Entschuldigung.
Yuk!	Igitt!	**Oh yes, you are!**	Oh doch!

Text Dead on the roof?

• **tour** [tʊə]	Trip from one place to another.	Tour, Fahrt, Reise
• **pilot** ['paɪlət]	A *pilot* flies a plane or a helicopter.	Pilot(in)
• **to relax** [rɪ'læks]	Are you worried? Just *relax*, everything's OK.	sich entspannen, sich ausruhen
• **nervous** ['nɜ:vəs]		nervös, aufgeregt
yeah [jeə]		*umgangsspr.*: ja
to **take off** [teɪk‿'ɒf]		abheben
soon [su:n]	in a short time from now; a short time later	bald
above [ə'bʌv]	Over. There's a nice picture *above* the table in Becky's room.	oben, über, oberhalb
immediately [ɪ'mi:diətli]	At once.	sofort, gleich
a bit [ə 'bɪt]		ein bisschen
beautiful ['bju:tɪfl]		wunderschön, hübsch
lady ['leɪdi]	Another word for woman.	Dame, Frau
• **camera** ['kæmrə]	Mr Dixon took his *camera* to Bamburgh Castle and came back with lots of pictures.	Kamera, Fotoapparat
to **take photos** [teɪk 'fəʊtəʊz]		fotografieren, Fotos machen
• **photo** ['fəʊtəʊ]		Foto, Fotografie
metre ['mi:tə]		Meter
to **weigh** [weɪ]	I can't carry these shopping bags, they *weigh* too much.	wiegen
ton [tʌn]	*AE:* 907 kg. A ton (*BE*) is 1000 kg, but an American *ton* doesn't weigh so much.	Tonne (*Gewicht*)

• **finger** ['fɪŋgə]	! Achtung Aussprache: das *g* wird mitgesprochen!	Finger
closed [kləʊzd]	open ↔ *closed*	geschlossen
2.45 (point) ['tu: pɔɪnt ˌfɔ: 'faɪv]	! Bei Zahlen wird statt eines Kommas im Englischen ein Punkt gesetzt und gesprochen. Two *point* four five = zwei Komma vier fünf	Komma (*bei Zahlenangaben*)
to **look like** ['lʊk laɪk]	The London Eye *looks like* a big wheel.	aussehen wie
to **lie** [laɪ]	! I like *lying* in the sun.	liegen
• **back** [bæk]		Rücken
• **exciting** [ɪk'saɪtɪŋ]	excited → *exciting*	spannend, aufregend
no longer [nəʊ 'lɒŋgə]	Not any more. We can *no longer* walk in that park. It's closed.	nicht mehr, nicht länger
gun [gʌn]	A man with a *gun* went into a shop and said, "Give me the money!"	Schusswaffe
• **gangster** ['gæŋkstə]	A *gangster* is a bad person.	Gangster, Verbrecher
• **to land** [lænd]	To bring a plane or helicopter down.	landen
emergency [ɪ'mɜ:dʒntsi]	That plane can't land, something's wrong with it – it's an *emergency*!	Notfall, Notlage
police [pə'li:s]	! The *police* **are** coming.	Polizei
• **slowly** ['sləʊli]	slow → *slowly*	langsam
to **move** [mu:v]	Mr Dixon's back hurts, he can't *move*.	(sich) bewegen
workman ['wɜ:kmən]	There are *workmen* in the kitchen and bathroom: we haven't got any water.	Handwerker
electric drill [ɪ'lektrɪk ˌdrɪl]	Mr Burton is making some shelves for the shop. He's using an *electric drill* to put them up.	elektrische Bohrmaschine
• **electric** [ɪ'lektrɪk]		elektrisch
drill [drɪl]		Bohrer, Bohrmaschine
to **faint** [feɪnt]	Sarah *fainted* after she hit her head.	ohnmächtig werden
to **be lucky** ['lʌki]	 *I'm lucky.* = Ich habe Glück. *I'm happy.* = Ich bin glücklich.	Glück haben
2 to **drive** [draɪv]		fahren
3 **newspaper** ['nju:sˌpeɪpə]	Mr Dixon reads the *newspaper* every morning while he's having breakfast.	Zeitung
• **journalist** ['dʒɜ:nlɪst]	A *journalist* writes for a newspaper.	Journalist(in)
to **arrive (at)** [ə'raɪv]		ankommen
beginning [bɪ'gɪnɪŋ]	*beginning* ↔ ending, end	Anfang, Beginn
• **life** [laɪf]	to live [lɪv] → *life* [laɪf]	Leben

1 Schreibe die folgenden Wörter auf und markiere die Buchstaben, die nicht gesprochen werden.

w̲rite, listen, answer, white, right, knife, car, half, know, chocolate, wreck, straight, weigh

2 Schreibe dir ein beliebiges Wort auf und versuche möglichst viele Reimwörter zu finden. Markiere Besonderheiten in der Schreibung, z. B. sa̲y̲ – we̲i̲g̲h̲.

Fallen dir weitere Beispiele von Wörtern mit besondes schwieriger Aussprache ein?

extra line

extra ['ekstrə]	zusätzlich; Zusatz

A Christmas time

1 Christmas ['krɪsməs]	Weihnachten
Christmas Eve [ˌkrɪsməs‿'i:v]	Heiligabend
stocking ['stɒkɪŋ]	Strumpf
present ['preznt]	Geschenk
Father Christmas [ˌfɑ:ðə 'krɪsməs]	Weihnachtsmann
mince pie [ˌmɪnts 'paɪ]	gefülltes Weihnachtsgebäck
a long way [lɒŋ 'weɪ]	von weit her
hungry ['hʌŋgri]	hungrig
December [dɪ'sembə]	Dezember
Christmas Day [ˌkrɪsməs 'deɪ]	Erster Weihnachtsfeiertag
dinner ['dɪnə]	Abendessen
turkey ['tɜ:ki]	Truthahn
Christmas pudding [ˌkrɪsməs 'pʊdɪŋ]	*brit. Weihnachtssüßspeise*
cracker ['krækə]	Knallbonbon
to pull [pʊl]	ziehen
Boxing Day ['bɒksɪŋ ˌdeɪ]	zweiter Weihnachtsfeiertag
pantomime ['pæntəmaɪm]	Weihnachtsmärchen
Aladdin [ə'lædɪn]	Aladin
2 to wish [wɪʃ]	wünschen
merry ['meri]	fröhlich
happy ['hæpi]	glücklich
New Year [ˌnju: 'jɪə]	Neujahr
good tidings [gʊd 'taɪdɪŋz]	frohe Botschaft
kin [kɪn]	Verwandtschaft, Familie
some [sʌm]	*hier:* etwas davon
we won't go ['wəʊnt gəʊ]	wir werden nicht gehen
until [ʌn'tɪl]	bis; erst wenn
for [fɔ:; fə]	denn

B Fun page

Fun page ['fʌn ˌpeɪdʒ]	Spaßseite
fun [fʌn]	Spaß
1 joke [dʒəʊk]	Witz
wings [wɪŋz]	Flügel
roast [rəʊst]	gebraten
turkey ['tɜ:ki]	Truthahn
everyone ['evriwʌn]	jeder, jedermann
dictionary ['dɪkʃnri]	Wörterbuch
beginning [bɪ'gɪnɪŋ]	(etwas), das ... beginnt
all right [ɔ:l 'raɪt]	in Ordnung; alles klar
2 riddle ['rɪdl]	Rätsel
3 vet [vet]	Tierarzt, Tierärztin
library ['laɪbrəri]	Bücherei
T-shirt ['ti:ʃɜ:t]	T-Shirt
elephant ['elɪfənt]	Elefant
bookworm ['bʊkwɜ:m]	Bücherwurm
ill [ɪl]	krank
through [θru:]	durch
hamburger ['hæmbɜ:gə]	Hamburger
4 class clown [ˌklɑ:s 'klaʊn]	Klassenclown, Klassenkasper
school [sku:l]	*hier*: Schwarm

C Poetry page

poetry ['pəʊətri]	Lyrik
1 to try, tried [traɪ; traɪd]	versuchen, probieren
store [stɔ:]	Laden, Geschäft
reason ['ri:zn]	Grund
any more [ˌeni 'mɔ:]	(nicht) mehr
fool [fu:l]	Dummkopf, Narr
bone [bəʊn]	Knochen
to order ['ɔ:də]	bestellen
rose [rəʊz]	Rose
violet ['vaɪələt]	Veilchen
sugar ['ʃʊgə]	Zucker
aloud [ə'laʊd]	laut
rhyme [raɪm]	Reim
rhythm ['rɪðm]	Rhythmus
1 stressed [strest]	betont
syllable ['sɪləbl]	Silbe

1 they are repeated [ɑ: rɪ'pi:tɪd]	sie werden wiederholt
to repeat [rɪ'pi:t]	wiederholen
to count [kaʊnt]	zählen
2 anti-smoking [ˌænti 'sməʊkɪŋ]	Nichtraucher-; Antiraucher-
rhyming ['raɪmɪŋ]	Reim-
to rhyme [raɪm]	sich reimen
to smoke [sməʊk]	rauchen
pack [pæk]	Päckchen
nothing ['nʌθɪŋ]	nichts
to bury ['beri]	begraben; beerdigen
beneath [bɪ'ni:θ]	unter, unterhalb
he'll [hi:l]	er wird
4 way [weɪ]	Art und Weise
that [ðæt; ðət]	die *(Relativpronomen)*
to begin, began [bɪ'gɪn; bɪ'gæn]	anfangen, beginnen
all right [ɔ:l 'raɪt]	in Ordnung; alles klar
to stress [stres]	betonen

D The paper bag princess

paper bag princess ['peɪpə ˌbæg prɪn'ses]	*hier:* Lumpenprinzessin
paper bag [ˌpeɪpə 'bæg]	Papiertüte
paper ['peɪpə]	Papier
princess [prɪn'ses]	Prinzessin
beautiful ['bju:tɪfl]	wunderschön, hübsch
was going to marry [wəz ˌgəʊɪŋ tə 'mæri]	wollte heiraten
to marry ['mæri]	heiraten
prince [prɪnts]	Prinz
dragon ['drægn]	Drachen
to smash [smæʃ]	zerschlagen, zertrümmern
to burn [bɜ:n]	verbrennen
could [kʊd]	konnte
finally ['faɪnli]	letztlich, zuletzt
cave [keɪv]	Höhle
large [lɑ:dʒ]	groß, riesig
to bang [bæŋ]	hämmern; fest (an)klopfen
whole [həʊl]	ganz
world [wɜ:ld]	Welt
breath [breθ]	Atem
deep [di:p]	tief
to breathe [bri:ð]	atmen
fire [faɪə]	Feuer
nothing ['nʌθɪŋ]	nichts
no longer [nəʊ 'lɒŋgə]	nicht länger
to cook [kʊk]	kochen
burger ['bɜ:gə]	Hamburger
second ['seknd]	Sekunde
to jump up [dʒʌmp‿'ʌp]	hochspringen
straight [streɪt]	gerade; direkt
to whisper ['wɪspə]	flüstern
to move [mu:v]	(sich) bewegen
ear [ɪə]	Ohr
you're a mess [mes]	du siehst total unordentlich aus
to smell, smelt [smel, smelt]	riechen
hair [heə]	Haar(e)
dirty ['dɜ:ti]	schmutzig
real [rɪəl]	richtig, echt
bum [bʌm]	Idiot, Depp
get married [get 'mærid]	heiraten

E A very cultured bird

cultured ['kʌltʃəd]	kultiviert
called [kɔ:ld]	(Buch), das … heißt
Fudge/ Fudgie [fʌdʒ; 'fʌdʒi]	*Kosename*
grade *(AE)* [greɪd]	Klasse
one night [wʌn 'naɪt]	eines Abends
Mom [mɒm]	Mama
to do well [du: 'wel]	gute Leistungen erbringen
would like [wʊd 'laɪk]	würde/hätte gerne
to repeat [rɪ'pi:t]	wiederholen
yo-yo ['jəʊjəʊ]	Jo-Jo
cage [keɪdʒ]	Käfig
tonight [tə'naɪt]	heute Abend
few [fju:]	einige
kind [kaɪnd]	Art
myna bird ['maɪnə ˌbɜ:d]	Hirtenstar, Beo
anything ['eniθɪŋ]	irgendetwas
to add [æd]	hinzufügen
Guess what? [ges 'wɒt]	Weißt du was?, Rate mal, was passiert ist.
pet store ['pet stɔ:]	Zoohandlung
to have to ['hæv tə]	müssen
to order ['ɔ:də]	bestellen
all [ɔ:l]	*hier:* ganz, vollkommen
to name [neɪm]	benennen
to expect [ɪk'spekt]	erwarten

as [æz; əz]	da, weil
feather ['feðə]	Feder
unusual [ʌn'ju:ʒl]	ungewöhnlich
definitely ['defɪnətli]	definitiv, bestimmt
to go down to [gəʊ 'daʊn tə]	hinuntergehen zu, gehen nach
cover ['kʌvə]	Abdeckung
to call [kɔ:l]	nennen
Bonjour ['bɒŋʒʊə]	*frz.:* Guten Tag!
over and over again [ˌəʊvər‿ənd‿ˌəʊvər‿ə'gen]	immer wieder
as if [əz‿'ɪf]	als ob
to bang [bæŋ]	hämmern; fest (an)klopfen
to greet [gri:t]	(be)grüßen
smart [smɑ:t]	schlau, klug
terrific [tə'rɪfɪk]	ausgezeichnet, hervorragend
worm [wɜ:m]	Wurm
insect ['ɪnsekt]	Insekt
plant [plɑ:nt]	Pflanze
to push [pʊʃ]	schieben, drücken

aside [ə'saɪd]	beiseite
conversation [ˌkɒnvə'seɪʃn]	Unterhaltung
Show and Tell [ˌʃəʊ‿ən 'tel]	*Unterrichtsteil, in dem Schüler etwas mitbringen und vorstellen*
permission [pə'mɪʃn]	Erlaubnis, Genehmigung
to miss [mɪs]	verpassen
half, *pl.* halves [hɑ:f; hɑ:vz]	die Hälfte
in case of problems [ɪn ˌkeɪs‿əv 'prɒbləmz]	für den Fall, dass es Probleme gibt
everyone ['evriwʌn]	jeder, jedermann
to pull [pʊl]	ziehen
to present [prɪ'zent]	präsentieren
to sound (like) [saʊnd]	sich anhören (wie)
robot ['rəʊbɒt]	Roboter
to bend over [ˌbend‿'əʊvə]	sich über etw. beugen
Parlez-vous francais? [pɑ:leɪ ˌvu: 'frɒŋseɪ]	*frz.:* Sprechen Sie Französisch?
to cock [kɒk]	(den Kopf) schief legen

1 Ordne diese Wörter in alphabetischer Reihenfolge:
castle – everybody – guitar – easy – exercise – biro – brilliant – ceiling.

2 Bilde Wortketten, zum Beispiel:

Ihr könnt zu zweit spielen. Wer nach einer festgelegten Zeit die längste Wortkette hat, gewinnt.

Natürlich kannst du auch ein Muster wie dieses legen:

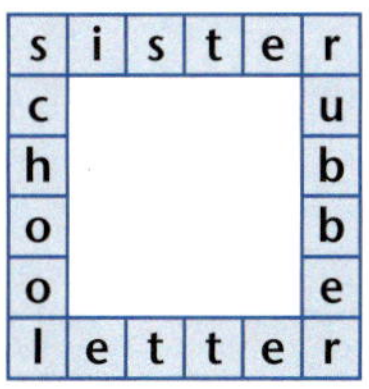

Suche Wörter für ein neues Viereck oder eine andere Form.

3 Im Englischen können manche Wörter in verschiedenen Zusammenhängen benutzt werden. Kannst du diese Gruppen ergänzen?

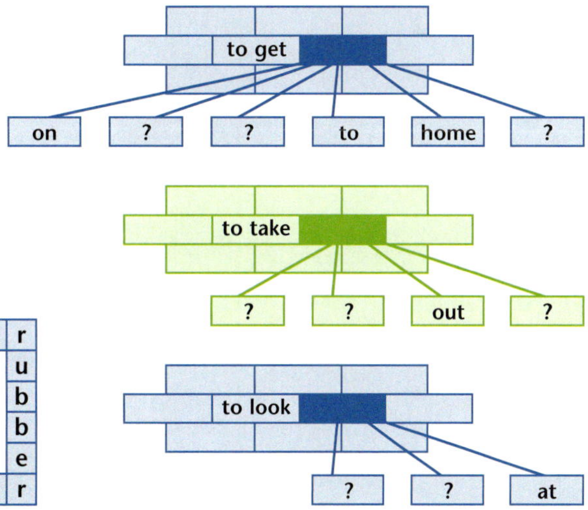

dictionary

In dieser alphabetischen Liste ist das gesamte Vokabular von *Green Line NEW Bayern 1* enthalten. Namen werden in gesonderten Listen nach dem Vokabular aufgeführt.
Die mit ° gekennzeichneten Einträge sollten bereits aus der Grundschule bekannt sein.
Die mit * gekennzeichneten Verben sind unregelmäßig (siehe S. 155). Die Wörter, deren Fundstellen in Spitzklammern stehen, gehören nicht zum aktiv zu beherrschenden Lernwortschatz und werden hier als fakultativ bezeichnet.

Die Angaben nach den Einträgen verweisen auf das erstmalige Vorkommen der Wörter, z. B.
to **start** [stɑ:t] anfangen **LS**, 10 – Let's start, Seite 10
family ['fæmli] Familie **F1**, 24 = Focus 1, Seite 24
U = Unit, EL = Extra Line

A

°**a(n)** [ə; ən] ein(e) **LS**, 10
a bit [ə 'bɪt] ein bisschen **U7**, 106
°a hundred [ə 'hʌndrəd] hundert **U2**, 44
⟨a long way⟩ [lɒŋ 'weɪ] von weit her **EL**, 114
a lot of [ə 'lɒt‿əv] viele, eine Menge **U5**, 78
a pair of [ə 'peər‿əv] ein Paar **F2**, 49
Aboriginal [ˌæbə'rɪdʒnl] Ureinwohner/-in Australiens **F4**, 99
about [ə'baʊt] über; wegen **LS**, 10
above [ə'bʌv] oben, über, oberhalb **U7**, 106
to **act something out** [ˌækt sʌmθɪŋ‿'aʊt] etwas durchspielen **U4**, 67
action ['ækʃn] Aktion, Handlung **U5**, 82
actually ['æktʃuəli] eigentlich; tatsächlich **U7**, 104
⟨to **add**⟩ [æd] hinzufügen **EL**, 120
African ['æfrɪkən] afrikanisch, Afrikaner/-in **F4**, 99
⟨**Afrikaans**⟩ [ˌæfrɪ'kɑ:ns] Afrikaans (*Sprache in Südafrika*) **F4**, 99
after ['ɑ:ftə] nach **U3**, 50
°**afternoon** [ˌɑ:ftə'nu:n] Nachmittag **U1**, 32
again [ə'gen] wieder **LS**, 15
again and again [ə'gen‿ənd‿ə'gen] immer wieder **U5**, 81
ago [ə'gəʊ] vor (*zeitlich*) **U6**, 90
air [eə] Luft **U4**, 68
°**airport** ['eəpɔ:t] Flughafen **U2**, 38
*to be **alive** [ə'laɪv] lebendig sein; leben **U5**, 80
all [ɔ:l] alle(s); ganz **U2**, 38
all the time [ˌɔ:l ðə 'taɪm] die ganze Zeit **U2**, 42
⟨**all**⟩ [ɔ:l] *hier*: ganz, vollkommen **EL**, 120
⟨all right⟩ [ɔ:l 'raɪt] in Ordnung; alles klar **EL**, 115
almost ['ɔ:lməʊst] fast, beinahe **U5**, 78
alone [ə'ləʊn] alleine **U1**, 30
⟨**aloud**⟩ [ə'laʊd] laut **EL**, 116
alphabet ['ælfəbet] Alphabet **LS**, 17
already [ɔ:l'redi] schon **U1**, 28
also ['ɔ:lsəʊ] auch **U7**, 101
always ['ɔ:lweɪz] immer, ständig **U1**, 30
am [ˌeɪ'em] vormittags (*Uhrzeit*) **U3**, 51
American [ə'merɪkən] amerikanisch; Amerikaner/-in **U7**, 100
and [ænd; ən(d)] und **LS**, 9
angry ['æŋgri] zornig, wütend **U3**, 54
°**animal** ['ænɪml] Tier **U1**, 28
°**anorak** ['ænəræk] Anorak **F2**, 49
another [ə'nʌðə] noch ein(e); ein(e) andere(-r/-s) **U4**, 66
answer ['ɑ:ntsə] Antwort **LS**, 19
to **answer** ['ɑ:ntsə] (be)antworten **LS**, 16
⟨**anti-smoking**⟩ [ˌænti 'sməʊkɪŋ] Nichtraucher-; Antiraucher- **EL**, 116
any ['eni] irgendein(-e/-er); irgendwelche **U5**, 78
⟨any more⟩ [ˌeni 'mɔ:] (nicht) mehr **EL**, 116
⟨**anything**⟩ ['eniθɪŋ] irgendetwas **EL**, 120
apart from [ə'pɑ:t frəm] außer, abgesehen von **U7**, 104
apartment *(AE)* [ə'pɑ:tmənt] Apartment, Wohnung **U7**, 103
°**apple** ['æpl] Apfel **U7**, 104
°**April** ['eɪprl] April **U4**, 62
°**arm** [ɑ:m] Arm **LS**, 21
around [ə'raʊnd] herum, umher **U4**, 68
to **arrive** (at) [ə'raɪv] ankommen **U7**, 108
article ['ɑ:tɪkl] Artikel (*in der Zeitung, etc.*) **U6**, 86
⟨**as**⟩ [æz; əz] da, weil **EL**, 121
⟨**aside**⟩ [ə'saɪd] beiseite **EL**, 121
⟨**as if**⟩ [əz‿'ɪf] als ob **EL**, 121
to **ask** [ɑ:sk] fragen **LS**, 16
Assembly [ə'sembli] Versammlung; Morgenappell **U3**, 52
shop **assistant** ['ʃɒp‿əˌsɪstnt] Verkäufer(in) **F2**, 49
at [æt; ət] in, auf, bei, an **LS**, 10
°at home [ət 'həʊm] zu Hause **U3**, 53
at last [ət 'lɑ:st] endlich **U5**, 81
at once [ət 'wʌnts] sofort, plötzlich **U3**, 56
at the seaside [ət ðə 'si:saɪd] am Meer **U5**, 74
to **attack** [ə'tæk] angreifen **U6**, 86
attraction [ə'trækʃn] Attraktion, Sehenswürdigkeit **U7**, 100
°**August** ['ɔ:gəst] August **U4**, 62
°**aunt** [ɑ:nt] Tante **F1**, 24
Australian ['ɒstreɪliən] australisch **F4**, 99
away [ə'weɪ] weg (von) **U3**, 57
right **away** [raɪt‿ə'weɪ] sofort, gleich **U6**, 92

B

back [bæk] Rücken **U7**, 106
back [bæk] zurück **U4**, 64
⟨**backbone**⟩ ['bækbəʊn] Rückgrat **F3**, 73
°**bad** [bæd] schlecht **U3**, 50
to be in a bad way [ɪn‿ə 'bæd ˌweɪ] in schlechter Verfassung sein **U6**, 92
°**bag** [bæg] Tasche **LS**, 14
mixed bag [ˌmɪkst 'bæg] buntes Allerlei **LS**, 23
⟨paper bag⟩ [ˌpeɪpə 'bæg] Papiertüte **EL**, 118
⟨paper bag princess⟩ ['peɪpə ˌbæg prɪn'‿ses] *hier*: Lumpenprinzessin **EL**, 118
school bag ['sku:l bæg] Schultasche **LS**, 14
bagpipes *pl.* ['bægpaɪps] Dudelsack **F3**, 72
°**ball** [bɔ:l] Ball **LS**, 14
⟨**banana**⟩ [bə'nɑ:nə] Banane **U4**, 63
⟨to **bang**⟩ [bæŋ] hämmern; fest (an)klopfen **EL**, 118
bar [bɑ:] Tafel; Riegel; Stück; Stange **U5**, 78
to **bark** (at) [bɑ:k] (an)bellen **U3**, 56
°**baseball** ['beɪsbɔ:l] Baseball **U7**, 100
basket ['bɑ:skɪt] Korb, Körbchen **U6**, 88
bath [bɑ:θ] Bad **U1**, 27
°**bathroom** ['bɑ:θrʊm] Badezimmer **U1**, 27
°*to **be** [bi:] sein **LS**, 12
to be alive [ə'laɪv] lebendig sein; leben **U5**, 80
to be frightened (of) ['fraɪtnd] Angst haben (vor) **U5**, 80
to be good at ['gʊd‿ət] gut sein in **LS**, 16
to be hurt [bi: 'hɜ:t] weh tun; verletzt sein **LS**, 12
to be in a bad way [ɪn‿ə 'bæd ˌweɪ] in schlechter Verfassung sein **U6**, 92
to be interested in [bi‿'ɪntrəstɪd‿ɪn] interessiert sein an, sich interessieren für **U7**, 104
to be late [bi: 'leɪt] zu spät sein, zu spät kommen **LS**, 20
to be lucky ['lʌki] Glück haben **U7**, 107
to be married to [bi: 'mærid tə] verheiratet sein mit **F1**, 24
to be on [ɒn] im Gange sein, laufen **U2**, 44
to be scared [bi: 'skeəd] Angst haben, erschrocken sein **U6**, 86
to be surprised [sə'praɪzd] überrascht sein **U6**, 87

to be worried ['wʌ:rid] besorgt, beunruhigt U6, 92
°**beach** [bi:tʃ] Strand F3, 72
*to **beat** [bi:t] besiegen; schlagen F3, 72
beautiful ['bju:tɪfl] wunderschön, hübsch U7, 106
because [bɪ'kɒz] weil U3, 50
°**bed** [bed] Bett LS, 14
bed and breakfast [ˌbed‿n 'brekfəst] Zimmer mit Frühstück U5, 75
°**bedroom** ['bedrʊm] Schlafzimmer U1, 27
before [bɪ'fɔ:] vor; bevor U3, 52
beginning [bɪ'gɪnɪŋ] Anfang, Beginn U7, 108
below [bɪ'ləʊ] unterhalb, unten U7, 105
⟨*to **bend**⟩ [bend] beugen; biegen LS, 21
⟨bend over⟩ [ˌbend‿'əʊvə] sich über etw. beugen EL, 121
⟨**beneath**⟩ [bɪ'ni:θ] unter, unterhalb EL, 116
best [best] beste(-r/-s) LS, 10
better ['betə] besser U3, 58
°**big** [bɪg] groß; dick U1, 32
°**bike** [baɪk] Fahrrad U1, 27
°**bird** [bɜ:d] Vogel U5, 75
⟨myna bird⟩ ['maɪnə ˌbɜ:d] Hirtenstar, Beo EL, 120
biro ['baɪrəʊ] Kugelschreiber, Kuli LS, 14
°**birthday** ['bɜ:θdeɪ] Geburtstag F1, 24
a **bit** [ə 'bɪt] ein bisschen U7, 106
°**black** [blæk] schwarz LS, 13
°**blackboard, board** ['blækbɔ:d; bɔ:d] Tafel LS, 21
⟨to **blindfold**⟩ ['blaɪndfəʊld] die Augen verbinden U4, 66
blonde [blɒnd] blond F1, 25
°**blue** [blu:] blau LS, 13
°**board, blackboard** [bɔ:d; 'blækbɔ:d] Tafel LS, 21
boat [bəʊt] Boot, Schiff U5, 75
°**body** ['bɒdi] Körper F3, 73
⟨**bone**⟩ [bəʊn] Knochen EL, 116
⟨**Bonjour**⟩ ['bɒŋʒʊə] *frz.*: Guten Tag! EL, 121
°**book** [bʊk] Buch; Heft LS, 10
exercise book ['eksəsaɪz ˌbʊk] Übungsheft LS, 10
bookshop ['bʊkʃɒp] Buchhandlung U2, 38
⟨**bookworm**⟩ ['bʊkwɜ:m] Bücherwurm EL, 115
boring ['bɔ:rɪŋ] langweilig U3, 52
both [bəʊθ] beide F1, 25
°**bottle** ['bɒtl] Flasche U1, 28
bowl [bəʊl] Schale, Schälchen U1, 30
°**box** [bɒks] Kiste, Schachtel; Kasten U1, 30
⟨**Boxing** Day⟩ ['bɒksɪŋ ˌdeɪ] zweiter Weihnachtsfeiertag EL, 114
°**boy** [bɔɪ] Junge LS, 12
boyfriend ['bɔɪfrend] Freund U2, 42
brave [breɪv] tapfer, mutig U5, 81
°**breakfast** ['brekfəst] Frühstück U1, 30
bed and breakfast [ˌbed‿n 'brekfəst] Zimmer mit Frühstück U5, 75
⟨**breath**⟩ [breθ] Atem EL, 118
⟨to **breathe**⟩ [bri:ð] atmen EL, 118
°**bridge** [brɪdʒ] Brücke U7, 101
brilliant ['brɪljənt] toll, prima; leuchtend LS, 16
*to **bring** [brɪŋ] bringen LS, 20
⟨**Brit**⟩ [brɪt] *umgangsspr.*: Engländer U7, 104
Made in **Britain** [ˌmeɪd‿ɪn 'brɪtn] Hergestellt in Großbritannien U2, 46
British ['brɪtɪʃ] britisch F2, 49
°**brother** ['brʌðə] Bruder F1, 24
°**brown** [braʊn] braun LS, 13
°**budgie** ['bʌdʒi] Wellensittich F2, 48
building ['bɪldɪŋ] Gebäude U7, 105
⟨**bum**⟩ [bʌm] Idiot, Depp EL, 119
*to give somebody the **bumps** [ˌgɪv ðə 'bʌmps] jemanden hochwerfen und wieder auffangen U4, 63
to **bump** [bʌmp] (an)stoßen U4, 63
burger ['bɜ:gə] Hamburger U7, 104
⟨burger⟩ ['bɜ:gə] Hamburger EL, 119
⟨to **burn**⟩ [bɜ:n] verbrennen EL, 118
⟨to **bury**⟩ ['beri] begraben; beerdigen EL, 116
°**bus** [bʌs] Bus U2, 38
°by (bus) [baɪ] mit (dem Bus), per U2, 38
bush [bʊʃ] Busch, Strauch U3, 54
business ['bɪznɪs] Geschäft; Branche U7, 102
on business [ɒn 'bɪznɪs] geschäftlich U7, 102
busy ['bɪzi] beschäftigt; belebt; voller Menschen U1, 28
but [bʌt; bət] aber LS, 12
°*to **buy** [baɪ] kaufen U2, 40
by [baɪ] bei; an F3, 72
by [baɪ] von U1, 28
°by (bus) [baɪ] mit (dem Bus), per U2, 38
°**Bye!** [baɪ] Tschüss! LS, 10

C

café ['kæfeɪ] Café U2, 42
⟨**cage**⟩ [keɪdʒ] Käfig EL, 120
cake [keɪk] Kuchen U4, 63
⟨sponge cake⟩ ['spʌndʒ ˌkeɪk] Rührkuchen, Biskuitboden U4, 63
°**calendar** ['kæləndə] Kalender U4, 62
call [kɔ:l] Anruf U6, 92
°⟨to **call**⟩ [kɔ:l] nennen EL, 121
to call [kɔ:l] (an)rufen; Bescheid geben U1, 32
camera ['kæmrə] Kamera, Fotoapparat U7, 106
°**can** [kæn; kən] kann, können LS, 12
°can't [kɑ:nt] nicht können U1, 28
candle ['kændl] Kerze U4, 63
capital ['kæpɪtl] Hauptstadt F3, 72
°**car** [kɑ:] Auto U2, 38
card [kɑ:d] Karte U4, 62
to **carry** ['kæri] tragen U2, 42
cartoon [kɑ:'tu:n] Cartoon; Zeichentrickfilm U2, 40
⟨in **case** of problems⟩ [ɪn ˌkeɪs‿əv 'prɒbləmz] für den Fall, dass es Probleme gibt EL, 121
°pencil case ['pentsl ˌkeɪs] Federmäppchen LS, 14
°**castle** ['kɑ:sl] Schloss; Burg U2, 38
°**cat** [kæt] Katze LS, 10
⟨**cave**⟩ [keɪv] Höhle EL, 118
CD [si:'di:] CD U1, 27
CD player [ˌsi:'di: ˌpleɪə] CD-Spieler U1, 28
ceiling ['si:lɪŋ] (Zimmer-)Decke U4, 69
centre ['sentə] Zentrum U1, 26
city centre [ˌsɪti 'sentə] Stadtzentrum, Stadtmitte U1, 26
shopping centre ['ʃɒpɪŋ ˌsentə] Einkaufszentrum U2, 38
°**chair** [tʃeə] Stuhl LS, 14
champion ['tʃæmpiən] Gewinner; Champion U2, 45
to **change** [tʃeɪndʒ] tauschen, wechseln; (sich) ändern U4, 66
to **chase** [tʃeɪs] verfolgen, jagen U3, 54
to **check** [tʃek] (über)prüfen; kontrollieren LS, 22
Let's check! [lets 'tʃek] Lass(t) uns überprüfen. LS, 22
°**cheese** [tʃi:z] Käse U7, 104
chick [tʃɪk] Küken U6, 95
°**chicken** ['tʃɪkɪn] Huhn, Hähnchen U6, 86
°**child**, *pl.* **children** ['tʃaɪld; 'tʃɪldrn] Kind F1, 25
chip *(AE)* [tʃɪp] Kartoffelchip U7, 104
chips *pl. (BE)* [tʃɪps] Pommes frites U7, 104
°fish and chips [ˌfɪʃ‿n‿'tʃɪps] Fisch und Pommes frites U7, 103
chocolate ['tʃɒklət] Schokolade U5, 78
*to **choose** [tʃu:z] (aus)wählen U6, 94
°⟨**Christmas**⟩ ['krɪsməs] Weihnachten EL, 114
⟨Christmas Day⟩ [ˌkrɪsməs 'deɪ] Erster Weihnachtsfeiertag EL, 114
⟨Christmas Eve⟩ [ˌkrɪsməs‿'i:v] Heiligabend EL, 114
⟨Christmas pudding⟩ [ˌkrɪsməs 'pʊdɪŋ] *brit. Weihnachtssüßspeise* EL, 114
⟨Father Christmas⟩ [ˌfɑ:ðə 'krɪsməs] Weihnachtsmann EL, 114
church [tʃɜ:tʃ] Kirche U2, 39
cinema ['sɪnəmə] Kino U2, 39
circle ['sɜ:kl] Kreis U4, 66
°**city** ['sɪti] Stadt; Großstadt U1, 26
city centre [ˌsɪti 'sentə] Stadtzentrum, Stadtmitte U1, 26
°to **clap** [klæp] klatschen LS, 19
°**class** [klɑ:s] Schulklasse, Klasse LS, 18
⟨class clown⟩ ['klɑ:s ˌklaʊn] Klassenclown, Klassenkasper EL, 115
in class [ɪŋ 'klɑ:s] in/vor der Klasse U4, 65
classroom ['klɑ:srʊm] Klassenzimmer LS, 18
to **clean** [kli:n] säubern, reinigen U6, 86
*to **cling** (to) ['klɪŋ] sich festhalten (an), sich festklammern (an) U5, 81
°o'**clock** [ə'klɒk] Uhr (*Zeitangabe bei vollen Stunden*) U3, 50
closed [kləʊzd] geschlossen U7, 106
°**clothes** *pl.* [kləʊðz] Kleider, Kleidung U1, 28
°**cloud** [klaʊd] Wolke U2, 45
⟨class **clown**⟩ ['klɑ:s ˌklaʊn] Klassenclown, Klassenkasper EL, 115
coast [kəʊst] Küste U7, 100
⟨to **cock**⟩ [kɒk] (den Kopf) schief legen EL, 121
°**cold** [kəʊld] kalt U5, 76

collage [kɒ'lɑ:ʒ] Collage **F4**, 99
to **collect** [kə'lekt] sammeln **U3**, 58
°**colour** ['kʌlə] Farbe **LS**, 13
°What colour is/are …? [ˌwɒt 'kʌlər‿ɪz/ɑ:] Welche Farbe hat/haben …? **LS**, 13
*to **come** [kʌm] kommen **LS**, 10
Come on! [kʌm‿'ɒn] Komm(t)! **LS**, 10
to come in [kʌm‿'ɪn] hereinkommen **U1**, 28
comic ['kɒmɪk] Comic(heft) **LS**, 14
community [kə'mju:nəti] Gemeinde; Gemeinschaft **F4**, 99
°**computer** [ˌkəm'pju:tə] Computer **U1**, 28
to **connect (to)** [kə'nekt] verbinden (mit) **U3**, 58
⟨**conversation**⟩ [ˌkɒnvə'seɪʃn] Unterhaltung **EL**, 121
⟨to **cook**⟩ [kʊk] kochen **EL**, 119
to **copy** ['kɒpi] abschreiben, kopieren **U3**, 59
to **correct** [kə'rekt] korrigieren, verbessern **LS**, 21
correct [kə'rekt] richtig, korrekt **U5**, 75
⟨**could**⟩ [kʊd] konnte **EL**, 118
⟨to **count**⟩ [kaʊnt] zählen **EL**, 116
country ['kʌntri] Land; ländliche Gegend, Landschaft **F3**, 72
of **course** [əv 'kɔ:s] natürlich, selbstverständlich **F1**, 25
°**cousin** ['kʌzn] Cousin, Cousine **F1**, 24
⟨**cover**⟩ ['kʌvə] Abdeckung **EL**, 121
°**cow** [kaʊ] Kuh **U6**, 87
⟨**cracker**⟩ ['krækə] Knallbonbon **EL**, 114
to **crash** [kræʃ] aufschlagen, gegen etwas krachen **U5**, 80
crash! [kræʃ] Krach! Bumm!; Zusammenstoß **U4**, 69
cream [kri:m] Creme; Sahne **U3**, 52
°ice cream [aɪs 'kri:m] Eis, Eiscreme **U3**, 52
crisp *(BE)* [krɪsp] Kartoffelchip **U7**, 104
to **cry** [kraɪ] schreien, rufen; weinen **U3**, 54
⟨**cultured**⟩ ['kʌltʃəd] kultiviert **EL**, 120
°**cup** [kʌp] Tasse **U1**, 30
°**cupboard** ['kʌbəd] Küchenschrank, Schrank **U1**, 32
⟨**custard**⟩ ['kʌstəd] Vanillepudding **U4**, 63
customer ['kʌstəmə] Kunde, Kundin **F2**, 49

D

dad [dæd] Papa **U1**, 27
°**dangerous** ['deɪndʒrəs] gefährlich **U5**, 81
dark [dɑ:k] dunkel **F1**, 25
date [deɪt] Datum **U4**, 62
°**day** [deɪ] Tag **LS**, 17
⟨Boxing Day⟩ ['bɒksɪŋ ˌdeɪ] zweiter Weihnachtsfeiertag **EL**, 114
⟨Christmas Day⟩ [ˌkrɪsməs 'deɪ] Erster Weihnachtsfeiertag **EL**, 114
every day [ˌevri 'deɪ] jeden Tag **LS**, 17
the day before yesterday [ðə ˌdeɪ bɪfɔ: 'jestədeɪ] vorgestern **U6**, 96
dead [ded] tot **U6**, 92
°Oh **dear!** ['əʊ ˌdɪə] Oje! **LS**, 14
°**dear** [dɪə] lieb **U3**, 52
°**December** [dɪ'sembə] Dezember **U4**, 62
⟨to **decorate**⟩ ['dekəreɪt] dekorieren, verzieren **U4**, 63
⟨**deep**⟩ [di:p] tief **EL**, 118
⟨**definitely**⟩ ['defɪnətli] definitiv, bestimmt **EL**, 120
°**desk** [desk] Schreibtisch **LS**, 14
dialect ['daɪəlekt] Dialekt **F4**, 99
dialogue ['daɪəlɒg] Dialog, Gespräch **U2**, 39
dictionary ['dɪkʃnri] Wörterbuch **U4**, 63
to **die** [daɪ] sterben **U6**, 93
different ['dɪfrnt] anders, verschieden **U2**, 41
°**dinner** ['dɪnə] Abendessen **U3**, 50
to have dinner [hæv 'dɪnə] zu Abend essen **U3**, 50
⟨**dirty**⟩ ['dɜ:ti] schmutzig **EL**, 119
°*to **do** [du:] tun, machen **LS**, 21
⟨to do well⟩ [du: 'wel] gute Leistungen erbringen **EL**, 120
°**dog** [dɒg] Hund **LS**, 10
⟨**dog-tired**⟩ [ˌdɒg 'taɪəd] hundemüde **U3**, 57
°**door** [dɔ:] Tür **U1**, 27
double ['dʌbl] Doppel-, zweimal **LS**, 17
°**down** [daʊn] entlang; herunter, hinunter, nach unten **U2**, 39
downtown *(AE)* [ˌdaʊn'taʊn] im Stadtzentrum **U7**, 103
⟨**dragon**⟩ ['drægn] Drachen **EL**, 118
°*to **draw** [drɔ:] zeichnen **LS**, 15
drawer [drɔ:] Schublade **LS**, 14
*to **dream** [dri:m] träumen **U4**, 69
°**dress** [dres] Kleid **F2**, 49
drill [drɪl] Bohrer, Bohrmaschine **U7**, 107
electric drill [ɪ'lektrɪk ˌdrɪl] elektrische Bohrmaschine **U7**, 107
°**drink** [drɪŋk] Getränk **U3**, 57
°*to **drink** [drɪŋk] trinken **U6**, 90
*to **drive** [draɪv] fahren **U7**, 109
driver ['draɪvə] Fahrer(in) **U2**, 44
°**duck** [dʌk] Ente **U6**, 95

E

each [i:tʃ] jede(-r/-s) **U2**, 46
⟨**ear**⟩ [ɪə] Ohr **EL**, 119
early ['ɜ:li] früh **U3**, 51
to **earn** [ɜ:n] verdienen **U3**, 56
east [i:st] Osten **F3**, 72
°**easy** ['i:zi] einfach, leicht **LS**, 15
°*to **eat** [i:t] essen **U4**, 68
°**egg** [eg] Ei **U6**, 86
°**eight** [eɪt] acht **LS**, 9
°**eighteen** [eɪ'ti:n] achtzehn **F2**, 48
eighteenth [eɪ'ti:nθ] achtzehnte (-r/-s) **U4**, 62
eighth [eɪtθ] achte (-r/-s) **U4**, 62
eight-hundred-year-old [ˌeɪt hʌndrəd 'jɪər‿əʊld] achthundert Jahre alt **U5**, 75
°**eighty** ['eɪti] achtzig **U2**, 44
electric [ɪ'lektrɪk] elektrisch **U7**, 107
electric drill [ɪ'lektrɪk ˌdrɪl] elektrische Bohrmaschine **U7**, 107
°⟨**elephant**⟩ ['elɪfənt] Elefant **EL**, 115
°**eleven** [ɪ'levn] elf **LS**, 8
eleventh [ɪ'levnθ] elfte (-r/-s) **U4**, 62
else [els] andere(-r/-s) **U7**, 104
°**e-mail** ['i:meɪl] E-mail **U2**, 42
emergency [ɪ'mɜ:dʒntsi] Notfall, Notlage **U7**, 107
empty ['empti] leer **U1**, 28
end [end] Ende, Schluss **U3**, 51
ending ['endɪŋ] Ende, Schluss *(einer Geschichte)* **U4**, 69
engaged [ɪŋ'geɪdʒd] besetzt, belegt **U2**, 42
engine ['endʒɪn] Motor **U5**, 80
°**English** ['ɪŋglɪʃ] englisch; Englisch **LS**, 14
°What's … in English? [ˌwɒts … ɪn‿'ɪŋglɪʃ] Was heißt … auf Englisch? **LS**, 14
enough [ɪ'nʌf] genug, genügend **U6**, 90
er [ɜ:] äh **LS**, 16
especially [ɪ'speʃli] besonders, vor allem **F3**, 72
⟨Christmas **Eve**⟩ [ˌkrɪsməs‿'i:v] Heiligabend **EL**, 114
°**evening** ['i:vnɪŋ] Abend **U3**, 50
event [ɪ'vent] Ereignis **U7**, 105
every ['evri] jede(-r/-s) **LS**, 17
every day [ˌevri 'deɪ] jeden Tag **LS**, 17
everybody ['evribɒdi] jeder; alle **U4**, 68
⟨**everyone**⟩ ['evriwʌn] jeder **EL**, 115
everything ['evriθɪŋ] alles **LS**, 13
everywhere ['evriweə] überall **U6**, 95
to **examine** [ɪg'zæmɪn] untersuchen, kontrollieren **U6**, 92
example [ɪg'zɑ:mpl] Beispiel **LS**, 11
for example [fər‿ɪg'zɑ:mpl] zum Beispiel **U3**, 52
except [ɪk'sept] außer **U4**, 68
excited [ɪk'saɪtɪd] aufgeregt **U4**, 68
exciting [ɪk'saɪtɪŋ] spannend, aufregend **U7**, 106
°**Excuse me!** [ɪk'skju:z mi] Entschuldigung! Entschuldigen Sie! **U2**, 39
°**exercise** ['eksəsaɪz] Übung **LS**, 10
exercise book ['eksəsaɪz ˌbʊk] Übungsheft **LS**, 10
⟨to **expect**⟩ [ɪk'spekt] erwarten **EL**, 120
to **explain** [ɪk'spleɪn] erklären, erläutern **U6**, 92
⟨**extra**⟩ ['ekstrə] zusätzlich; Zusatz **EL**, 114
°**eye** [aɪ] Auge **LS**, 13

F

°**face** [feɪs] Gesicht **U3**, 56
to **faint** [feɪnt] ohnmächtig werden **U7**, 107
fair [feə] gerecht, fair **U1**, 34
falls *(pl.)* [fɔ:lz] Wasserfall **U7**, 101
*to **fall** (over) [fɔ:l‿'əʊvə] (hin)fallen; umfallen **U3**, 57
false [fɔ:ls] falsch **LS**, 21
°**family** ['fæmli] Familie **F1**, 24
⟨family tree⟩ ['fæmli tri:] Familienstammbaum **F1**, 24
fantastic [fæn'tæstɪk] fantastisch, großartig **U7**, 102
far [fɑ:] weit **U2**, 39
far more interesting [ˌfɑ: mɔ:r‿'ɪntrəstɪŋ] weitaus interessanter **U7**, 101
farm [fɑ:m] Farm, Bauernhof **U6**, 86

farmer ['fɑ:mə] Farmer, Landwirt(in) U7, 101
farmyard ['fɑ:mjɑ:d] Hof *(auf einem Bauernhof)* U6, 88
fast [fɑ:st] schnell LS, 12
°father ['fɑ:ðə] Vater F1, 24
⟨Father Christmas⟩ [ˌfɑ:ðə 'krɪsməs] Weihnachtsmann EL, 114
°favourite ['feɪvrɪt] Lieblings- LS, 17
⟨feather⟩ ['feðə] Feder EL, 120
°February ['februri] Februar U4, 62
°*to feed [fi:d] füttern U6, 86
*to feel [fi:l] (sich) fühlen U5, 76
to fetch [fetʃ] (ab)holen U2, 42
⟨few⟩ [fju:] einige EL, 120
field [fi:ld] Feld; Acker U6, 87
°fifteen [fɪf'ti:n] fünfzehn F2, 48
fifteenth [fɪf'ti:nθ] fünftzehnte (-r/-s) U4, 62
fifth [fɪfθ] fünfte (-r/-s) U4, 62
°fifty ['fɪfti] fünfzig U2, 44
*to fight [faɪt] streiten, kämpfen U1, 30
⟨finally⟩ ['faɪnli] letztlich, zuletzt EL, 118
*to find [faɪnd] finden LS, 14
Find the odd word out! [ˌɒd wɜ:d‿'aʊt] Finde das Wort, das nicht in die Gruppe passt! *(Wortschatzübung)* U1, 30
°fine [faɪn] gut, in Ordnung; schön LS, 12
°I'm fine. [aɪm 'faɪn] Mir geht es gut. LS, 12
°finger ['fɪŋgə] Finger U7, 106
to finish ['fɪnɪʃ] fertig machen; aufhören U3, 52
⟨fire⟩ [faɪə] Feuer EL, 118
first [fɜ:st] erste(-r/-s); zuerst U3, 58
°fish and chips [ˌfɪʃ‿n‿'tʃɪps] Fisch und Pommes frites U7, 103
°five [faɪv] fünf LS, 9
flag [flæg] Flagge U7, 100
°flat [flæt] Wohnung U1, 27
flight [flaɪt] Flug U7, 103
°floor [flɔ:] Fußboden; Stockwerk LS, 14
°*to fly [flaɪ] fliegen U3, 54
to fly on [flaɪ‿'ɒn] weiterfliegen U7, 102
focus ['fəʊkəs] Blickpunkt F1, 24
°folder ['fəʊldə] Ordner, Mappe LS, 14
to follow ['fɒləʊ] hinterher gehen; (be)folgen U6, 92
°food [fu:d] Essen, Nahrung; Lebensmittel U4, 63
⟨fool⟩ [fu:l] Dummkopf, Narr EL, 116
°foot, *pl.* feet [fʊt; fi:t] Fuß, Füße LS, 14
°football ['fʊtbɔ:l] Fußball LS, 14
football magazine ['fʊtbɔ:l mægəˌzi:n] Fußballzeitschrift LS, 14
for [fɔ:; fə] für U1, 30
for example [fər‿ɪg'zɑ:mpl] zum Beispiel U3, 52
⟨for⟩ [fɔ:; fə] denn EL, 114
forest ['fɒrɪst] Wald U1, 27
*to forget [fə'get] vergessen F4, 98
°fork [fɔ:k] Gabel U1, 30
form [fɔ:m; fɔ:mz] Form LS, 12
°forty ['fɔ:ti] vierzig U2, 44
°four [fɔ:] vier LS, 9
°fourteen [fɔ:'ti:n] vierzehn F2, 48
fourteenth [fɔ:'ti:nθ] vierzehnte (-r/-s) U4, 62
fourth [fɔ:θ] vierte (-r/-s) U4, 62
⟨Franconian⟩ [fræŋ'kəʊniən] fränkisch F4, 99
free [fri:] frei U3, 50
French [frentʃ] französisch; Französisch F4, 99
fresh [freʃ] frisch U6, 86
°Friday ['fraɪdeɪ] Freitag U1, 30
°friend [frend] Freund(in) LS, 10
fries *pl. (AE)* [fraɪz] Pommes frites U7, 104
*to be frightened (of) ['fraɪtnd] Angst haben (vor) U5, 80
frog [frɒg] Frosch U1, 32
from [frɒm; frəm] aus, von LS, 8
°Where are you from? [ˌweər‿ə jə 'frɒm] Woher kommst du/kommt ihr/ kommen Sie? LS, 9
°Where ... from? [ˌweə ... 'frɒm] Woher ...? LS, 9
in front of [ɪn 'frʌnt‿əv] vor, davor U2, 38
⟨fruit⟩ [fru:t] Obst, Frucht U4, 63
full [fʊl] voll U5, 75
⟨fun⟩ [fʌn] Spaß EL, 115
fun [fʌn] Freude, Spaß U2, 46
°funny ['fʌni] komisch, lustig LS, 18

G

°game [geɪm] Spiel LS, 15
gangster ['gæŋkstə] Gangster, Verbrecher U7, 106
°garage ['gærɑ:ʒ] Garage U1, 27
°garden ['gɑ:dn] Garten U1, 27
gate [geɪt] Tor, Pforte U6, 95
geography [dʒi'ɒgrəfi] Geographie, Erdkunde U7, 101
°German ['dʒɜ:mən] deutsch; Deutsche(r); Deutsch LS, 16
gerund ['dʒernd] Gerundium U7, 105
*to get [get] (be)kommen U1, 32
to get into [get‿'ɪntə] in etwas hineingelangen U1, 32
to get lost [get 'lɒst] verloren gehen, sich verirren U3, 56
⟨to get married⟩ [get 'mærid] heiraten EL, 119
to get off (the bus) [get‿'ɒf] aussteigen (aus dem Bus) U2, 44
to get on (the bus) [get‿'ɒn] einsteigen (in den Bus) U2, 44
°to get up [get‿'ʌp] aufstehen U3, 52
to get wet [get 'wet] nass werden U2, 42
°girl [gɜ:l] Mädchen LS, 12
°*to give [gɪv] geben; schenken U4, 64
to give somebody the bumps [ˌgɪv ðə 'bʌmps] jemanden hochwerfen und wieder auffangen U4, 63
to give up [gɪv‿'ʌp] aufgeben U5, 81
°glass [glɑ:s] Glas U1, 30
glasses *pl.* ['glɑ:sɪz] Brille U4, 69
gm (= gram) [græm] Gramm U4, 63
°*to go [gəʊ] gehen LS, 10
Let's go! [lets 'gəʊ] Lass(t) uns gehen! LS, 10
⟨to go down to⟩ [gəʊ 'daʊn tə] hinuntergehen zu, gehen nach EL, 121
to go for a walk [ˌgəʊ fər‿ə 'wɔ:k] spazieren gehen U3, 50
°to go on [gəʊ‿'ɒn] weitermachen, weiterführen U2, 45
to go shopping [ˌgəʊ 'ʃɒpɪŋ] einkaufen gehen U2, 38
to go to sleep [gəʊ tə 'sli:p] einschlafen U3, 57
°good [gʊd] gut LS, 16
⟨good tidings⟩ [gʊd 'taɪdɪŋz] frohe Botschaft EL, 114
to be good at ['gʊd‿ət] gut sein in LS, 16
°Goodbye! [gʊd'baɪ] Auf Wiedersehen! LS, 15
°*to have (got) [hæv 'gɒt] besitzen, haben U1, 28
to grab [græb] greifen; schnappen U4, 68
⟨grade *(AE)*⟩ [greɪd] Klasse EL, 120
grammar ['græmə] Grammatik U2, 42
°grandma ['grændmɑ:] Oma F1, 24
°grandpa ['grændpɑ:] Opa F1, 24
°great [greɪt] großartig, toll LS, 12
°green [gri:n] grün LS, 13
⟨to greet⟩ [gri:t] (be)grüßen EL, 121
°grey [greɪ] grau LS, 13
group [gru:p] Klasse; Gruppe LS, 10
tutor group ['tju:tə ˌgru:p] Klasse *(in einer englischen Schule)* LS, 10
°*to grow [grəʊ] anbauen; wachsen U7, 101
to guess [ges] raten, vermuten U4, 65
⟨Guess what?⟩ [ges 'wɒt] Weißt du was? Rate mal, was passiert ist. EL, 120
guitar [gɪ'tɑ:] Gitarre U2, 40
gun [gʌn] Schusswaffe U7, 106

H

⟨hair⟩ [heə] Haar(e) EL, 119
⟨half, *pl.* halves⟩ [hɑ:f; hɑ:vz] die Hälfte EL, 121
half past (two) ['hɑ:f pɑ:st] halb (drei) U3, 51
hall [hɔ:l] Flur, Diele, Korridor U1, 27
⟨hamburger⟩ ['hæmbɜ:gə] Hamburger EL, 115
°hamster ['hæmstə] Hamster F2, 48
°hand [hænd] Hand LS, 19
to happen ['hæpn] geschehen, passieren U3, 54
°happy ['hæpi] glücklich U4, 62
harbour ['hɑ:bə] Hafen U5, 75
°to hate [heɪt] hassen, nicht mögen U3, 52
°*to have (got) [hæv 'gɒt] besitzen, haben U1, 28
to have a race [ˌhæv‿ə 'reɪs] ein Rennen veranstalten U2, 44
to have dinner [hæv 'dɪnə] zu Abend essen U3, 50
⟨to have to⟩ ['hæv tə] müssen EL, 120
°he [hi:] er LS, 10
⟨he'll⟩ [hi:l] er wird EL, 116
°head [hed] Kopf F3, 73
heading ['hedɪŋ] Überschrift U6, 94
*to hear [hɪə] hören U2, 42
⟨hear us rap⟩ [ˌhɪər‿ʌs 'ræp] Hör(t) uns rappen. LS, 17

heart [hɑ:t] Herz **F3**, 73
°**helicopter** ['helɪˌkɒptə] Helikopter, Hubschrauber **U7**, 105
°**Hello!** [hə'ləʊ] Hallo **LS**, 8
to say hello [seɪ hə'ləʊ] Hallo sagen, sich begrüßen **U6**, 91
help [help] Hilfe, Rettung **U5**, 81
°to **help** [help] helfen **U2**, 43
helpless ['helpləs] hilflos **U5**, 80
°**her** [hɜ:] ihr(e); sie; ihr **LS**, 10
here [hɪə] hier **LS**, 10
°Here you are! [ˌhɪə ju:‿'ɑ:] Hier bitte! Bitteschön! **U2**, 44
Hey! [heɪ] He! **LS**, 10
Hi! [haɪ] Hi! Hallo! **LS**, 9
highest ['haɪɪst] (der, die, das) höchste; größte **U7**, 105
°**hill** [hɪl] Hügel **U3**, 54
him [hɪm] ihm; ihn **U2**, 42
°**his** [hɪz] sein(e) **LS**, 10
*to **hit** [hɪt] schlagen; treffen; *hier*: gegen etwas fahren **U3**, 54
°**holiday** ['hɒlədeɪ] Urlaub, Feiertag **U6**, 86
°**home** [həʊm] Heim; nach Hause **U1**, 32
°at home [ət 'həʊm] zu Hause **U3**, 53
°**homework** ['həʊmwɜ:k] Hausaufgaben **LS**, 20
to **hope** [həʊp] hoffen **U7**, 102
°**horse** [hɔ:s] Pferd **U1**, 28
white horses [waɪt 'hɔ:sɪz] *hier*: Schaumkronen **U5**, 80
°**hot** [hɒt] heiß **U5**, 76
opening **hours** ['əʊpnɪŋ‿ˌaʊəz] Öffnungszeiten **U3**, 51
°**house** [haʊs] Haus **LS**, 12
°**how** [haʊ] wie **LS**, 9
How about ...? ['haʊ‿əˌbaʊt] Wie ist es mit ...? **U7**, 104
°How are you? [ˌhaʊ‿'ɑ: ju:] Wie geht es dir/euch/Ihnen? **LS**, 12
°how many [haʊ 'meni] wie viele **U1**, 33
°How much is/are ...? [ˌhaʊ 'mʌtʃ‿ɪz/ɑ:] Wie viel kostet/kosten ...? **F2**, 49
°How old are you? [haʊ‿'əʊld‿ə ju:] Wie alt bist du/sind Sie? **LS**, 9
⟨How to write ...⟩ [ˌhaʊ tə 'raɪt] Wie man ... schreibt. **U3**, 58
huge [hju:dʒ] riesig, gewaltig **U4**, 69
Huh? [hʌ; hə] Was? Hä? **U2**, 45
°a **hundred** [ə'hʌndrəd] hundert **U2**, 44
°**hungry** ['hʌŋgri] hungrig **U4**, 68
*to be **hurt** [bi: 'hɜ:t] weh tun; verletzt sein **LS**, 12

I

°**I** [aɪ] ich **LS**, 8
°I'm fine. [aɪm 'faɪn] Mir geht es gut. **LS**, 12
°**ice** [aɪs] Eis **U3**, 52
°ice cream [aɪs 'kri:m] Eis, Eiscreme **U3**, 52
idea [aɪ'dɪə] Einfall, Idee; Ahnung **LS**, 21
No idea! [ˌnəʊ‿aɪ'dɪə] Keine Ahnung! **LS**, 21
if [ɪf] wenn, falls; ob **U4**, 66
⟨**ill**⟩ [ɪl] krank **EL**, 115
immediately [ɪ'mi:diətli] sofort, gleich **U7**, 106
important [ɪm'pɔ:tnt] wichtig; einflussreich **U6**, 94
°**in** [ɪn] in; rein, herein **LS**, 9
⟨in case of problems⟩ [ɪn ˌkeɪs‿əv 'prɒbləmz] für den Fall, dass es Probleme gibt **EL**, 121
in class [ɪŋ 'klɑ:s] in/vor der Klasse **U4**, 65
in front of [ɪn 'frʌnt‿əv] vor, davor **U2**, 38
Indian ['ɪndiən] indisch; Inder(in); indianisch; Indianer(in) **F1**, 25
information [ˌɪnfə'meɪʃn] Information(en) **U2**, 39
⟨**insect**⟩ ['ɪnsekt] Insekt **EL**, 121
inside [ɪn'saɪd] innen, drin; nach drinnen **U1**, 27
instrument ['ɪntstrəmənt] Instrument **U3**, 59
*to be **interested** in [bi‿'ɪntrəstɪd‿ɪn] interessiert sein an, sich interessieren für **U7**, 104
interesting ['ɪntrestɪŋ] interessant **U5**, 75
far more interesting [ˌfɑ: mɔ:r‿'ɪntrəstɪŋ] weitaus interessanter **U7**, 101
international [ˌɪntə'næʃnl] international **F1**, 25
°**Internet** ['ɪntənet] Internet **U5**, 74
interview ['ɪntəvju:] Interview; Befragung **U4**, 71
into ['ɪntu; 'ɪntə] in, hinein **U1**, 32
invitation [ˌɪnvɪ'teɪʃn] Einladung **U4**, 62
to **invite** [ɪn'vaɪt] einladen **U4**, 63
Irish ['aɪrɪʃ] irisch; Irisch **F4**, 98
irregular [ɪ'regjələ] unregelmäßig **U6**, 89
island ['aɪlənd] Insel **F3**, 73
°**it** [ɪt] es **LS**, 10
It's your turn. ['jɔ: tɜ:n] Du bist/Sie sind dran. **LS**, 10
Italian [ɪ'tæliən] italienisch; Italiener(in); Italienisch **F1**, 25
its [ɪts] sein(e); ihr(e) **LS**, 18

J

°**January** ['dʒænjuri] Januar **U4**, 62
°**jeans** *pl.* [dʒi:nz] Jeans **F2**, 49
jelly ['dʒeli] Wackelpudding, Gelee **U4**, 63
°**job** [dʒɒb] Arbeitsstelle, Job **U3**, 56
jogging ['dʒɒgɪŋ] Jogging **U7**, 104
⟨**joke**⟩ [dʒəʊk] Witz **EL**, 115
journalist ['dʒɜ:nlɪst] Journalist(in) **U7**, 108
⟨**juice**⟩ ['dʒu:s] Saft **U4**, 63
°**July** [dʒʊ'laɪ] Juli **U4**, 62
°to **jump** [dʒʌmp] springen **U5**, 81
⟨to jump up⟩ [dʒʌmp‿'ʌp] hochspringen **EL**, 119
°**June** [dʒu:n] Juni **U4**, 62
just [dʒʌst] gerade; nur **U2**, 40

K

keeper ['ki:pə] Wärter, Aufseher **U5**, 80
kid [kɪd] Kind; Kitz **U6**, 86
⟨**kin**⟩ [kɪn] Verwandtschaft, Familie **EL**, 114
⟨**kind**⟩ [kaɪnd] Art **EL**, 120
kindergarten ['kɪndəgɑ:tn] Kindergarten **U3**, 59
°**king** [kɪŋ] König **U4**, 66
°**kitchen** ['kɪtʃɪn] Küche **U1**, 27
⟨**knee**⟩ [ni:] Knie **LS**, 21
°**knife**, *pl.* **knives** [naɪf; naɪvz] Messer **U1**, 30
°*to **know** [nəʊ] wissen; kennen **U4**, 66

L

°**lady** ['leɪdi] Dame, Frau **U7**, 106
lamb [læm] Lamm, Lämmchen **U6**, 90
to **land** [lænd] landen **U7**, 106
landscape ['lændskeɪp] Landschaft **U7**, 101
lane [leɪn] Gasse; Fahrspur **U1**, 27
language ['læŋgwɪdʒ] Sprache **U1**, 28
⟨**large**⟩ [lɑ:dʒ] groß, riesig **EL**, 118
largest ['lɑ:dʒɪst] (der, die, das) größte **U7**, 100
last [lɑ:st] letzte(-r/-s) **U2**, 43
at last [ət 'lɑ:st] endlich **U5**, 81
late [leɪt] spät **U3**, 54
to be late [bi: 'leɪt] zu spät sein, zu spät kommen **LS**, 20
later ['leɪtə] später **U1**, 32
to **laugh** [lɑ:f] lachen **LS**, 18
⟨**layer**⟩ ['leɪə] Schicht, Lage **U4**, 63
lazy ['leɪzi] faul **U1**, 30
°*to **learn** [lɜ:n] lernen **U6**, 86
°**left** [left] links; linke(-r/-s) **LS**, 21
on somebody's right/left [ɒn ˌsʌmbədiz 'raɪt/'left] zur Rechten/zur Linken von jemandem **F1**, 24
°**leg** [leg] Bein **LS**, 21
°**lesson** ['lesn] Unterrichtsstunde, Schulstunde **LS**, 20
*to **let** [let] lassen **LS**, 8
Let's check! [lets 'tʃek] Lass(t) uns überprüfen. **LS**, 22
Let's go! [lets 'gəʊ] Lass(t) uns gehen! **LS**, 10
Let's start! [lets 'stɑ:t] Lass(t) uns anfangen! **LS**, 8
°**letter** ['letə] Buchstabe; Brief **U2**, 43
thank you letter ['θæŋk jʊ ˌletə] Dankschreiben **U4**, 63
⟨**library**⟩ ['laɪbrəri] Bücherei **EL**, 115
*to **lie** [laɪ; leɪ] liegen **U7**, 106
life, *pl.* **lives** [laɪf] Leben **U7**, 108
lighthouse ['laɪthaʊs] Leuchtturm **U5**, 80
°to **like** [laɪk] mögen, gern haben **LS**, 12
like (this/that) [laɪk 'ðɪs/ðæt] so wie (hier/dort) **LS**, 18
line [laɪn] Zeile; Linie **U1**, 33
list [lɪst] Liste **LS**, 14
°to **listen** (to) ['lɪsn] zuhören, (an)hören **LS**, 11
listening ['lɪsnɪŋ] Hören, *hier:* Hörübung **LS**, 11
°**little** [lɪtl] klein **U1**, 32
°to **live** [lɪv] wohnen, leben **U3**, 59

°**living** room ['lɪvɪŋ rʊm] Wohnzimmer U1, 27
lock [lɒk] (Fahrrad-)Schloss U1, 30
°**long** [lɒŋ] lang LS, 12
⟨a long way⟩ [lɒŋ 'weɪ] von weit her EL, 114
⟨no longer⟩ [nəʊ 'lɒŋgə] nicht länger EL, 119
no longer [nəʊ 'lɒŋgə] nicht mehr, nicht länger U7, 106
to **look** [lʊk] (aus)sehen; schauen LS, 10
to look after [lʊk‿'ɑ:ftə] aufpassen auf; hüten U3, 56
to look at ['lʊk‿ət] anschauen LS, 18
to look like ['lʊk laɪk] aussehen wie U7, 106
*to **lose** [lu:z] verlieren U2, 44
*to get **lost** [get 'lɒst] verloren gehen, sich verirren U3, 56
a **lot** of [ə 'lɒt‿əv] viele, eine Menge U5, 78
lots of ['lɒts‿əv] viel(e) U2, 38
you lot ['ju: ˌlɒt] ihr alle U7, 102
loud [laʊd] laut LS, 18
love [lʌv] Liebe; Herzliche Grüße *(am Briefende)* U3, 52
to **love** [lʌv] lieben, gern mögen U3, 52
lovely ['lʌvli] schön, hübsch; herrlich U4, 64
luck [lʌk] Glück U4, 63
*to be **lucky** ['lʌki] Glück haben U7, 107
°**lunch** [lʌntʃ] Mittagessen U1, 30
lunchbox ['lʌntʃbɒks] Pausenbrotbehälter U1, 30

M

madam ['mædəm] Gnädige Frau *(Anrede)* F2, 49
Made in Britain [ˌmeɪd‿ɪn 'brɪtn] Hergestellt in Großbritannien U2, 46
magazine [mægə'zi:n] Zeitschrift, Magazin LS, 14
football magazine ['fʊtbɔ:l mægəˌzi:n] Fußballzeitschrift LS, 14
*to **make** [meɪk] machen, tun LS, 11
Made in Britain [ˌmeɪd‿ɪn 'brɪtn] Hergestellt in Großbritannien U2, 46
°**man**, *pl.* **men** [mæn; men] Mann U1, 27
°how **many** [haʊ 'meni] wie viele U1, 33
°**map** [mæp] Stadtplan, Landkarte U2, 39
mind map ['maɪnd mæp] Wörternetz *(eine Art Schaubild)* LS, 17
°**March** [mɑ:tʃ] März U4, 62
to **mark** [mɑ:k] markieren U1, 35
°**market** ['mɑ:kɪt] Markt U2, 38
*to be **married** to [bi: 'mærid tə] verheiratet sein mit F1, 24
⟨to get married⟩ [get 'mærid] heiraten EL, 119
⟨to **marry**⟩ ['mæri] heiraten EL, 118
mouse **mat** ['maʊs mæt] Mauspad U5, 78
match [mætʃ] Wettkampf; Spiel; Match U3, 53
to **match** [mætʃ] zusammenbringen, zusammenfügen LS, 18
Maths [mæθs] Mathematik LS, 16
°What's the **matter**? [ˌwɒts ðə 'mætə] Was ist los? Was hast du? U1, 32
°**May** [meɪ] Mai U4, 62
maybe ['meɪbi] vielleicht LS, 14
me [mi:] mich; mir LS, 13
*to **mean** [mi:n] bedeuten; meinen U4, 66
media *pl.* ['mi:diə] Medien U2, 40
*to **meet** [mi:t] (sich) treffen U3, 51
⟨**merry**⟩ ['meri] fröhlich EL, 114
⟨you're a **mess**⟩ [mes] du siehst total unordentlich aus EL, 119
message ['mesɪdʒ] Nachricht U7, 105
metre ['mi:tə] Meter U7, 106
middle ['mɪdl] Mitte; Mittel- U3, 57
mile [maɪl] Meile *(brit. Längenmaß)* U5, 81
°**milk** [mɪlk] Milch U6, 87
to **milk** [mɪlk] melken U6, 87
⟨**mince** pie⟩ [ˌmɪnts 'paɪ] gefülltes Weihnachtsgebäck EL, 114
mind map ['maɪnd mæp] Wörternetz *(eine Art Schaubild)* LS, 17
to **mind** [maɪnd] etwas dagegen haben U7, 104
minus ['maɪnəs] minus; weniger F2, 48
minute ['mɪnɪt] Minute U2, 40
⟨to **miss**⟩ [mɪs] verpassen EL, 121
What's missing? [ˌwɒts 'mɪsɪŋ] Was fehlt? LS, 11
⟨to **mix**⟩ [mɪks] mischen U4, 63
mixed bag [ˌmɪkst 'bæg] buntes Allerlei LS, 23
ml (= millilitre) ['mɪlɪli:tə] Milliliter U4, 63
mobile ['məʊbaɪl] Handy, Mobiltelefon U2, 42
⟨**Mom**⟩ [mɒm] Mama EL, 120
moment ['məʊmənt] Moment, Augenblick U6, 93
°**Monday** ['mʌndeɪ] Montag U3, 50
°**money** ['mʌni] Geld U2, 38
pocket money ['pɒkɪt ˌmʌni] Taschengeld U2, 40
monster ['mɒntstə] Monster LS, 9
°**month** [mʌnθ] Monat U4, 62
more [mɔ:] mehr U4, 63
⟨any more⟩ [ˌeni 'mɔ:] (nicht) mehr EL, 116
°**morning** ['mɔ:nɪŋ] Morgen; Vormittag LS, 21
°**mother** ['mʌðə] Mutter F1, 24
°**mountain** ['maʊntɪn] Berg U7, 100
°**mouse**, *pl.* **mice** [maʊs; maɪs] Maus U5, 78
mouse mat ['maʊs mæt] Mauspad U5, 78
to **move** [mu:v] (sich) bewegen U7, 107
⟨to move⟩ [mu:v] (sich) bewegen EL, 119
°**Mr** ['mɪstə] Herr *(Anrede)* LS, 16
°**Mrs** ['mɪsɪz] Frau *(Anrede)* LS, 16
much [mʌtʃ] viel U4, 63
°How much is/are ...? [ˌhaʊ 'mʌtʃ‿ɪz/ɑ:] Wieviel kostet/kosten ...? F2, 49
muesli ['mju:zli] Müsli U3, 56
mug [mʌg] Becher; Krug U5, 78
Mum [mʌm] Mama LS, 14
museum [mju:'zi:əm] Museum U5, 75
music ['mju:zɪk] Musik U2, 38
must [mʌst; məst] müssen U1, 28
°**my** [maɪ] mein(e) LS, 8
°My name is ... [maɪ 'neɪm‿ɪz] Ich heiße ... LS, 8
⟨**myna** bird⟩ ['maɪnə ˌbɜ:d] Hirtenstar, Beo EL, 120

N

°**name** [neɪm] Name LS, 8
°My name is ... [maɪ 'neɪm‿ɪz] Ich heiße ... LS, 8
°What's your name? [ˌwɒts jə 'neɪm] Wie heißt du/heißen Sie? LS, 9
⟨to **name**⟩ [neɪm] benennen EL, 120
national ['næʃnl] national, landesweit U7, 101
national park [ˌnæʃnl 'pɑ:k] Nationalpark, Naturpark U7, 101
near [nɪə] nahe, in der Nähe von U4, 64
°to **need** [ni:d] brauchen, benötigen U1, 30
negative ['negətɪv] negativ, verneint U6, 90
neighbour ['neɪbə] Nachbar(in) U1, 31
nervous ['nɜ:vəs] nervös, aufgeregt U7, 106
never ['nevə] nie, niemals U3, 52
new [nju:] neu LS, 9
⟨New Year⟩ [ˌnju: 'jɪə] Neujahr EL, 114
newspaper ['nju:sˌpeɪpə] Zeitung U7, 108
next [nekst] nächste(-r/-s) U4, 67
°**next to** ['nekst tə] neben LS, 14
nice [naɪs] nett LS, 10
°**night** [naɪt] Nacht U5, 80
⟨one night⟩ [wʌn 'naɪt] eines Abends EL, 120
°**nine** [naɪn] neun LS, 9
°**nineteen** [naɪn'ti:n] F2, 48
nineteenth [naɪn'ti:nθ] neunzehnte (-r/-s) U4, 62
°**ninety** ['naɪnti] neunzig U2, 44
ninth [naɪnθ] neunte (-r/-s) U4, 62
no [nəʊ] kein(e) LS, 21
No idea! [ˌnəʊ‿aɪ'dɪə] Keine Ahnung! LS, 21
no longer [nəʊ 'lɒŋgə] nicht mehr, nicht länger U7, 106
°**no** [nəʊ] nein LS, 12
noise [nɔɪz] Geräusch, Lärm U6, 92
noisy ['nɔɪzi] laut U4, 64
north [nɔ:θ] Norden F3, 72
°**nose** [nəʊz] Nase LS, 19
not [nɒt] nicht LS, 12
notes *pl.* [nəʊts] Notizen, Anmerkungen U6, 91
⟨**nothing**⟩ ['nʌθɪŋ] nichts EL, 116
°**November** [nəʊ'vembə] November U4, 62
now [naʊ] jetzt, nun LS, 20
°**number** ['nʌmbə] Zahl, Nummer LS, 11

O

°**o'clock** [ə'klɒk] Uhr *(Zeitangabe bei vollen Stunden)* U3, 50
°**October** [ɒk'təʊbə] Oktober U4, 62
odd [ɒd] seltsam, nicht passend U1, 30
Find the odd word out! [ˌɒd wɜ:d‿'aʊt] Finde das Wort, das nicht in die Gruppe passt! *(Wortschatzübung)* U1, 30

of [ɒv; əv] von **U1**, 27
of course [əv 'kɔ:s] natürlich, selbstverständlich **F1**, 25
off [ɒf] von ... weg/ab/herunter **U3**, 54
off to ['ɒf tə] auf nach **U7**, 100
Off to the USA! [ˌɒf tə ðə ˌju:es‿'eɪ] Auf in die USA! **U7**, 100
offer ['ɒfə] Angebot **F2**, 49
special offer [ˌspeʃl‿'ɒfə] Sonderangebot **F2**, 49
office ['ɒfɪs] Büro **U7**, 105
often ['ɒfn] oft **U3**, 52
oh [əʊ] oh; null **LS**, 11
°Oh dear! ['əʊ ˌdɪə] Oje! **LS**, 14
°**OK** [əʊ'keɪ] OK **LS**, 12
°**old** [əʊld] alt **LS**, 9
°How old are you? [haʊ‿'əʊld‿ə ˌju:] Wie alt bist du/sind Sie? **LS**, 9
omelette ['ɒmlət] Omelett **U6**, 89
*to be **on** [ɒn] im Gange sein, laufen **U2**, 44
°**on** [ɒn] auf **LS**, 14
on business [ɒn 'bɪznɪs] geschäftlich **U7**, 102
on somebody's right/left [ɒn ˌsʌmbədiz 'raɪt/'left] zur Rechten/zur Linken von jemandem **F1**, 24
⟨on top⟩ [ɒn 'tɒp] oben; obendrauf **U4**, 63
once [wʌnts] einmal; einst **U6**, 93
at once [ət 'wʌnts] sofort, plötzlich **U3**, 56
°**one** [wʌn] eins; ein(e) **LS**, 9
⟨one night⟩ [wʌn 'naɪt] eines Abends **EL**, 120
onion ['ʌnjən] Zwiebel **U7**, 104
only ['əʊnli] nur; erst; bloß **LS**, 23
Oops! [u:ps] Hoppla! Huch! **U2**, 45
°to **open** ['əʊpn] öffnen, aufmachen **LS**, 19
open ['əʊpn] offen; geöffnet **U3**, 51
opening hours ['əʊpnɪŋ‿ˌaʊəz] Öffnungszeiten **U3**, 51
or [ɔ:] oder **LS**, 14
°**orange** ['ɒrɪndʒ] orange **LS**, 13
⟨to **order**⟩ ['ɔ:də] bestellen **EL**, 116
other ['ʌðə] anders; andere(-r/-s) **U2**, 44
otherwise ['ʌðəwaɪz] sonst **U4**, 66
°**our** ['aʊə] unser(e) **LS**, 12
out [aʊt] raus, (nach) draußen **LS**, 19
out of ['aʊt‿əv] aus ... heraus **U3**, 54
outside [aʊt'saɪd] (nach) (dr)außen; außerhalb **U1**, 27
over ['əʊvə] (hin)über **U6**, 88
⟨over and over again⟩ [ˌəʊvər‿ənd ˌəʊvər‿ə'gen] immer wieder **EL**, 121
over there [ˌəʊvə 'ðeə] da drüben **LS**, 12
Ow! [aʊ] Autsch! **LS**, 10
(my) **own** [əʊn] (mein) eigen(-e/-r/-s) **U1**, 27

P

⟨**pack**⟩ [pæk] Päckchen **EL**, 116
⟨**packet**⟩ ['pækɪt] Päckchen; Paket **U4**, 63
page [peɪdʒ] Seite **LS**, 21
pair [peə] Paar **LS**, 15
a pair of [ə 'peər‿əv] ein Paar **F2**, 49
⟨**pantomime**⟩ ['pæntəmaɪm] Weihnachtsmärchen **EL**, 114
⟨**paper**⟩ ['peɪpə] Papier **EL**, 118
⟨paper bag⟩ [ˌpeɪpə 'bæg] Papiertüte **EL**, 118
⟨paper bag princess⟩ ['peɪpə ˌbæg prɪn'ses] *hier*: Lumpenprinzessin **EL**, 118
°**parents** *pl.* ['peərənts] Eltern **F1**, 25
°**park** [pɑ:k] Park **U1**, 27
national park [ˌnæʃnl 'pɑ:k] Nationalpark, Naturpark **U7**, 101
⟨**Parlez-vous francais?**⟩ [pɑ:leɪˌ vu: 'frɒŋseɪ] *frz.*: Sprechen Sie Französisch? **EL**, 121
part [pɑ:t] Teil **F3**, 72
partner ['pɑ:tnə] Partner(in) **U2**, 39
party ['pɑ:ti] Party, Feier **U4**, 63
past [pɑ:st] Vergangenheit **U6**, 89
past [pɑ:st] vorbei, vorüber **U2**, 45
°⟨**peach**⟩ [pi:tʃ] Pfirsich **U4**, 63
°**pen** [pen] Füller **LS**, 14
°**pencil** ['pentsl] Bleistift; Buntstift **LS**, 14
°pencil case ['pentsl ˌkeɪs] Federmäppchen **LS**, 14
°**penny**, *pl.* **pence** [peni; pents] Pence (*brit. Währungseinheit*) **F2**, 49
people ['pi:pl] Leute, Menschen **U2**, 38
⟨**permission**⟩ [pə'mɪʃn] Erlaubnis, Genehmigung **EL**, 121
person ['pɜ:sn] Person **F1**, 24
°**pet** [pet] Haustier; Liebling **U3**, 56
⟨**pet** store⟩ ['pet stɔ:] Zoohandlung **EL**, 120
to **phone** [fəʊn] telefonieren **U2**, 42
photo ['fəʊtəʊ] Foto, Fotografie **U7**, 106
to take photos [teɪk 'fəʊtəʊz] fotografieren, Fotos machen **U7**, 106
phrase [freɪz] Redewendung, Ausdruck **U2**, 39
to **pick up** [pɪk‿'ʌp] aufheben; abholen **U3**, 54
picnic ['pɪknɪk] Picknick **U3**, 57
°**picture** ['pɪktʃə] Bild **LS**, 15
⟨**mince pie**⟩ [ˌmɪnts 'paɪ] gefülltes Weihnachtsgebäck **EL**, 114
°**pig** [pɪg] Schwein **U6**, 86
pigsty ['pɪgstaɪ] Schweinestall **U6**, 86
pilot ['paɪlət] Pilot(in) **U7**, 106
°**pink** [pɪŋk] pink, rosa **LS**, 13
place [pleɪs] Platz, Stelle, Ort **F1**, 24
plan [plæn] Plan **U1**, 27
°**plane** [pleɪn] Flugzeug **U2**, 38
⟨**plant**⟩ [plɑ:nt] Pflanze **EL**, 121
°**plate** [pleɪt] Teller **U1**, 30
play [pleɪ] Spiel, Theaterstück **LS**, 13
role play ['rəʊl pleɪ] Rollenspiel **LS**, 13
°to **play** [pleɪ] spielen **LS**, 15
°**player** ['pleɪə] Spieler, Mitspieler **U4**, 66
CD player [ˌsi:'di: ˌpleɪə] CD-Spieler **U1**, 28
°**playground** ['pleɪgraʊnd] Schulhof, Pausenhof **LS**, 16
°**please** [pli:z] bitte **LS**, 20
plural ['plʊərl] Plural, Mehrzahl **U1**, 31
plus [plʌs] plus **F2**, 48
pm [ˌpi:'em] nachmittags (*Uhrzeit*) **U3**, 51
pocket ['pɒkɪt] Hosen- oder Jackentasche **U2**, 40
pocket money ['pɒkɪt ˌmʌni] Taschengeld **U2**, 40
poem ['pəʊɪm] Gedicht **U2**, 38
⟨**poetry**⟩ ['pəʊətri] Lyrik **EL**, 116
point [pɔɪnt] Punkt **LS**, 21
2.45 (point) ['tu: pɔɪnt ˌfɔ: 'faɪv] Komma (*bei Zahlenangaben*) **U7**, 106
police [pə'li:s] Polizei **U7**, 107
pony ['pəʊni] Pony **F2**, 48
Pooh! [pu:] Pfui! Bäh! **U6**, 86
swimming **pool** ['swɪmɪŋ ˌpu:l] Schwimmbecken; Schwimmbad **U1**, 27
poor [pɔ:; pʊə] arm **U2**, 45
pop star ['pɒp stɑ:] Popstar **U3**, 59
port [pɔ:t] Hafen **F3**, 72
post [pəʊst] Post **U6**, 88
postcard ['pəʊstkɑ:d] Postkarte **U6**, 88
°**poster** ['pəʊstə] Poster **U1**, 28
°**pound** [paʊnd] Pfund (*brit. Währungseinheit*) **F2**, 49
power ['paʊə] Kraft, Stärke, Macht **LS**, 17
Word power ['wɜ:d ˌpaʊə] *Besondere Wortschatzübung* **LS**, 17
practice ['præktɪs] Übung **LS**, 11
sound practice ['saʊnd ˌpræktɪs] *Hör-/Ausspracheübung* **LS**, 11
°**present** ['preznt] Gegenwart, Präsens **U3**, 55; Geschenk **U4**, 63
⟨to **present**⟩ [prɪ'zent] präsentieren **EL**, 121
°⟨**prince**⟩ [prɪnts] Prinz **EL**, 118
°⟨**princess**⟩ [prɪn'ses] Prinzessin **EL**, 118
⟨paper bag princess⟩ ['peɪpə ˌbæg prɪn'ses] *hier*: Lumpenprinzessin **EL**, 118
problem ['prɒbləm] Problem, Schwierigkeit **U6**, 92
⟨in case of problems⟩ [ɪn ˌkeɪs‿əv 'prɒbləmz] für den Fall, dass es Probleme gibt **EL**, 121
promise ['prɒmɪs] Versprechen **U6**, 88
⟨Christmas **pudding**⟩ [ˌkrɪsməs 'pʊdɪŋ] *brit. Weihnachtssüßspeise* **EL**, 114
⟨to **pull**⟩ [pʊl] ziehen **EL**, 114
⟨to pull⟩ [pʊl] ziehen **EL**, 121
pump [pʌmp] Pumpe, Luftpumpe **U1**, 30
°**pupil** ['pju:pl] Schüler(in) **U3**, 52
purple ['pɜ:pl] lila, violett **LS**, 13
⟨to **push**⟩ [pʊʃ] schieben, drücken **EL**, 121
°*to **put** [pʊt] setzen, stellen, legen **LS**, 21
to put in [pʊt‿'ɪn] einsetzen **LS**, 12
puzzle ['pʌzl] Rätsel; Puzzle **F1**, 24

Q

quarter past/to ['kwɔ:tə pɑ:st/tə] Viertel nach/vor **U3**, 51
question ['kwestʃn] Frage **LS**, 16
quiet ['kwaɪət] leise **LS**, 20
quite [kwaɪt] ziemlich; ganz, völlig **U4**, 64
quiz [kwɪz] Quiz, Rätsel **F3**, 73

R

°**rabbit** ['ræbɪt] Kaninchen F2, 48
race [reɪs] Wettlauf, Rennen U2, 44
to have a race [ˌhæv_ə 'reɪs] ein Rennen veranstalten U2, 44
racket ['rækɪt] Schläger U1, 28
radio ['reɪdiəʊ] Radio U4, 69
°**rain** [reɪn] Regen U2, 42
°to **rain** [reɪn] regnen U2, 42
°⟨**rainbow**⟩ ['reɪnbəʊ] Regenbogen LS, 13
rap [ræp] Rap LS, 17
⟨hear us **rap**⟩ [ˌhɪər_ʌs 'ræp] Hör(t) uns rappen. LS, 17
⟨**raspberry**⟩ ['rɑ:zbəri] Himbeere U4, 63
°*to **read** [ri:d] lesen U2, 39
ready ['redi] fertig, bereit LS, 20
⟨**real**⟩ [rɪəl] richtig, echt EL, 119
really ['rɪəli] wirklich LS, 12
⟨**reason**⟩ ['ri:zn] Grund EL, 116
°**red** [red] rot LS, 13
regular ['regjələ] regelmäßig; gleichmäßig U6, 86
relative ['relətɪv] Verwandte(r) U4, 63
to **relax** [rɪ'læks] sich entspannen, sich ausruhen U7, 106
to **remember** [rɪ'membə] sich erinnern (an); sich merken U4, 65
⟨to **repeat**⟩ [rɪ'pi:t] wiederholen EL, 116
⟨they are **repeated**⟩ [ɑ: rɪ'pi:tɪd] sie werden wiederholt EL, 116
rest [rest] Rest F3, 72
restaurant ['restərənt] Restaurant, Gaststätte U4, 63
⟨**rhyme**⟩ [raɪm] Reim EL, 116
⟨to **rhyme**⟩ [raɪm] (sich) reimen EL, 116
⟨**rhyming**⟩ ['raɪmɪŋ] Reim- EL, 116
⟨**rhythm**⟩ ['rɪðm] Rhythmus EL, 116
rich [rɪtʃ] reich U7, 102
⟨**riddle**⟩ ['rɪdl] Rätsel EL, 115
°*to **ride** [raɪd] fahren; reiten U3, 50
°**right** [raɪt] rechts; rechte(-r/-s) LS, 21
right [raɪt] richtig, korrekt LS, 14
⟨all right⟩ [ɔ:l 'raɪt] in Ordnung; alles klar EL, 115
on somebody's right/left [ɒn ˌsʌmbədiz 'raɪt/'left] zur Rechten/zur Linken von jemandem F1, 24
right away [raɪt_ə'weɪ] sofort, gleich U6, 92
°**river** ['rɪvə] Fluss F3, 72
°**road** [rəʊd] Straße U1, 27
⟨**roast**⟩ [rəʊst] gebraten EL, 115
⟨**robot**⟩ ['rəʊbɒt] Roboter EL, 121
rock [rɒk] Fels, Stein U5, 75
rodeo [rəʊ'deɪəʊ; 'rəʊdiəʊ] Rodeo U7, 100
role [rəʊl] Rolle LS, 13
role play ['rəʊl pleɪ] Rollenspiel LS, 13
°**roof** [ru:f] Dach U1, 27
°**room** [ru:m] Zimmer; Platz U1, 27
°living room ['lɪvɪŋ rʊm] Wohnzimmer U1, 27
°⟨**rose**⟩ [rəʊz] Rose EL, 116
round [raʊnd] um ... herum U4, 66
row [rəʊ] Sträßchen; Reihe U2, 39
to **row** [rəʊ] rudern U5, 81
°**rubber** ['rʌbə] Radiergummi LS, 14
rugby ['rʌgbi] Rugby F3, 72
rule [ru:l] Regel U1, 31
°**ruler** ['ru:lə] Lineal LS, 14
⟨**rump**⟩ [rʌmp] Hinterteil F3, 73
*to **run** [rʌn] rennen, laufen U2, 44
to **rush** [rʌʃ] sich beeilen U3, 54

S

°**sad** [sæd] traurig, schmerzlich U6, 93
safe [seɪf] sicher U5, 81
the **same** [seɪm] derselbe (die-/das-) U6, 86
sand [sænd] Sand U5, 75
°**sandwich** ['sændwɪdʒ] Sandwich, belegtes Brot U5, 76
°**Saturday** ['sætədeɪ] Samstag U3, 50
saucer ['sɔ:sə] Untertasse U1, 30
to **save** [seɪv] retten, bergen U5, 80
*to **say** [seɪ] sagen, sprechen LS, 11
to say hello [seɪ hə'ləʊ] Hallo sagen, sich begrüßen U6, 91
*to be **scared** [bi: 'skeəd] Angst haben, erschrocken sein U6, 86
scene [si:n] Szene; Schauplatz U5, 82
°⟨**school**⟩ [sku:l] *hier*: Schwarm EL, 115
school [sku:l] Schule LS, 10
school bag ['sku:l bæg] Schultasche LS, 14
scooter ['sku:tə] Roller U3, 54
to **scream** [skri:m] schreien, kreischen U4, 69
screen [skri:n] Bildschirm U7, 104
°**sea** [si:] Meer U5, 74
°**seal** [si:l] Seehund U5, 75
seaside ['si:saɪd] Küste, Meeresküste U5, 74
at the seaside [ət ðə 'si:saɪd] am Meer U5, 74
⟨**second**⟩ ['seknd] Sekunde EL, 119
second ['seknd] zweite(-r/-s) U4, 62
secret ['si:krət] Geheimnis U4, 66
°*to **see** [si:] sehen LS, 13
See you! ['si: ju:] Bis dann! Bis ... LS, 21
⟨whole **self**⟩ [ˌhəʊl 'self] *hier*: ganzer Körper LS, 21
*to **send** [send] schicken U7, 102
sentence ['sentənts] Satz LS, 11
°**September** [sep'tembə] September U4, 62
*to **set** the table [ˌset ðə 'teɪbl] den Tisch decken U1, 30
°**seven** [sevn] sieben LS, 9
°**seventeen** [ˌsevn'ti:n] siebzehn F2, 48
seventeenth [ˌsevn'ti:nθ] siebzehnte (-r/-s) U4, 62
seventh ['sevntθ] siebte (-r/-s) U4, 62
°**seventy** ['sevnti] siebzig U2, 44
°*to **shake** [ʃeɪk] schütteln U4, 69
⟨ to shake it all about⟩ [ˌʃeɪk_ɪt_ɔ:l_ə'baʊt] ihn *(den Arm)* herumschütteln LS, 21
°**she** [ʃi:] sie LS, 10
shed [ʃed] Schuppen, Stall U6, 87
°**sheep**, *pl.* **sheep** [ʃi:p] Schaf U6, 88
sheepdog ['ʃi:pdɒg] Hütehund; Schäferhund U6, 88
shelf, *pl.* **shelves** [ʃelf; ʃelvz] Regal, Regalbrett U1, 30
°*to **shine** [ʃaɪn] scheinen; glänzen U2, 45
°**ship** [ʃɪp] Schiff U5, 80
shirt [ʃɜ:t] Hemd F2, 49
°**shoe** [ʃu:] Schuh F2, 49
°**shop** [ʃɒp] Geschäft, Laden U1, 27
shop assistant ['ʃɒp_əˌsɪstnt] Verkäufer(in) F2, 49
shopping ['ʃɒpɪŋ] Einkaufen; Einkäufe U2, 38
shopping centre ['ʃɒpɪŋ ˌsentə] Einkaufszentrum U2, 38
to go shopping [ˌgəʊ 'ʃɒpɪŋ] einkaufen gehen U2, 38
°**short** [ʃɔ:t] kurz LS, 12
°**shoulder** ['ʃəʊldə] Schulter F3, 73
to **shout** [ʃaʊt] schreien, rufen U3, 54
°to **show** [ʃəʊ] zeigen U3, 54
⟨Show and Tell⟩ [ˌʃəʊ_ən 'tel] *Unterrichtsteil, in dem Schüler etwas mitbringen und vorstellen* EL, 121
Shsh! [ʃ] Pssst! U4, 66
°*to **shut** [ʃʌt] zumachen, schließen LS, 19
sightseeing ['saɪtsi:ɪŋ] Besichtigungstour U7, 105
silly ['sɪli] Dummkopf LS, 16
silly ['sɪli] dumm, doof, albern LS, 20
°*to **sing** [sɪŋ] singen LS, 13
to sing along [ˌsɪŋ_ə'lɒŋ] mitsingen LS, 13
sir [sɜ:] mein Herr *(Anrede)* F2, 49
°**sister** ['sɪstə] Schwester F1, 24
*to **sit** [sɪt] sitzen U2, 42
°to sit (down) [sɪt 'daʊn] sich (hin)setzen LS, 19
°**six** [sɪks] sechs LS, 9
°**sixteen** [ˌsɪk'sti:n] sechzehn F2, 48
sixteenth [ˌsɪk'sti:nθ] sechzehnte (-r/-s) U4, 62
sixth [sɪksθ] sechste (-r/-s) U4, 62
°**sixty** ['sɪksti] sechzig U2, 44
size [saɪz] Größe, Kleidergröße F2, 49
skateboard ['skeɪtbɔ:d] Skateboard U1, 28
skates *pl.* [skeɪts] Inlineskates, Rollschuhe, Schlittschuhe LS, 12
°**skating** ['skeɪtɪŋ] Inlineskate/ Schlittschuh fahren U4, 63
skiing ['ski:ɪŋ] Ski fahren F3, 72
skin [skɪn] Haut, Fell U6, 93
°**skirt** [skɜ:t] Rock F2, 49
°**sky** [skaɪ] Himmel U2, 45
skyscraper ['skaɪskreɪpə] Wolkenkratzer U7, 103
*to go to **sleep** [gəʊ tə 'sli:p] einschlafen U3, 57
*to **sleep** [sli:p] schlafen U3, 57
slow [sləʊ] langsam U5, 81
slowly ['sləʊli] langsam U7, 107
°**small** [smɔ:l] klein U3, 54
⟨**smart**⟩ [smɑ:t] schlau, klug EL, 121
⟨to **smash**⟩ [smæʃ] zerschlagen, zertrümmern EL, 118
smell [smel] Geruch, Gestank U6, 86
⟨*to **smell**⟩ [smel] riechen EL, 119
smile [smaɪl] Lächeln U6, 99
to **smile** [smaɪl] lächeln U4, 68
⟨to **smoke**⟩ [sməʊk] rauchen EL, 116
°**snake** [sneɪk] Schlange U1, 35
so [səʊ] so LS, 18

so [səʊ] also, deshalb **U4**, 64
so (that) ['səʊ ðət] damit; so dass **U3**, 56
⟨to **soak**⟩ [səʊk] tränken; durchweichen **U4**, 63
soap [səʊp] Seife **U5**, 78
soccer *(AE)* ['sɒkə] Fußball **U7**, 104
°**sock** [sɒk] Socke **F2**, 49
some [sʌm] einige; etwas **U3**, 53
⟨**some**⟩ [sʌm] *hier*: etwas davon **EL**, 114
somebody ['sʌmbədi] jemand **F1**, 24
something ['sʌmθɪŋ] etwas **U3**, 54
sometimes ['sʌmtaɪmz] manchmal **F1**, 25
°**song** [sɒŋ] Lied, Song **LS**, 12
soon [su:n] bald **U7**, 106
°**sorry** ['sɒri] Tut mir Leid, Entschuldigung **LS**, 20
sound [saʊnd] Ton, Geräusch **LS**, 11
sound practice ['saʊnd ˌpræktɪs] *Hör-/Ausspracheübung* **LS**, 11
⟨to **sound** (like)⟩ [saʊnd] sich anhören (wie) **EL**, 121
south [saʊθ] Süden **F3**, 72
souvenir [ˌsu:vn'ɪə] Souvenir, Andenken **U5**, 78
space [speɪs] Raum; Weltraum **U7**, 100
Spanish ['spænɪʃ] spanisch; Spanisch **F4**, 98
°*to **speak** [spi:k] sprechen **F4**, 98
special ['speʃl] besonders, speziell **F2**, 49
special offer [ˌspeʃl‿'ɒfə] Sonderangebot **F2**, 49
*to **spell** [spel] buchstabieren **LS**, 17
*to **spend** ['spend] ausgeben; verbringen **U2**, 38
⟨**spine**⟩ [spaɪn] Wirbelsäule **F3**, 73
splash [splæʃ] Spritzer, Planscher **U4**, 69
⟨**sponge** cake⟩ ['spʌndʒ ˌkeɪk] Rührkuchen, Biskuitboden **U4**, 63
°**spoon** [spu:n] Löffel **U1**, 30
°**sport** [spɔ:t] Sport **U7**, 105
square [skweə] Platz **U2**, 38
stable ['steɪbl] Stall **U6**, 87
°*to **stand** (up) [stænd‿'ʌp] (auf)stehen **LS**, 19
°**star** [stɑ:] Star; Stern **LS**, 17
pop star ['pɒp stɑ:] Popstar **U3**, 59
to **start** [stɑ:t] anfangen, starten **LS**, 8
Let's start! [lets 'stɑ:t] Lass(t) uns anfangen! **LS**, 8
state [steɪt] Staat, Land **U7**, 100
°**station** ['steɪʃn] Haltestelle, Bahnhof **U7**, 102
statue ['stætʃu:] Statue, Standbild **U2**, 38
to **stay** [steɪ] bleiben **U3**, 52
stereo ['steriəʊ] Stereoanlage **U1**, 28
still [stɪl] noch, immer noch **U4**, 68
⟨**stocking**⟩ ['stɒkɪŋ] Strumpf **EL**, 114
stone [stəʊn] Stein **U3**, 54
to **stop** [stɒp] aufhören; anhalten **U2**, 42
⟨**store**⟩ [stɔ:] Laden, Geschäft **EL**, 116
⟨pet store⟩ ['pet stɔ:] Zoohandlung **EL**, 120
storm [stɔ:m] Sturm **U5**, 80
°**story** ['stɔ:ri] Geschichte, Erzählung **U1**, 33
°**straight** [streɪt] gerade, geradewegs, direkt **U7**, 102
°**street** [stri:t] Straße **U2**, 39
⟨to **stress**⟩ [stres] betonen **EL**, 117
⟨**stressed**⟩ [strest] betont **EL**, 116
⟨to **stretch**⟩ [stretʃ] strecken; dehnen **LS**, 21
strong [strɒŋ] stark **U5**, 76
stupid ['stju:pɪd] dumm, blöd **U2**, 44
subject ['sʌbdʒɪkt] Schulfach; Thema **U3**, 52
suddenly ['sʌdnli] plötzlich, auf einmal **U3**, 54
⟨**sugar**⟩ ['ʃʊgə] Zucker **EL**, 116
suggestion [sə'dʒestʃn] Vorschlag, Anregung **U7**, 105
°**summer** ['sʌmə] Sommer **U7**, 102
°**sun** [sʌn] Sonne **U2**, 42
°**Sunday** ['sʌndeɪ] Sonntag **U1**, 32
°**sunny** ['sʌni] sonnig **U2**, 44
sunscreen ['sʌnskri:n] Sonnencreme **U5**, 76
°**supermarket** ['su:pəˌmɑ:kɪt] Supermarkt **U1**, 27
sure [ʃʊə; ʃɔ:] sicher **U1**, 30
surfing ['sɜ:fɪŋ] Wellenreiten, Surfen **F3**, 72
surprise [sə'praɪz] Überraschung **U4**, 69
*to be **surprised** [sə'praɪzd] überrascht sein **U6**, 87
°**sweatshirt** ['swetʃɜ:t] Sweatshirt **F2**, 49
sweets *pl.* [swi:ts] Süßigkeiten, Bonbons **U5**, 78
sweet [swi:t] süß **U4**, 63
°*to **swim** [swɪm] schwimmen **U5**, 75
°**swimming** ['swɪmɪŋ] Schwimmen **U4**, 63
swimming pool ['swɪmɪŋ ˌpu:l] Schwimmbecken; Schwimmbad **U1**, 27
⟨**syllable**⟩ ['sɪləbl] Silbe **EL**, 116
⟨**syrup**⟩ ['sɪrəp] Sirup **U4**, 63

T

2.45 (point) ['tu: pɔɪnt ˌfɔ: 'faɪv] Komma *(bei Zahlenangaben)* **U7**, 106
°**table** ['teɪbl] Tisch **F1**, 24
to set the table [ˌset ðə 'teɪbl] den Tisch decken **U1**, 30
°*to **take** [teɪk] (mit)nehmen; bringen **U1**, 32
to take off [teɪk‿'ɒf] abheben **U7**, 106
to take photos [teɪk 'fəʊtəʊz] fotografieren, Fotos machen **U7**, 106
to **talk** [tɔ:k] sprechen, reden **U1**, 27
°**tall** [tɔ:l] groß; hoch **F1**, 25
taxi ['tæksi] Taxi **U2**, 38
°**tea** [ti:] Tee; Abendessen **U1**, 32
*to **teach** [ti:tʃ] unterrichten, lehren **U3**, 56
°**teacher** ['ti:tʃə] Lehrer(in) **LS**, 14
team [ti:m] Gruppe, Team **LS**, 21
teatime ['ti:taɪm] Zeit für Nachmittagstee; Abendessen **U1**, 32
telephone ['telɪfəʊn] Telefon **LS**, 11
telescope ['telɪskəʊp] Teleskop; Fernrohr **U5**, 80
°**television** ['telɪvɪʒn] Fernsehen; Fernseher **U2**, 40
*to **tell** (somebody) [tel] (jemandem) sagen, mitteilen **U2**, 39
°**ten** [ten] zehn **LS**, 9
°**tennis** ['tenɪs] Tennis **U1**, 28
tense [tens] Zeit, Zeitform *(grammatisch)* **U5**, 82
tenth [tenθ] zehnte (-r/-s) **U4**, 62
terrible ['terəbl] schrecklich, furchtbar **LS**, 18
⟨**terrific**⟩ [tə'rɪfɪk] ausgezeichnet, hervorragend **EL**, 121
text [tekst] Text; Textnachricht (SMS) **LS**, 21
than [ðæn; ðən] als *(bei Vergleichen)* **F4**, 99
thank you letter ['θæŋk ju: ˌletə] Dankschreiben **U4**, 63
°Thank you very much! [ˌθæŋk ju: veri 'mʌtʃ] Vielen Dank! Herzlichen Dank! **LS**, 18
°**thanks** [θæŋks] danke **LS**, 12
°**that** [ðæt; ðət] dass **F3**, 72
that [ðæt] das; jenes **LS**, 10
⟨**that**⟩ [ðæt; ðət] die *(Relativpronomen)* **EL**, 117
the [ðə; ði] der, die *(auch pl.)*, das **LS**, 9
theatre ['θɪətə] Theater **U3**, 50
their [ðeə] ihr, ihre *(Plural)* **LS**, 12
them [ðem; ðəm] sie; ihnen **U2**, 39
then [ðen] dann **U2**, 44
there [ðeə] dort **LS**, 12
over there [ˌəʊvə 'ðeə] da drüben **LS**, 12
there are [ðeər‿'ɑ:] da sind; es gibt **LS**, 14
°there's [ðeəz] (= there is) da ist, es gibt **LS**, 14
these [ði:z] diese (hier) **LS**, 14
°**they** [ðeɪ] sie *(Plural)* **LS**, 12
⟨they are repeated⟩ [ɑ: rɪ'pi:tɪd] sie werden wiederholt **EL**, 116
°they're (= they are) sie sind **LS**, 12
thing [θɪŋ] Sache, Ding **LS**, 14
*to **think** (of) ['θɪŋk‿əv] denken (an) **U4**, 64
third [θɜ:d] dritte (-r/-s) **U4**, 62
°**thirteen** [θɜ:'ti:n] dreizehn **LS**, 23
thirteenth [θɜ:'ti:nθ] dreizehnte (-r/-s) **U4**, 62
°**thirty** ['θɜ:ti] dreißig **U2**, 44
°**this** [ðɪs] diese(-r/-s) **LS**, 10
those [ðəʊz] diese dort, jene **LS**, 14
°**three** [θri:] drei **LS**, 9
through [θru:] durch **U5**, 80
*to **throw** [θrəʊ] werfen **U3**, 56
°**Thursday** ['θɜ:zdeɪ] Donnerstag **U3**, 50
ticket ['tɪkɪt] Ticket, Fahrschein, Eintrittskarte **U2**, 38
⟨good **tidings**⟩ [gʊd 'taɪdɪŋz] frohe Botschaft **EL**, 114
tidy ['taɪdi] sauber, ordentlich **U1**, 28
°**time** [taɪm] Mal **U4**, 64; Zeit **U1**, 32
all the time [ˌɔ:l ðə 'taɪm] die ganze Zeit **U2**, 42
What time ...? [wɒt 'taɪm] Um wieviel Uhr ...? **U3**, 51
tin [tɪn] Dose, Büchse **U5**, 78
tip [tɪp] Tipp **U5**, 74
°**tired** ['taɪəd] müde **U3**, 57
title ['taɪtl] Titel, Überschrift **U6**, 92
to [tʊ; tə] bis **U3**, 51

to [tʊ; tə] nach; zu; in **LS**, 12
°**today** [tə'deɪ] heute **U1**, 30
together [tə'geðə] zusammen, miteinander **U1**, 30
°**tomorrow** [tə'mɒrəʊ] morgen **LS**, 21
ton [tʌn] Tonne (*Gewicht*) **U7**, 106
⟨**tonight**⟩ [tə'naɪt] heute Abend **EL**, 120
too [tu:] auch **LS**, 10
too [tu:] zu **LS**, 18
°**tooth**, *pl.* **teeth** [tu:θ; ti:θ] Zahn, Zähne **U4**, 68
⟨**on top**⟩ [ɒn 'tɒp] oben; obendrauf **U4**, 63
°to **touch** [tʌtʃ] berühren; antippen **LS**, 19
tour [tʊə] Tour, Fahrt, Reise **U7**, 106
tourist ['tʊərɪst] Tourist **U7**, 100
towards [tə'wɔ:dz] auf zu, darauf zu **U2**, 44
towel ['taʊəl] Handtuch **U5**, 76
°**town** [taʊn] Stadt **U2**, 38
tradition [trə'dɪʃn] Tradition **U4**, 63
°**train** [treɪn] Zug **U2**, 38
°**tree** [tri:] Baum **F1**, 24
⟨family tree⟩ ['fæmli tri:] Familienstammbaum **F1**, 24
tribe [traɪb] Stamm **U7**, 100
trick [trɪk] Trick; Streich **U1**, 32
to **trick** [trɪk] austricksen, täuschen **U6**, 93
trifle ['traɪfl] *englischer Nachtisch* **U4**, 63
trip [trɪp] Trip, Reise, Ausflug **U5**, 75
°**trousers** *pl.* ['traʊzəz] Hose **F2**, 49
true [tru:] wahr **LS**, 19
⟨**trunk**⟩ [trʌŋk] Rumpf **F3**, 73
to **try** (on) [traɪ‿'ɒn] (an)probieren; versuchen **F2**, 49
⟨**T-shirt**⟩ ['ti:ʃɜ:t] T-Shirt **EL**, 115
°**Tuesday** ['tju:zdeɪ] Dienstag **U3**, 50
turkey ['tɜ:ki] Truthahn **U6**, 86
It's your **turn.** ['jɔ: tɜ:n] Du bist/Sie sind dran. **LS**, 10
to **turn** [tɜ:n] einbiegen, abbiegen; drehen, wenden **U2**, 39
⟨to turn around⟩ [,tɜ:n‿ə'raʊnd] wenden; umdrehen **LS**, 21
tutor ['tju:tə] Klassenlehrer(in) **LS**, 10
tutor group ['tju:tə ,gru:p] Klasse (*in einer englischen Schule*) **LS**, 10
TV [ti:'vi:] Fernsehen; Fernseher **U2**, 40
to watch TV [,wɒtʃ ti:'vi:] fernsehen **U2**, 40
twelfth [twelfθ] zwölfte (-r/-s) **U4**, 62
°**twelve** [twelv] zwölf **LS**, 9
twentieth ['twentiɪθ] zwanzigste (-r/-s) **U4**, 62
°**twenty** ['twenti] zwanzig **U2**, 44
°**twenty-one** [,twenti'wʌn] einundzwanzig **U2**, 44
°**two** [tu:] zwei **LS**, 9
typical (of) ['tɪpɪkl] typisch (für) **U6**, 89

U

Ugh! [ɜ:] Igitt! (*Ausruf des Ekels*) **LS**, 16
°**uncle** ['ʌŋkl] Onkel **F1**, 24
°**under** ['ʌndə] unter **LS**, 14
°*to **understand** [,ʌndə'stænd] verstehen **F4**, 99
°**uniform** ['ju:nɪfɔ:m] Uniform **F2**, 49
unit ['ju:nɪt] Kapitel; Einheit **U1**, 26
until [ʌn'tɪl; n'tɪl] bis; erst wenn **U3**, 52
⟨**unusual**⟩ [ʌn'ju:ʒl] ungewöhnlich **EL**, 120
°**up** [ʌp] hoch, (hin)auf **LS**, 19
°**upstairs** [ʌp'steəz] (nach) oben, im Obergeschoss **U4**, 68
us [ʌs] wir; uns **LS**, 8
US [ju:'es] Vereinigte Staaten; US-amerikanisch **U7**, 100
to **use** [ju:z] benutzen, verwenden **U1**, 29
usually ['ju:ʒli] normalerweise, gewöhnlich **U3**, 51

V

°**vegetable** ['vedʒtəbl] Gemüse **U6**, 86
°**very** ['veri] sehr **LS**, 16
vet [vet] Tierarzt, Tierärztin **U6**, 92
video ['vɪdiəʊ] Video **U2**, 40
view [vju:] Aussicht, Sicht **F3**, 72
village ['vɪlɪdʒ] Dorf **U2**, 39
⟨**violet**⟩ ['vaɪələt] Veilchen **EL**, 116
to **visit** ['vɪzɪt] besuchen; besichtigen **U5**, 74
visitor ['vɪzɪtə] Besucher **U6**, 86
voice [vɔɪs] Stimme **U4**, 66

W

to **wait (for)** [weɪt] warten (auf) **U2**, 40
*to **wake** (somebody) up [weɪk‿'ʌp] (jemanden) aufwecken; aufwachen **U3**, 56
walk [wɔ:k] Spaziergang **U3**, 50
to go for a walk [,gəʊ fər‿ə 'wɔ:k] spazieren gehen **U3**, 50
to **walk** [wɔ:k] gehen, laufen **U2**, 44
°**wall** [wɔ:l] Wand; Mauer **U1**, 27
to **want** (to) ['wɒnt tə] wollen, mögen **U4**, 64
warm [wɔ:m] warm **U6**, 90
⟨**was going to marry**⟩ [wəz ,gəʊɪŋ tə 'mæri] wollte heiraten **EL**, 118
°to **wash** [wɒʃ] (sich) waschen; spülen **U3**, 56
°to **watch** [wɒtʃ] beobachten, (sich) ansehen **U2**, 40
to watch TV [,wɒtʃ ti:'vi:] fernsehen **U2**, 40
Watch out! [wɒtʃ‿'aʊt] Achtung! Pass(t) auf! **LS**, 17
water ['wɔ:tə] Wasser **U5**, 76
wave [weɪv] Welle **U5**, 80
to **wave** [weɪv] winken; schwenken **U3**, 54
way [weɪ] Weg; Art und Weise **U2**, 39
⟨a long way⟩ [lɒŋ 'weɪ] von weit her **EL**, 114
to be in a bad way [ɪn‿ə 'bæd ,weɪ] in schlechter Verfassung sein **U6**, 92
°**we** [wi:] wir **LS**, 12
°we're [wɪə] (= we are) wir sind **LS**, 12
⟨we won't go⟩ ['wəʊnt gəʊ] wir werden nicht gehen **EL**, 114
weak [wi:k] schwach **U6**, 93
°*to **wear** [weə] anhaben, tragen **U3**, 52
°**weather** ['weðə] Wetter **U5**, 75
°**Wednesday** ['wenzdeɪ] Mittwoch **U3**, 50
week [wi:k] Woche **U3**, 50
weekend ['wi:kend] Wochenende **U3**, 51
to **weigh** [weɪ] wiegen **U7**, 106
°**Welcome!** ['welkəm] Willkommen! **LS**, 12
°**well** [wel] gut **U4**, 64
⟨to do well⟩ [du: 'wel] gute Leistungen erbringen **EL**, 120
welly ['weli] Gummistiefel **U6**, 86
west [west] Westen **F3**, 72
°**wet** [wet] nass **U2**, 42
to get wet [get 'wet] nass werden **U2**, 42
°**what** [wɒt] was **LS**, 9
What about you? [,wɒt‿ə,baʊt 'ju:] Und dir/euch/Ihnen? Und du/ihr/Sie? **LS**, 12
°What colour is/are …? [,wɒt 'kʌlər‿ɪz/ɑ:] Welche Farbe hat/haben …? **LS**, 13
⟨what it's all about⟩ [,wɒt‿ɪts‿ɔ:l‿ə'baʊt] worum es geht **LS**, 21
°What's … in English? [,wɒts … ɪn‿'ɪŋglɪʃ] Was heißt … auf Englisch? **LS**, 14
What's missing? [,wɒts 'mɪsɪŋ] Was fehlt? **LS**, 11
°What's the matter? [,wɒts ðə 'mætə] Was ist los? Was hast du? **U1**, 32
°What's your name? [,wɒts jə 'neɪm] Wie heißt du/heißen Sie? **LS**, 9
What time …? [wɒt 'taɪm] Um wie viel Uhr …? **U3**, 51
wheat [wi:t] Weizen **U7**, 100
wheel [wi:l] Rad **F3**, 72
°**when** [wen] wann; als; wenn **U3**, 51
°**where** [weə] wo; wohin **LS**, 9
°Where are you from? [,weər‿ə jə 'frɒm] Woher kommst du/kommt ihr/kommen Sie? **LS**, 9
°Where … from? [,weə … 'frɒm] Woher …? **LS**, 9
which [wɪtʃ] welche(-r/-s) **U2**, 45
while [waɪl] während **U4**, 68
⟨**to whip**⟩ [wɪp] schlagen **U4**, 63
whisky ['wɪski] Whisky **F3**, 72
⟨**to whisper**⟩ ['wɪspə] flüstern **EL**, 119
°**white** [waɪt] weiß **LS**, 13
white horses [waɪt 'hɔ:sɪz] *hier*: Schaumkronen **U5**, 80
°**who** [hu:] wer **LS**, 16
who [hu:] wer, wen **U4**, 66
⟨**whole**⟩ [həʊl] ganz **EL**, 118
⟨whole self⟩ [,həʊl 'self] *hier*: ganzer Körper **LS**, 21
whose [hu:z] wessen **U4**, 66
why [waɪ] warum **U1**, 27
wide [waɪd] groß; breit; weit **U7**, 101
*to **win** [wɪn] gewinnen, siegen **U2**, 45
°**wind** ['wɪnd] Wind **U5**, 76
°**window** ['wɪndəʊ] Fenster **LS**, 21
⟨**wings** *pl.*⟩ [wɪŋz] Flügel **EL**, 115
⟨**to wish**⟩ [wɪʃ] wünschen **EL**, 114
with [wɪð] mit **LS**, 13
without [wɪð'aʊt] ohne **U3**, 52
°**woman**, *pl.* **women** ['wʊmən; 'wɪmɪn] Frau **F1**, 25
Woof! [wʊf] Wau! **LS**, 10
°**word** [wɜ:d] Wort **LS**, 15
Find the odd word out! [,ɒd wɜ:d‿'aʊt] Finde das Wort, das nicht in die Gruppe passt! (*Wortschatzübung*) **U1**, 30

Word power ['wɜ:d ˌpaʊə] *Besondere Wortschatzübung* **LS**, 17
work [wɜ:k] Arbeit **U4**, 66
to **work** [wɜ:k] arbeiten **U1**, 28
workman, *pl.* **workmen** ['wɜ:kmən] Handwerker **U7**, 107
world [wɜ:ld] Erde, Welt **F4**, 98
⟨**worm**⟩ [wɜ:m] Wurm **U7**, 104
*to be **worried** ['wʌrid] besorgt, beunruhigt **U6**, 92
to **worry** ['wʌri] (sich) Sorgen machen **U4**, 63
⟨**would like**⟩ [wʊd 'laɪk] würde/hätte gerne **EL**, 120
°**wow!** [waʊ] Wow! Toll! **LS**, 10
wreck [rek] Wrack **U5**, 80
°*to **write** [raɪt] schreiben **LS**, 10
°**wrong** [rɒŋ] falsch **F2**, 48

Y

yard [jɑ:d] Hof **U6**, 88
yeah [jeə] *umgangsspr.*: ja **U7**, 106
year [jɪə] Jahr; Jahrgang **U4**, 63
⟨New Year⟩ [ˌnju: 'jɪə] Neujahr **EL**, 114
°**yellow** ['jeləʊ] gelb **LS**, 13
°**yes** [jes] ja **LS**, 10
°**yesterday** ['jestədeɪ] gestern **U6**, 88
the day before yesterday [ðə ˌdeɪ bɪfɔ: 'jestədeɪ] vorgestern **U6**, 96
you [ju:; jə] du, ihr, Sie **LS**, 9
you [ju:; jə] man **U4**, 62
you lot ['ju: ˌlɒt] ihr alle **U7**, 102
⟨you're a mess⟩ [mes] du siehst total unordentlich aus **EL**, 119
°**young** [jʌŋ] jung **LS**, 20
your [jɔ:; jə] dein(e); euer/eure; Ihr(e) **LS**, 9
It's your turn. ['jɔ: tɜ:n] Du bist/Sie sind dran. **LS**, 10
⟨**yo-yo**⟩ ['jəʊjəʊ] Jo-Jo **EL**, 120
Yuk! [jʌk] Igitt! **U3**, 56
yummy ['jʌmi] lecker **U4**, 64
⟨Yummy!⟩ ['jʌmi] Lecker! **U4**, 63

Z

zoo [zu:] Zoo, **U3**, 51
⟨**Zulu**⟩ ['zu:lu:] Zulu **F4**, 99

Boys' names

Alan ['ælən] **U6**, 92
Anil [æ'ni:l] **F1**, 25
Arthur ['ɑ:θə] **F1**, 24
Balujee ['bɑ:luˌdʒi:] **F1**, 25
Brooklyn ['brʊklɪn] **U4**, 71
Colin ['kɒlɪn] **U1**, 26
Daniel ['dænjəl] **U1**, 19
David ['deɪvɪd] **LS**, 10
Eddy ['edi] **U1**, 26
⟨**Farley**⟩ ['fɑ:li] **EL**, 120
Frank [fræŋk] **U7**, 106
⟨**Fudge/Fudgie**⟩ [fʌdʒ; 'fʌdʒi] *Kosename* **EL**, 120
Hanif [hæ'ni:f] **F4**, 99
Jack [dʒæk] **F1**, 24
José [heʊ'zeɪ] **F4**, 98
Joshua ['dʒɒʃjuə] **F3**, 72
Lenny ['leni] **U6**, 88
Mark [mɑ:k] **U1**, 26
Paul [pɔ:l] **F1**, 24
⟨**Peter**⟩ [pi:tə] **EL**, 117
Rajiv [rə'dʒi:v] **F1**, 25
Robert ['rɒbət] **LS**, 9
Romeo ['rəʊmiəʊ] **U4**, 71
⟨**Ronald**⟩ ['rɒnld] **EL**, 118
Ryan ['raɪən] Ryan **F3**, 72
Sam [sæm] **U6**, 88
Tejinder [tə'dʒɪndə] **F1**, 25
Tom [tɒm] **U6**, 94
Tommy ['tɒmi] **U3**, 58

Girls' names

Anuja [æ'nu:dʒə] **F1**, 25
Becky ['beki] **LS**, 10
⟨**Elizabeth**⟩ [ɪ'lɪzəbəθ] **EL**, 118
Emily ['emɪli] **F3**, 72
Fiona [fi'əʊnə] **F3**, 72
Gemma ['dʒemə] **U6**, 86
Grace [greɪs] **U5**, 80
Helen ['helɪn] **F1**, 25
Jamila [dʒə'mi:lə] **F3**, 72
Janet ['dʒænɪt] **U1**, 26
Jenny ['dʒeni] **U1**, 26
Kim [kɪm] **U1**, 26
Lizzy ['lɪzi] **F1**, 24
Margaret ['mɑ:grət] **LS**, 16
Mary ['meəri] **U6**, 92
Mary-Beth [ˌmeəri 'beθ] **U7**, 102
Meg [meg] **U7**, 103
Noreen [nɒ'ri:n] **F4**, 98
Pat [pæt] **U1**, 26
Peggy ['pegi] **F1**, 24
Rita ['ri:tə] **F1**, 25
Rosa ['rəʊzə] **F1**, 25
Sarah ['seərə] Sarah **LS**, 8
Sue [su:] **F1**, 26
Vanessa [və'nesə] **F4**, 99
Victoria [vɪk'tɔ:riə] **U4**, 71

Surnames

Burton ['bɜ:tn] **LS**, 10
Cooper ['ku:pə] **LS**, 16
Croft [krɒft] Croft **LS**, 9
Dane [deɪn] Dane **LS**, 16
Dixon ['dɪksən] **LS**, 8
⟨**Green**⟩ [gri:n] **EL**, 121
Jones [dʒəʊnz] **F1**, 24
MacDonald [mək'dɒnld] **U6**, 95
Penrose ['penrəʊz] **LS**, 10
Pilewski [pɪ'levski] **U7**, 106
Potter ['pɒtə] **U6**, 94
Rudd [rʌd] **U6**, 89
Singh [sɪŋ] **F1**, 25
Smith [smɪθ] **U6**, 92
Wallace ['wɒlɪs] **U7**, 108
Wray [reɪ] **U6**, 87

Place names

Alaska [ə'læskə] **U7**, 100
America [ə'merɪkə] **F4**, 98
Arndale Road [ˌɑ:ndeɪl 'rəʊd] **U1**, 26
Arnot Hill Park [ˌɑ:nət hɪl 'pɑ:k] **U1**, 27
Australia ['ɒstreɪliə] **F4**, 99
Bamburgh ['bæmbrə] **U5**, 75
Beastmarket Hill [ˌbi:stmɑ:kɪt 'hɪl] **U2**, 39
Belfast [bel'fɑ:st] **F3**, 72
Berwick-upon-Tweed [ˌberɪk‿əpɒn 'twi:d] **U5**, 75
Big Harcar Rock [bɪg ˌhɑ:kə 'rɒk] **U5**, 81
Birmingham ['bɜ:mɪŋəm] **U6**, 86
Blackpool ['blækpu:l] **U7**, 103
Boston ['bɒstn] **U7**, 101
Broadway ['brɔ:dweɪ] **U7**, 105
California [ˌkælɪ'fɔ:niə] **F4**, 98
Cardiff ['kɑ:dɪf] **F3**, 72
Castle Road [ˌkɑ: sl 'rəʊd] **U2**, 39
Central Park [ˌsentrl 'pɑ:k] **U7**, 104
Chapel Bar [ˌtʃæpl 'bɑ:] **U2**, 39
Chinatown ['tʃaɪnətaʊn] **U7**, 106
Colorado [ˌkɒlr'ɑ:dəʊ] **U7**, 100
Cornwall ['kɔ:nwɔ:l] **F3**, 72
Delhi ['deli] **F4**, 99
Denver ['denvə] **U7**, 100
Devon ['devn] **U6**, 87
Dundee [dʌn'di:] **U5**, 80
Edinburgh ['edɪnbrə] **F3**, 72
Edwards Lane [ˌedwədz 'leɪn] **U1**, 27
°**England** ['ɪŋglənd] **U3**, 52
Everglades National Park [ˌevəgleɪdz ˌnæʃnl 'pɑ:k] **U7**, 101
Exchange Walk [ɪksˌtʃeɪndʒ 'wɔ:k] **U2**, 39
Farne Islands [fɑ:n‿'aɪləndz] **U5**, 74
Florida ['flɒrɪdə] **U7**, 101
France [frɑ:nts] **U7**, 106
Friar Lane [ˌfraɪə 'leɪn] **U2**, 39
Germany ['dʒɜ:məni] **U1**, 29
Grand Canyon [ˌgrænd 'kænjən] **U7**, 100
Haywood ['heɪwʊd] **LS**, 10
Heathrow [ˌhi:θ'rəʊ] **U7**, 109
Hudson River [ˌhʌdsn 'rɪvə] **U7**, 106
Hull [hʌl] **U5**, 80
India ['ɪndiə] **F1**, 25
Ireland ['aɪələnd] **F3**, 72
Johannesburg [dʒəʊ'hænɪsbɜ:g] **F4**, 99
King Street ['kɪŋ ˌstri:t] **U2**, 39
Larwood Grove [ˌlɑ:wʊd 'grəʊv] **U1**, 26
Leytonstone ['leɪtnstəʊn] **U4**, 71
Liverpool ['lɪvəpu:l] **U3**, 59
°**London** ['lʌndən] **LS**, 9
Long Row [ˌlɒŋ 'rəʊ] **U2**, 39
Los Angeles [lɒs‿'ændʒɪli:z] **U7**, 100
Madison Square Garden [ˌmædɪsn ˌskweə 'gɑ:dn] **U7**, 105
Maid Marian Way [ˌmeɪd ˌmæriən 'weɪ] **U2**, 39
Manchester ['mæntʃɪstə] **U6**, 86
Manhattan [mæn'hætn] **U7**, 106
Mansfield ['mænsfi:ld] **LS**, 9
Mansfield Road [ˌmænsfi:ld 'rəʊd] **U1**, 27
Market Square [ˌmɑ:kɪt 'skweə] **U2**, 39
Market Street ['mɑ:kɪt ˌstri:t] **U2**, 42
Mexico ['meksɪkəʊ] **F4**, 99
Mississippi River [ˌmɪsɪsɪpi 'rɪvə] **U7**, 100
Mount Street ['maʊnt ˌstri:t] **U2**, 39
Munich ['mju:nɪk] **U3**, 51
Nethercott ['neðəkət] **U6**, 86

Newcastle-upon-Tyne [ˌnjuːkɑːsl‿əpɒn ˈtaɪn] U5, 75
New York [ˌnjuː ˈjɔːk] U7, 100
New York City [ˌnjuː jɔːk ˈsɪti] U7, 104
Niagara Falls [naɪˌægrə ˈfɔːlz] U7, 109
Northern Ireland [ˌnɔːðn‿ˈaɪələnd] F3, 72
North Sea [ˌnɔːθ ˈsiː] U5, 76
Northumbria [nɔːˈθʌmbriə] U5, 74
Nottingham [ˈnɒtɪŋəm] LS, 8
Nottingham Road [ˌnɒtɪŋəm ˈrəʊd] U1, 27
Old Market Square [ˌəʊld ˌmɑːkɪt ˈskweə] U2, 38
Oxclose Lane [ˌɒkskləʊs ˈleɪn] U1, 27
Parliament Street [ˈpɑːləmənt ˌstriːt] U2, 39
Philadelphia [ˌfɪləˈdelfiə] U7, 101
Republic of Ireland [rɪˌpʌblɪk‿əv‿ˈaɪələnd] F3, 72
Rocky Mountains [ˌrɒki ˈmaʊntɪnz] U7, 100
San Diego [ˌsæn diˈeɪgəʊ] F4, 98
Scotland [ˈskɒtlənd] F3, 72
Seahouses [ˈsiːhaʊzɪz] U5, 74
Sherwood [ˈʃɜːwʊd] U1, 26
Sherwood Forest [ˌʃɜːwʊd ˈfɒrɪst] U1, 27
Smithy Row [ˌsmɪði ˈrəʊ] U2, 39
South Africa [ˌsaʊθ‿ˈæfrɪkə] F4, 99
South Parade [ˌsaʊθ pəˈreɪd] U2, 39
South Street Seaport [ˌsaʊθ striːt ˈsiːpɔːt] U7, 105
St Peter's Gate [snt ˈpiːtəz ˌgeɪt] U2, 39
Texas [ˈteksəs] U7, 102
the Thames [temz] F3, 72
Thoresby Park [ˌθɔːzbi ˈpɑːk] R2, 60
UK [juːˈkeɪ] F3, 72
United Kingdom [juːˌnaɪtɪd ˈkɪŋdəm] F3, 72
United States of America [juːˌnaɪtɪd ˈsteɪts‿əv‿əˈmerɪkə] U7, 100
the USA [ˌjuːesˈeɪ] USA U7, 100
Wales [weɪlz] F3, 72
Washington [ˈwɒʃɪŋtən] U7, 100
Washington, D.C. [ˌwɒʃɪŋtən ˌdiːˈsiː] U7, 101
Wheeler Gate [ˈwiːlə ˌgeɪt] U2, 39
Yorkshire [ˈjɔːkʃə] U6, 88

Other names

⟨Aladdin⟩ [əˈlædɪn] Aladin EL, 114
Bamburgh Castle [ˌbæmbrə ˈkɑːsl] U5, 75
Barker [ˈbɑːkə] LS, 10
Big Apple [ˌbɪg‿ˈæpl] U7, 104
Bluebell [ˈbluːbel] U6, 87
Burtons' Bike Shop [ˌbɜːtnz ˈbaɪk ʃɒp] U1, 30
City Information Centre [ˌsɪti‿ɪnfəˈmeɪʃn ˌsentə] U2, 39
David Beckham [ˌdeɪvɪd ˈbekəm] U4, 71
Day Rider Ticket [ˌdeɪ ˈraɪdə ˌtɪkɪt] U2, 38
Disney World [ˈdɪzni ˌwɜːld] U7, 109
Empire State Building [ˌempaɪə ˈsteɪt ˌbɪldɪŋ] U7, 105
Forfarshire [ˈfɔːfəʃə] U5, 80
Giants [ˈdʒaɪənts] U7, 104
Golden Gate Bridge [ˌgəʊldn ˌgeɪt ˈbrɪdʒ] U7, 101
Grace Darling [ˌgreɪs ˈdɑːlɪŋ] U5, 80
Grace Darling Museum [ˌgreɪs ˌdɑːlɪŋ mjuːˈziːəm] U5, 81
Greenfield Farm [ˌgriːnfiːld ˈfɑːm] U6, 91
Haywood School [ˌheɪwʊd ˈskuːl] LS, 10
Hillside Farm [ˌhɪlsaɪd ˈfɑːm] U6, 94
Hokey Cokey [ˌhəʊki ˈkəʊki] LS, 21
Information Centre [ɪnfəˈmeɪʃn ˌsentə] U2, 39
Jon Bon Jovi [ˌdʒɒn bɒn ˈdʒəʊvi] U7, 100
⟨Judy Blume⟩ [ˌdʒuːdi ˈbluːm] EL, 120
Kennedy Space Center [ˌkenədi ˈspeɪs ˌsentə] U7, 101
King Ethelred [kɪŋ‿ˈeθlred] *brit. Spiel* U4, 66
Lenny Kravitz [ˌleni ˈkrævɪts] U7, 108
London Eye [ˌlʌndən‿ˈaɪ] F3, 72
Longstone Lighthouse [ˌlɒŋstəʊn ˈlaɪthaʊs] U5, 80
Madonna [məˈdɒnə] U7, 100
Manchester United [ˌmæntʃɪstə juːˈnaɪtɪd] U7, 104
Martins Media [ˌmɑːtɪnz ˈmiːdiə] U2, 40
Monny [ˈmɒni] LS, 9
National Museum of the American Indian [ˌnæʃnl mjuːˈziːəm‿əv ði‿əˌmerɪkn‿ˈɪndiən] U7, 105
Robbie Williams [ˌrɒbi ˈwɪljəmz] LS, 17
Robin Hood [ˌrɒbɪn ˈhʊd] U2, 38
Rockefeller Center [ˌrɒkəfelə ˈsentə] U7, 105
Simon says [ˌsaɪmən ˈsez] LS, 19
Springfield Farm [ˌsprɪŋfiːld ˈfɑːm] U6, 88
Statue of Liberty [ˌstætʃuː‿əv ˈlɪbəti] U7, 105
St Peter's Church [snt ˌpiːtəz ˈtʃɜːtʃ] U2, 39
Tabby [ˈtæbi] LS, 10
The Bell Inn [ðə ˌbel‿ˈɪn] U2, 39
The Underdogs [ðɪ ˈʌndədɒgz] U1, 28
Victoria Shopping Centre [vɪkˌtɔːriə ˈʃɒpɪŋ ˌsentə] U2, 38

Bildquellen: US1: Getty Images (1–2); Mauritius/Fergusson (3)/Stock Image (4); VVS4: S. 3: Ernst Klett Verlag/Smith; S. 8: Profile Nottingham (1–3); Ernst Klett Verlag/Smith (4); S. 9: OKAPIA KG/Toshibata (1); Helga Lade Fotoagentur GmbH (2–3); Ernst Klett Verlag/Smith (4); S. 11: Helga Lade/Weiss (1); Ernst Klett Verlag/Smith (2–5); S. 12, S. 16, S. 17, S. 23: Ernst Klett Verlag/Smith; S. 25: Greenhill, London (1–4,7); Getty Images/PhotoDisc (5–6)/Stone (8); S. 26: Ernst Klett Verlag/Smith (1–6); M. Kunhar (7); Getty Images (8); S. 27: Ernst Klett Verlag/Smith; S. 38: Greenhill, London/Smith (1–2); Nottingham City Transport (3+5); Klett-Archiv/Smith (4); S. 39: MEV (1–4); S. 46: Corbis/ Bettmann; S. 48: MEV (1,6); Reinhard-Tierfoto (2); Angermayer/Reinhard (3); ZEFA (4); Getty Images/Photodisc (5); S. 49: Superbild/Zscharnack (1); MEV (2); Mauritius/Pöhlmann (3); Ernst Klett Verlag/Silberzahn (4); Mauritius/Kumicak (5); Mauritius/Ley (6); S. 50: Ernst Klett Verlag/ Smith (1–4); M. Kunhar (5); S. 51: Corbis/Beebe (1); Ernst Klett Verlag/ Smith (2); S. 52: Klett-Archiv; S. 59: Getty Images/Eye Wire; S. 63: C. Handwerker; S. 64: Getty Images/foodpix; S. 70: © The Spectator, 1995; S. 71: dpa; S. 72: Mauritius (1–2); The J. A. Cash Photolibrary (73); Greenhill, London (4–5); Nevis Range, Scotland (6); S. 3: Mauritius/Vidler (1); dpa (2); The Irish Image Collection/Munday (3); Britain on View (4); Superbild/Ducke (5); S. 74: Ernst Klett Verlag/Smith; S. 75: Robert Harding Picture Library Ltd./Harding (1–2,5); OKAPIA KG/Janfot/Naturbild (3–4); Corbis/Busselle (6); S. 76: Ernst Klett Verlag/Smith; S. 77: Helga Lade/ Thompson; S. 84: Regeneration and Tourism, East Lindsey District Council; S. 86 (turkey) Greenhill, London; S. 86–87: © The Sunday Times; S. 87: (horse) Okapia/Klein & Hubert; S. 88: Corbis/Woolfitt; S. 89: Ernst Klett Verlag/Smith (1–2); S. 96: Punch Library/Hewison; S. 98: MEV (1–2); Mauritius (3, 5); Das Fotoarchiv/Meyer (4); S. 99: Superbild/Esbin-Anderson (1); Corbis/Dean; Eye Ubiquitous (2); MEV (3); Corbis/C. & A. Purcell (4); Timmermann Foto-Presse (5); Corbis (6); Mauritius (7); S. 100: Comstock (1); ©) Corel Corporation (2); S. 101: Getty Images (1,4); Getty Images PhotoDisc (2–3); Bilderberg/Schmid (5); S. 102. S. 103, 106: Getty Images/PhotoDisc; S. 104: Corbis/Krist; S. 108: dpa; S. 109: IMAGO; S. 114: Topham Picturepoint, Edenbridge, Kent (1); Getty Images/Buchholz; S. 115: © Punch Limited; S. 116: ZEFA (1); Juniors Bildarchiv/Wegler (2); MEV (3–4); Getty Images/Stone (5); S. 117: ZEFA/Davey (1); Klett-Archiv (2); S. 118: Annick Press Ltd./Martchenko; S. 122: Ernst Klett Verlag/Smith; S. 123: MEV (1); Profile Nottingham (2); S. 125: M. Kunhar; S. 127: Corbis/Boys; S. 129: © Corel Corporation (1–3); HVS1: © Mit freundlicher Genehmigung der Bank of England; S. 212: Image Bank, München.

Textquellen: S. 13: Sing a rainbow, Neue Welt Musikverlag GmbH, München; S. 21: The Hokey Cokey, Connelly-Musikverlag Dr. Hans Sikorski KG, Hamburg; S. 46: Singin' in the rain/1929 EMI Catalogue Partnership/Robbins Cat. Inc. USA. Reprinted by permission of CPP Belwin Europe, Surrey, England; S. 50: © Extra-Musikverlag Ralph Siegel GmbH & Co. KG München; S. 73: Islandman, Sony/ATV Music Publishing (Germany) GmbH; S. 77: Summer holiday, Edition Accord GmbH; S. 108: Fly away, Lenny Kravitz/EMI Virgin Music Publishing GmbH; S. 86: © Times Newspapers Ltd.; S. 116: W.R. Espy (1); Meadowbrook Press (2–5); S. 118: The Paper Bag Princess (abridged) by Robert N. Munsch © 1980 Bob Munsch Enterprises Ltd., Annick Press Ltd. Toronto, New York, Vancouver; S. 120: Superfudge by Judy Blume, © 1980 Judy Blume, reprinted by permission of William Morris Agency, Inc. on behalf of the Author.

What you can say to your friends or to the teacher …

Before and after the lesson	
Good morning, Mr / Mrs … .	Guten Morgen, Herr / Frau … .
I'm sorry I'm late.	Tut mir Leid, dass ich mich verspätet habe.
What's for homework?	Was haben wir als Hausaufgabe auf?
Good-bye. Bye.	Auf Wiedersehen. Tschüs.

Asking for help	
What's that in English / German?	Was heißt das auf Englisch / Deutsch?
Can I say: …? What does … mean?	Kann ich sagen: …? Was bedeutet …?
How do you do this exercise?	Wie macht man / geht diese Übung?
Is this right? I'm not sure.	Ist das richtig? Ich bin mir nicht sicher.
Sorry, I don't know.	Tut mir Leid, das weiß ich nicht.
Pardon? Can you repeat the question / sentence, please?	Wie bitte? Können Sie / Kannst du bitte die Frage / den Satz wiederholen?
Can you play the CD again, please?	Können Sie die CD bitte noch mal abspielen?
Can we do another example, please?	Können wir noch ein Beispiel machen?
Thanks. Thank you (very much).	Danke. Vielen Dank.

Working together	
Can I work with …?	Kann ich mit … zusammenarbeiten?
Can I have your crayon / ruler …?	Kann ich mal deinen Buntstift / dein Lineal … haben?
Whose turn is it?	Wer ist dran?
Let's write … on our poster.	Schreiben wir … auf unser Poster.
Let's put this picture there.	Setzen / Kleben wir das Bild da hin.

Talking about your ideas	
I like / don't like this story / song / game … .	Diese Geschichte / dieses Lied / dieses Spiel gefällt mir / gefällt mir nicht.
I don't think this is right / wrong.	Ich glaube nicht, dass dies richtig / falsch ist.
Let's act the story / play a game.	Wir möchten die Geschichte / ein Spiel spielen.

… and what the teacher says to you

Open your books at page … .	Öffnet eure Bücher auf Seite … .
Turn to page … .	Schlagt Seite … auf.
Read the text on page … .	Lies den Text auf Seite … .
Would you collect the exercise books / worksheets / workbooks, please?	Würdest du bitte die Übungshefte / Arbeitsblätter / Arbeitsbücher einsammeln?
Do this exercise for homework.	Macht diese Übung als Hausaufgabe.
Who would like to write on a transparency?	Wer möchte auf Folie schreiben?
Be quiet. Sit down, please.	Sei / Seid ruhig. Setz dich / Setzt euch, bitte.
Please speak up.	Sprich / Sprecht lauter, bitte.
No prompting, please.	Nicht vorsagen, bitte.
Good. Very good. That's good.	Gut! Sehr gut! Das ist gut.
You can do better. Try again.	Das kannst du besser. Versuch es noch einmal.
That's it. Well done.	So ist es richtig. Gut gemacht.

Souvenirs, souvenirs ...
EMPIRE STATE BUILDING, NEW YORK CITY
CALIFORNIA
ACROSS THE COLORADO RIVER AT LEE'S FERRY
PARIS PALACE
NEW YORK
LONDON
Greetings from
FORNIA
PLACE STAMP HERE
THE SUNSHINE

BRITISH MONEY

Notes (reduced in size)

£1 = a pound
1p = 1 penny
10p = 10 pence
There are 100 pence in a pound.

Coins

ALASKA
WASHINGTON
Seattle
OREGON
IDAHO
MONTANA
NORTH DAKOTA
SOUTH DAKOTA
WYOMING
NEBRASKA
CALIFORNIA
NEVADA
UTAH
COLORADO
Denver
KANSAS
ROCKY MOUNTAINS
San Francisco
Grand Canyon
Los Angeles
San Diego
PACIFIC OCEAN
ARIZONA
USA
NEW MEXICO
TEXAS
OK
HAWAII
MEXICO